Introduction to Statistics in Pharmaceutical Clinical Trials

Introduction to Statistics in Pharmaceutical Clinical Trials

Todd A Durham MS
Senior Director of Biostatistics and Data Management
Inspire Pharmaceuticals
Durham, North Carolina, USA

J Rick Turner PhD
Chairman, Department of Clinical Research
Campbell University School of Pharmacy
Research Triangle Park, North Carolina, USA
and
Consulting Executive Director of Operations
CTMG, Inc.
Greenville and Wilson, North Carolina, USA

Pharmaceutical Press

Published by the Pharmaceutical Press
66-68 East Smithfield, London E1W 1AW, UK

(P.P) is a trade mark of RPS Publishing
RPS Publishing is the publishing organisation of the Royal
Pharmaceutical Society of Great Britain

First Published 2008

Typeset by J&L Composition, Filey, North Yorkshire
Printed on demand by TJ International, Padstow, Cornwall

ISBN 978 0 85369 714 5

Disclaimer

**The drug selections and doses given in this book are for illustration only. The authors and publishers
take no responsibility for any actions consequent upon following the contents of this book without
first checking current sources of reference.**

All doses mentioned are checked carefully. However, no stated dose should be relied on as the basis for
prescription writing, advising or monitoring. Recommendations change constantly, and a current copy of
an official formulary, such as the British National Formulary or the Summary of Product Characteristics,
should always be consulted. Similarly, therapeutic selections and profiles of therapeutic and adverse activities are based upon the authors' interpretation of official recommendations and the literature at the time of
publication. The most current literature must always be consulted.

Contents

Foreword

With this introductory text, the authors have managed to de-mystify Statistics for students of pharmacy and clinical research who may be taking their first, or one of their earliest, courses in the subject. Three fundamental departures from the standard treatment of statistics are evident from the start – the way in which "Statistics" is defined, the organization of the book itself, and the use of a single, unifying disease area for illustration throughout the book. The reference to Statistics as "an experimental approach to gaining knowledge" at the start of the first chapter sets the tone for the rest of the book. Statistical concepts are defined and explained relative to their usefulness in clinical decision making. A unique operational definition of the discipline of Statistics is presented that consists of six components, beginning with the posing of a research question and concluding with both a regulatory submission and peer-reviewed publication. This is a far cry from the standard definitions used in most Statistics texts and alerts the reader to the fact that applications and discussions of utility will be intertwined with mathematical concepts and methodologies for the duration of their reading.

Rather than simply providing an exposition of mathematical terms and operators followed by a canvassing of the usual array of statistical tools and techniques, the authors choose instead to follow the product development pathway in organizing their book, showing how statistics plays an important role in providing the ability to move from step to step with objectivity and sound decision making. After an overview of the drug development paradigm that includes the nonclinical, manufacturing, and marketing aspects, the reader is introduced to the fundamentals of experimental design, probability distributions, and hypothesis testing. The reader is then guided through each phase of pharmaceutical clinical trials. From early phase to confirmatory trials, the questions that need to be addressed and the types of data and statistical tools needed to address them are explained and fully illustrated with an antihypertensive treatment example. Note, however, that the straightforward nature of the exposition does not equate to simplicity of subject matter. Nonparametric statistics, noninferiority trials, and adaptive designs all receive mention as the text covers the majority of situations these future researchers are likely to encounter. And unlike many basic statistics texts with a focus on efficacy occupying the majority of the pages, safety analyses receive nearly equal treatment here. Timely safety topics of particular clinical interest, such as QT/QTc interval prolongation and how to design a study to test for this adverse effect, are covered.

Focusing on a potential treatment of hypertension for illustration throughout the book provides consistency and really makes the product development pathway come alive. The reader has the sense of helping move this product from phase to phase, and the example serves to not only illustrate the statistical methods, but also the clinical decision making surrounding the product's development. In addition, the reader is able to accumulate the medical background required to appreciate the data examples in a minimum number of pages, and the example is rich enough so as to not afford any loss of generality with this singular focus.

The dialogue between clinician and statistician is of the utmost importance in the successful execution of a product development program today. The need for strong communication skills, verbal and written, among those involved in this complex process has never been greater. The authors have provided a text that fully equips students to engage in clear and meaningful dialogue with their clinical colleagues and regulatory counterparts. By focusing on the common goal of learning essential information about experimental products through well-designed and well-conducted studies, and accurately collected and appropriately analyzed data, the reader never loses sight of the fact that statistics are the means to the end, and not the end in themselves. As the authors note on page 191, "Our interest in Statistics, then, is a pragmatic one: The discipline provides the best way currently available to conduct clinical development programs."

I have had the pleasure of working with Todd Durham for over 10 years and I am not surprised in the least with his clear and concise treatment of Statistics in this text. He is known among friends, colleagues, and students for his thoughtful approach to study design and analysis problems, his excellent communication skills, and his great capacity for mentoring and tutoring others. His contributions through this text will enable other classrooms to benefit from his winning style of teaching even when he is not present to lead the discussion himself. Todd is an Adjunct Professor of Clinical Research at the Campbell University School of Pharmacy, and teaches Statistics to students in the Master of Science in Clinical Research program. I am delighted that this collaboration with Rick Turner, the Chairman of the Department of Clinical Research, has proved so successful.

Lisa M. LaVange, Ph.D.
Professor and Director, Collaborative
Studies Coordinating Center
Department of Biostatistics,
School of Public Health
University of North Carolina at Chapel Hill
Chapel Hill, NC, USA
January 2008

Preface

This book is an introductory statistics textbook designed primarily for students of pharmacy, clinical research, and allied health professions. It takes a novel approach by not only teaching you how to conduct individual statistical analyses, but also placing these analyses in the context of the clinical research activities needed to develop a new pharmaceutical drug. By taking this approach, we are able to provide you with a unified theme throughout the book and, in addition, to teach you the computational steps needed to conduct these analyses and provide you with a powerful conceptual understanding of why these analyses are so informative. This approach also makes the book well suited to professionals entering the pharmaceutical, biotechnology, and contract research organization (CRO) industries who wish to gain a broader understanding of study design and research methodology in clinical trials. Both target audiences will find this book a useful introduction to the central role of the discipline of Statistics in the clinical development of pharmaceutical drugs that improve the human condition. Important concepts are reinforced with review questions at the end of chapters.

By focusing on the statistical analyses most commonly used in drug development and employing an organizational structure that follows the order in which these statistical analyses are commonly used in clinical drug development, the book shows you how the discipline of Statistics facilitates the acquisition of optimum quality data, that is, numerical representations of relevant information, which form the basis of rational decision-making throughout the drug development process.

Although this book meaningfully integrates the computational aspects of statistics with the overall conceptual objectives for which they are used, we have not included some topics that are traditionally included in introductory statistics textbooks, including linear regression and correlation. We believe that the selected topics and the depth at which they are discussed are appropriate and unique for our intended audience. While we are very happy with the title of the book as it is, the title *The Statistical Basis of Decision-making in Pharmaceutical Clinical Trials* would capture one of the book's major themes extremely well.

The motivation to write this book is directly related to our professional activities. Both of us teach Statistics in the Department of Clinical Research at the Campbell University School of Pharmacy (TD, a professional biostatistician, is also an Adjunct Professor of Clinical Research, and RT is Chairman of this department). The department is located in the heart of North Carolina's Research Triangle Park, one of the world's leading pharmaceutical and biotechnology research centers. Statistics courses in this department are therefore taught in the context of the development of new pharmaceutical and biopharmaceutical products, with the goal of providing a solid knowledge and understanding of the nature, methods, applications, and importance of the discipline of Statistics. It should be emphasized that we are not training our students to be professional statisticians. Rather, we wish them to become familiar with the basics of design, methodology, and analysis as used in the development of new drugs. We aim to convey the following information:

- why, and how, data are collected in clinical studies (to investigate a specific question, using appropriate study design and research methodology)

- how these data are summarized and analyzed (descriptive statistics, hypothesis testing and inferential statistics, statistical significance)
- what the results mean in the context of the clinical research question (interpretation, estimation, and clinical significance)
- how the results are communicated to regulatory agencies and to the scientific and medical communities.

By presenting statistical analysis in a meaningful, integrated, and relevant manner, our students' knowledge and retention of the material is markedly improved. Moreover, their understanding and appreciation of the discipline of Statistics in all of their future scientific endeavors (both academically while studying, and professionally once in the workforce) is considerably enhanced. This book will become the text for the first of two Statistics courses in our Master of Science in Clinical Research program.

It is appropriate to acknowledge here that neither author is a clinician. The first author is a professional statistician and the second a professional educator, medical writer, and research methodologist. We are also both clinical trialists: The first author is experienced in statistical aspects of clinical trials, and the second in writing regulatory clinical documentation. At various points throughout this book, we discuss how the discipline of Statistics provides the rational evidence for making clinical decisions. On several occasions we use hypothetical data, show how statistical analyses of these data and the associated statistical interpretations can form the rational basis for clinical decision-making, and illustrate what the hypothetical

clinical decision might be. This is done for educational purposes. Please remain aware, when reading our hypothetical clinical interpretations, that we are not clinicians: We are conveying the logic and importance of incorporating statistical information in the process of clinical decision-making. The crucial role that the discipline of Statistics plays in clinical practice is to provide the information upon which evidence-based clinical practice is based. The most effective drug development programs, one facet of the larger field of clinical research, result from the collaboration of many specialists, including statisticians and clinicians. Actual clinical decisions are, of course, the province of clinicians.

We express our thanks to professional colleagues and students who have supported and informed us during the preparation of this book. Christina De Bono and Kevin Tuley at Pharmaceutical Press have provided constant support and assistance throughout this project, and we are very grateful. Richard Zink provided detailed reviews of several drafts of the manuscript. Finally, our previous students have provided invaluable feedback on lecture material and initial drafts of this book.

Views expressed in this book are those of the authors and Turner Medical Communications LLC, and not necessarily those of Inspire Pharmaceuticals and/or the Campbell University School of Pharmacy.

Todd Durham and Rick Turner
Research Triangle Park, NC, USA
August 2007

Dedications

This book is dedicated to Heidi Durham and Karen Turner, who have been there for us every step of the way. We also thank Rachel, Daisy, Misty, and Mishadow for their wonderful companionship.

1

The discipline of Statistics: Introduction and terminology

1.1 Introduction

It is common to start a textbook with a definition of the book's topic. However, in the case of the discipline of Statistics (indicated in this book with a capital "S"), it is difficult to find a universally accepted definition. Different textbooks are written for different target audiences, and their goals can therefore be quite different. So, before going any further, it is appropriate to identify our target audiences, and to provide you with a definition of Statistics that is informative and meaningful in the context of this book.

The discipline of Statistics is discussed in the context of pharmaceutical clinical trials because two of the primary target audiences for this book are students of pharmacy and students of clinical research. A clinical trial can be defined as an experiment testing a medical treatment on humans (Piantadosi, 2005). In this definition, the words "human" and "clinical" are closely linked. However, this definition also makes it clear that clinical trials can be performed to test a variety of medical treatments. In addition to pharmaceutical trials, the focus of this book, clinical trials are conducted to test medical devices (see Becker and Whyte, 2006) and some surgical practices.

In addition to being suitable for students of both pharmacy and clinical research this book is also suitable for other students who are interested in the development of new pharmaceutical drugs, including students of medicine, nursing, and other health-related professions where pharmacotherapy is of relevance. Statistics courses are typically part of such degree programs, and we have designed this book so that these students will also benefit from the material presented and taught. Our goal in this book is to introduce you to basic statistical methodology and analysis in a meaningful and very relevant context, the conduct of pharmaceutical clinical trials. We use the phrase "clinical trials" from now on with the understanding that all discussions are about the development of pharmaceutical drugs.

By teaching Statistics in a context that is very relevant to you, the statistical analyses that you will learn about will not simply be abstract ideas: They will be techniques that meaningfully collect and analyze numerical information of importance in your profession. The development of new drugs, whether brand-new chemical entities (NCEs), biologics, or new forms of existing drugs, requires three steps:

1. collection of numerical representations of information
2. analysis and interpretation of this numerical information
3. decision-making based on this analysis and interpretation.

By the end of this book you will have a solid conceptual knowledge and understanding of the experimental methods and statistical analyses used in new drug development. In addition, you will have gained computational knowledge: You will have learned how to conduct the most commonly used statistical analyses and how to interpret the results of these analyses. This combination of conceptual and computational knowledge and understanding is a powerful one that will serve you well in the rest of your studies.

A couple of conceptual points are useful here. First, there is much more to the discipline of Statistics than "obligatory calculations" at the end of a study. Rather, the discipline of Statistics is an integral component throughout the entire new drug process. Second, conducting the statistical analyses most commonly employed in new drug development is really not that hard. The hard parts of new drug development are asking the correct research questions, making sure that the correct study design is used in each clinical trial, and making sure that the correct experimental methodologies are used to acquire optimum quality data during the clinical trial (we talk more about these issues in Chapters 3 and 4). If good research questions are asked, and the correct study designs and experimental methodologies used to collect optimum quality data, performing the statistical analyses is not really that difficult. As Piantadosi (2005) commented, "good trials are usually simple to analyze correctly."

1.2 The discipline of Statistics

The discipline of Statistics is a well-developed and powerful discipline that involves much more than simply number crunching. Crunching numbers is certainly part of it, but, unless those numbers have been carefully and meaningfully collected, crunching them is not going to provide any useful information.

Statistics is a scientific discipline because it adopts the scientific method: A method of thinking and conducting business in a certain way. You are very likely familiar with the sciences of biology, chemistry, and physics, but these are not the only sciences. Individual fields of investigation can be called a science, or a scientific discipline, if they adopt the scientific method of inquiry. In this method, theories lead to hypotheses, and these hypotheses are then tested in the scientific manner. A key characteristic of scientific hypotheses is that they need to be able to be disproved. If repeated evaluations of a theory via appropriate hypothesis testing do not disprove the theory, compelling evidence starts to accumulate that the theory may have merit. It is then deemed reasonable to proceed on the basis that the theory does indeed have merit, but with the knowledge and acceptance that future investigations may provide evidence that the theory does not have merit (see Turner, 2007).

In this book we have adopted the broad operational definition of Statistics provided by Turner (2007). In this definition, Statistics is regarded as a multi-faceted scientific discipline that comprises the following activities:

- Identifying a research question that needs to be answered.
- Deciding upon the design of the study, the methodology that will be employed, and the numerical information (data) that will be collected.
- Presenting the design, methodology, and data to be collected in a study protocol. This study protocol specifies the manner of data collection and addresses all methodological considerations necessary to ensure the collection of optimum quality data for subsequent statistical analysis.
- Identifying the statistical techniques that will be used to describe and analyze the data in an associated statistical analysis plan that is written in conjunction with the study protocol.
- Describing and analyzing the data. This includes analyzing the variation in the data to see if there is compelling evidence that the drug is safe and effective. This process includes evaluation of the statistical significance of the results obtained and, of critical importance, their clinical significance.
- Presenting the results of a clinical study to a regulatory agency in a clinical study report, and presenting the results to the clinical community in journal publications.

This functional definition makes clear that the discipline of Statistics is indeed multi-faceted and essential throughout clinical trials. It is critical at the start of the clinical trial process so that a study can be designed appropriately to facilitate the collection of optimum quality data, which then need to be organized and managed correctly. These data are then described and analyzed, and the numerical results of these analyses are interpreted in the context of the particular study. Finally, the numerical results of the analyses and the authors' interpretation of these results are presented to regulatory agencies to request permission to market the drug, and published in clinical communications to provide information to physicians.

This functional definition of Statistics may well contain some concepts and terms with which you are not familiar at this point, and that is fine. This book's goal is to make you familiar with these terms and concepts so that you will understand the statistical processes and procedures that are used in clinical trials. Individual chapters address different parts of this definition. However, it is important for us to emphasize here that the individual aspects presented in the chapters are really seamless components of one overall experimental approach to gaining knowledge, the discipline of Statistics. These components act together to ensure that high-quality data acquisition, correct analysis, and appropriate interpretations provide optimal answers to good research questions.

1.3 The term "statistic" and the plural form "statistics"

Having operationally defined the discipline of Statistics, we will now operationally define the terms "statistic" and "statistics," each written with a lower case "s." A statistic typically involves one piece of numerical information. For example, the number of states in the United States of America is 50, and the number of countries comprising the United Kingdom is 4. In some circumstances, however, a statistic can usefully involve more than one piece of numerical information. Consider how you might describe a sports team's performance in a season. A simple numerical representation of this success might be the number of games they won, perhaps 17. However, it is probably more useful to provide information about wins and losses (assume no draws), and therefore to provide the total number of games as well. In this context, a "17-3" summary of the season's performance (a winning season) is quite different from a "17-23" summary of performance (a losing season), even though the number of wins is the same. So, if you want to regard 17-3 as a single statistic, even though it contains two numbers, this seems perfectly reasonable to us. Indeed, one medical example of a single statistic involving two pieces of numerical information, a person's blood

pressure, is particularly relevant for the discussions in this book concerning the development of a new investigational drug that is intended to reduce high blood pressure. This point is discussed further in Section 1.10.

The word "statistics" with a lower case "s" is used throughout the book as simply the plural of the term statistic. A listing of the sports team's wins and losses for the last 10 seasons, perhaps along with similar details for every other team in the same division or conference, would very adequately be described as statistics.

1.4 The term "statistical analysis"

The term "statistical analysis" has two meanings. Statistical analysis, used in a general sense, can be regarded as a global description or plan of how data collected will be analyzed. The term "a statistical analysis" refers to an individual analytical technique that is used to describe and analyze numerical information. This book teaches you how to conduct a collection of statistical analyses that are appropriate for use in analyzing the results of clinical trials.

1.5 Association versus causation

If we were to measure a number of characteristics (for example, age, height, and bone mineral density) in a large group of individuals we would undoubtedly find that they were related in some sense. For example, as we age from infants to young adults, our height increases from 18 inches (or 45 cm) or so to 50 inches (1.27 m) or more. If we were to examine the age and height of children aged less than 17 years, we would not find many (if any) 17-year-old children who were 18 inches (45 cm) tall, and we would not find many (if any) 2-year-old children who were 60 inches (1.52 m) tall. Biological and medical traits with such a relationship are said to be associated.

When someone suffers an acute injury such as a cut from a kitchen knife the immediate bodily response *may* include bleeding and sharp stinging pain. Various biological responses to the trauma can lead to a number of measurable effects. Had the trauma not occurred at this time the finger would not have bled and nor would the sharp stinging pain have occurred. Some cuts are so minor that they do not result in either bleeding or pain so the occurrence of the trauma does not perfectly predict the effects bleeding and pain. The philosophical description of causative effects is controversial. Without delving into this controversy we can think of cause-and-effect relationships as being established on the basis of:

- biological plausibility
- temporal relationship between the antecedent (cause) and the result (effect)
- some quantitative demonstration that occurrence of the "cause" increases the likelihood of observing the effect.

The two concepts association and causation occur throughout this text and they should not be confused. Association of two characteristics is a requirement to establish causation, but the converse is not true. It is truer to say that aging "causes" human growth than to say that growth causes aging. There are a number of research methods, especially in the field of epidemiology, that may be used to study the relationship among various health risks (including the use of medical treatments) and health outcomes. However, the randomized clinical trial is considered the gold standard when it comes to establishing cause-and-effect relationships. In this book we discuss the likely causative effects of new drugs on health outcomes of interest.

1.6 Variation and systematic variation

The study of the biological sciences has major differences from the physical and mathematical sciences. In the physical sciences, the same operation done under the same conditions always produces the same result. For example, a ball dropped off the same building always accelerates towards the earth at the same rate, a rate governed by the gravitational pull between the earth and the ball. In the biological sciences, including the clinical sciences, this is simply not the case. The same dose of medicine (even dose adjusted for weight) will not have an identical effect on two different people. In a large group of people there will typically be considerable variation in response. Similarly, the optimum clinical care of one patient will likely involve a different combination of therapeutic interventions than the optimum care of another. In clinical research we have to deal with variation, and examining data for systematic variation falls squarely within the province of Statistics. The topic of variation is discussed further in Chapter 5.

1.7 Compelling evidence

Compelling evidence in Statistics might be thought of as the inverse of 'reasonable doubt' in the legal system, but with the advantage that it can be quantified according to the precise rules of Statistics. The discipline of Statistics has been developed as a widely accepted method of conducting scientific investigation in many fields, including drug development. Data are collected, analyzed, interpreted, and presented in a certain way such that the scientific and clinical communities at large recognize the validity of the study.

In the practice of law, each attorney presents his or her evidence in a certain manner to a jury under the scrutiny of a judge, who makes sure that each component of the evidence is legitimate in that it meets an acknowledged level of acceptance. It is often true in legal cases that absolute proof is not possible (unless there is incredibly strong evidence such as a video of the crime, and even then the defense lawyer will probably argue the existence of extenuating circumstances), so the prosecutor's arguments have to be demonstrated to be likely true beyond a reasonable doubt. In the context of clinical trials the discipline of Statistics incorporates accepted methods of data collection and data analysis that can provide compelling evidence that an investigational drug does indeed do what it is intended to do. A clinical trial may provide compelling evidence that an investigational drug does indeed lower blood pressure. The term "compelling evidence" is not the same as the term "proof" because a single clinical trial cannot prove that a drug is effective. However, it can certainly provide compelling evidence.

1.8 The terms "datum" and "data"

The word data is a plural word indicating more than one piece of numerical information. The singular form of the term is datum. As the statistical analyses described in this book always analyze more than one data point the term "data" is used throughout. Accordingly, accompanying plural words are used in conjunction with the word data. Examples are "the data are, the data were, these data, the data show."

If you have any uncertainty as to how to construct a phrase including the word data, replace the word data in your mind with the word results. While the words data and results are not synonymous, the word results is a plural construct, as is the word data. This strategy will likely help you express a phrase including the word data correctly.

The word datum does not occur again in this book.

1.9 Results from statistical analyses as the basis for decision-making

Many decisions have to be made throughout the drug development process. A lot of these decisions concern whether it is prudent to continue to the next phase of development, as outlined in Chapter 2. To allow rational decisions to be made we need reliable, quantitative information upon which to base our decisions. In a very real sense the main contribution of the discipline of Statistics in research endeavors is providing numerical representations of information that facilitate good decision-making.

Data are numerical representations of individual pieces of information. Once data have been collected in a clinical trial that employed the appropriate study design and experimental methodology, statistical analysis utilizes these individual pieces of numerical information to obtain a numerical representation of the "big picture." The results of a statistical analysis and, very importantly, the interpretation of these results in the context of the specific research question being asked provide the empirical information upon which decisions can be made. We talk a lot about decision-making in this book.

1.10 Blood pressure and blood pressure medication

We have deliberately chosen to focus on one particular therapeutic area for the worked examples throughout this book: This strategy provides a unified approach in all of the discussions about clinical trials and statistical analyses. Our discussion and worked examples focus on the development of a new investigational drug for the treatment of high blood pressure. The term hypertension is used for this condition, and drugs intended for the treatment of hypertension are called antihypertensive drugs, or simply antihypertensives.

1.10.1 Blood pressure and its measurements

The measurement of blood pressure usually involves the joint measurement of two aspects of arterial blood pressure, systolic blood pressure (SBP) and diastolic blood pressure (DBP). The SBP provides a representation of the pressure of blood as it is ejected from the heart into the body's arteries at each heart beat. The DBP provides a representation of the blood pressure in the arteries in between each heart beat. A healthy blood pressure for a young adult is often represented as "120/80." This is pronounced "one twenty over eighty." In this case, the "/" symbol does not represent the division of 120 by 80 to get a value of 1.5: It is simply used to separate the two blood pressure readings. The units of blood pressure are millimeters of mercury (mmHg), so the actual blood pressure values in this case are an SBP of 120 mmHg and a DBP of 80 mmHg.

Suppose now that we measured someone's blood pressure five times, once every 5 minutes. The average blood pressure could be represented by calculating the average SBP (say 124 mmHg) and the average DBP (say 82 mmHg) and then writing this average blood pressure as 124/82.

1.10.2 Medical management of blood pressure

The Seventh Report of the Joint National Committee on Prevention, Detection, Evalution, and Treatment of High Blood Pressure (JNC 7: National Institutes of Health, 2004) is a definitive publication concerning the treatment of hypertension. It provides the following blood pressure classifications for adult blood pressures:

- Normal: SBP < 120 mmHg and DBP < 80 mmHg.
- Pre-hypertension: SBP 120–139 mmHg or DBP 80–89 mmHg.
- Stage 1 hypertension: SBP 140–159 mmHg or DBP 90–99 mmHg.
- Stage 2 hypertension: SBP ≥ 160 mmHg or DBP ≥ 100 mmHg.

These classifications are related to management strategies for hypertension. This report is the first of the JNC's series of reports to use the term "pre-hypertension," a term introduced to signal the need for increased awareness and education among healthcare professionals and the general public of the benefits of reducing blood pressure before it reaches the levels in the hypertensive categories. The relationship between blood pressure and risk of cardiovascular events is "continuous, consistent, and independent of other risk factors. The higher the BP, the greater is the chance of heart attack, heart failure, stroke, and kidney disease" (National Institutes of Health, 2004, p 2). These classifications are provided as a very useful means of directing the management of blood pressure by clinicians, who have to make a decision whether or not to treat a patient. If they decide that pharmacological treatment is warranted they need to decide what regimen should be prescribed. There

are several classes of antihypertensive drugs on the market, and clinicians typically follow the recommendations in this report.

1.11 Organization of the book

As noted in Section 1.1, reading this book provides you with a solid conceptual knowledge and understanding of the experimental methods and statistical analyses used in new drug development, teaches you how to conduct statistical analyses commonly used in clinical trials, and shows you how to interpret the results of these analyses to facilitate rational, information-based decision-making. This information is taught in the context of a particular category of clinical trials that are conducted during the development of a new drug. As you will see in Chapter 2, clinical drug development programs typically consist of a progressive series of clinical trials. These range from the first trials in which the investigational drug is administered to humans to much larger trials that are conducted as the last item before requesting marketing approval for the drug from a regulatory agency. This book focuses on these larger trials, frequently called Phase III trials and also known as therapeutic confirmatory trials.

This book, therefore, is a self-contained introduction to the discipline of Statistics and its use in therapeutic confirmatory clinical trials. The first part of the book provides introductory comments about the discipline of Statistics and lays the foundations for our later discussions in the context of pharmaceutical trials. Chapter 2 presents an overview of the process of new drug development and the role of clinical trials in this process. The categories of different types of clinical trials are identified and discussed so that you will understand the types of data collected in them.

Chapters 3 and 4 discuss how research questions are asked and answered in statistical language during clinical trials, and introduce the study designs and experimental methodologies that are used to acquire optimum quality data with which to answer our research questions. Chapter 5 discusses statistical ways of describing and summarizing these data. Chapter 6 introduces hypothesis testing and estimation, two important ways of analyzing data from clinical trials.

The concepts and techniques discussed in these chapters are then developed and extended in later chapters, in which we teach you how to conduct statistical analyses commonly employed in preapproval clinical trials, that is, clinical trials that are conducted before applying for marketing approval from a regulatory agency. Chapter 7 discusses clinical trials that are conducted at the beginning of a clinical development program. While these trials are not the major focus of this book, it is appropriate to consider them briefly. The statistical challenges in early phase trials are different from those in Phase III trials, and it is appropriate to highlight these differences.

Chapters 8–11 discuss clinical trials that are conducted later during the clinical development program. These chapters address both safety data and efficacy data. Throughout these chapters, each new statistical analysis taught is addressed in the following way:

- identification of the research question (what is the decision to be made?)
- identification of data that will provide an answer to the research question
- identification of the appropriate study design (how to conduct a trial that will provide data capable of answering the research question as accurately as possible)
- identification of the best methodologies to collect optimum quality data during the study with which to answer the research question as accurately as possible
- identification of the appropriate statistical analysis to be employed
- computational steps necessary to conduct the statistical analysis chosen
- inference and decision-making: Interpreting the results in the light of the specific research question asked.

Chapters 12 and 13 then conclude the book by providing an overarching discussion of the topics covered in previous chapters, and discussing further the philosophical rationales for the employment of Statistics in new drug development.

1.12 Some context before reading Chapters 2–11

The purpose of this section is to provide you with a conceptual framework within which to assimilate the statistical material presented in Chapters 2–11. While this book teaches you the computational skills to conduct some statistical analyses, as an introductory statistics textbook should, we also want to provide you with a conceptual knowledge and understanding of why these analyses are undertaken. Rephrasing this last point, we want to provide you with a conceptual knowledge and understanding of how the information gained from a clinical trial is used in various forms of decision-making.

1.12.1 Decision-making during a clinical development program

The process of developing a new drug is an extremely expensive one. While we do not know the precise exchange rate on the day that you are reading this, estimates of US$1bn and £600m are certainly very meaningful at the time of writing. A related and highly relevant observation is that most drugs fail to reach marketing approval. For every 10 000 potential drug compounds only 10 make it to initial clinical trials in which the investigational drug is administered to humans for the first time. Of these ten, only one, or maybe two, will successfully make it through all phases of clinical trials and be approved by a regulatory agency for marketing. Given that the other eight or nine investigational drugs will not receive marketing approval, that is, they will "fail," it makes sense from many perspectives that they fail as early as possible.

This statement may initially (and very reasonably) seem counterintuitive to you: Isn't the goal to approve a new drug? It certainly is, but, to get a drug approved, we need to provide a regulatory agency with compelling evidence that the drug is both safe and efficacious. If a drug is not safe and efficacious, the sooner we find out the better, for various reasons. First, money spent on a drug that fails cannot be spent on developing another drug that might receive marketing approval – that is, from a business perspective, it is not optimal. Second, and more importantly, individuals volunteer to be in clinical trials.

In later phase clinical trials, individuals with the disease or condition of interest, that is, the desired indication for the investigational drug under development, volunteer for these trials. One crucial ethical aspect of preclinical trials is that we must be uncertain about whether the investigational drug works. If we know that the drug works we should not be giving a placebo to half of our participants. If we know (or arguably even strongly suspect) that the drug does not work we should not administer it to clinical trial participants. In addition, in the case of relatively less common diseases, there are only so many individuals who can participate in clinical trials, and we would prefer that they participate in a trial employing an investigational drug with a relatively higher chance of being approved than in one employing a drug with a relatively lower chance. Therefore, we should be constantly looking for evidence that our investigational drug does *not* work, and we should stop the clinical development program at that point. The discipline of Statistics provides the information that forms the rational basis for making the decision to stop the clinical development program, that is, to kill the drug.

1.12.2 Decision-making during evidence-based clinical practice

Evidence-based clinical practice has two components:

1. Providing the evidence: This is the domain of clinical research and, in the case of drug development, the province of clinical trialists. The discipline of Statistics is a central and critical component of the planning, conduct, analysis, and interpretation of clinical trials.
2. Using the evidence to decide on the best treatment for individual patients on a case-by-case basis. This is the domain of clinical practice.

Both components are vital to evidence-based clinical practice. Katz (2001, p xvii) has written persuasively and eloquently on this issue:

All of the art and all of the science of medicine depend on how artfully and scientifically we as practitioners reach our decisions. The art of clinical decision making is judgment, an even more difficult concept to grapple with than evidence.

1.12.3 Summary

This book introduces you to the statistical methodology employed in drug development at both a conceptual and a computational level. Statistical methodology provides numerical representations of information that facilitate rational, information-based decision-making during regulatory considerations and clinical practice.

1.13   Review

1. When studying the effect of an investigational antihypertensive drug, what sources of background variation might we be concerned with in measurements of blood pressure?

2. Describe three cases where two biological or health traits are associated.

3. Describe three cases where two biological or health traits represent a cause and effect.

1.14   References

Becker KM, Whyte JJ (eds) (2006). *Clinical Evaluation of Medical Devices: Principles and case studies*, 2nd edn. Totowa, NJ: Humana Press.

Katz DL (2001). *Clinical Epidemiology and Evidence-based Medicine: Fundamental principles of clinical reasoning & research*. Thousand Oaks, CA: Sage Publications.

National Institutes of Health (2004). *The Seventh Report of the Joint National Committee on Prevention, Detection, Evaluation, and Treatment of High Blood Pressure*. NIH Publication 04-5230. Bethesda, MD: National Institutes of Health.

Piantadosi S (2005). *Clinical Trials: A methodologic perspective*, 2nd edn. Chichester: John Wiley & Sons.

Turner JR (2007). *New Drug Development: Design, methodology, and analysis*. Hoboken, NJ: John Wiley & Sons.

2

The role of clinical trials in new drug development

2.1 Introduction

This chapter provides an overview of the process of new drug development. It introduces you to this process in a relatively succinct way, but still provides enough details for you to understand the relevance and importance of the statistical methodologies discussed in the following chapters.

As well as evaluating how well a new drug does its job (for example, how well an investigational antihypertensive drug lowers blood pressure), it is vital to evaluate the safety of the drug. Both safety and efficacy are investigated very thoroughly in preapproval clinical trials, and the discipline of Statistics provides the tools to conduct these investigations. As you will see in due course the types of statistical analyses used in the assessment of safety and of efficacy are quite different. Moreover, the evaluation of data collected during postmarketing surveillance once the drug has been approved for marketing employs additional types of statistical analyses. Hence, there is a wide variety of statistical analyses, and it is critical to use the appropriate methodologies and statistical analyses in each case.

New drug development is a very long, complex, and expensive undertaking. The process starts with the identification of a drug molecule, a chemical compound that may become an approved drug many years later. Extensive formulation and chemistry research must be undertaken to put the drug molecule in a form that may be used in nonclinical (animal) and clinical studies. The characteristics of a new drug that make it useful include the following (Norgrady and Weaver, 2005):

- It is safe.
- It is efficacious.
- It can successfully navigate all necessary regulatory oversight, including those that govern nonclinical trials and preapproval clinical trials, and be approved by regulatory agencies for marketing.
- It can be manufactured in sufficiently large quantities by processes that can comply with all necessary regulatory oversight and that are financially viable for the sponsor.

This list of attributes provides a good map for our discussions in this chapter.

2.2 Drug discovery

Drug discovery is the first part of the process of drug development. It can be conceptualized as the research done from the time of the recognition of a therapeutic need to the time that a drug candidate is selected for initial nonclinical testing. A drug candidate may be a small molecule or a biological macromolecule such as a protein or nucleic acid. Drug discovery activities vary between small molecules and biological macromolecules but the way in which preapproval clinical trials are structured is very similar in both cases. The descriptions here address small molecule drug discovery.

The ultimate goals of drug discovery are to identify a lead compound, a drug molecule that is the first choice candidate for the next stage of the drug development process, and then to optimize the molecule. This latter activity is called lead optimization. It refers to searching for a closely related molecule or chemically engineering modifications in the lead drug molecule to produce the molecule that is best suited to progress to nonclinical testing. Contemporary disciplines such as genomics and proteomics, bioinformatics, structural–activity relationships, and *in silico* computer modeling (see Turner, 2007) are used to maximize the chance of an identified molecule producing the desired biological result (having beneficial pharmacodynamic activity) while simultaneously minimizing its chance of producing unwanted side-effects (having pharmacotoxic activity). Once a drug molecule that appears to have a 'good' chance of being suitable for human pharmacotherapy is identified (someone has to make this decision) the candidate drug is tested extensively in nonclinical research.

2.3 Regulatory guidance and governance

Once a certain point in a nonclinical development program is reached, compliance with regulatory governance becomes necessary. From that point on all aspects of the drug development process – manufacturing, the remaining nonclinical studies, and clinical trials – are conducted following regulatory guidance and governance. This section provides an overview of regulatory agencies and their work and responsibilities.

There are many regulatory agencies around the world, each charged to be responsible for public health within their respective countries. While there are some differences among these agencies, there are also many similarities: The activities of the International Conference on Harmonisation of Technical Requirements for Registration of Pharmaceuticals for Human Use, a long name that is usefully represented by the acronym ICH, have led to greater homogeneity. The ICH is an amalgamation of expertise from regulatory agencies and trade associations in Europe, Japan, and the USA. This chapter includes overviews of two regulatory agencies, the US Food and Drug Administration (FDA) and European Medicines Agency (EMEA), and of the regulatory dossiers submitted to them during the development of a new drug.

2.3.1 The Food and Drug Administration

The US FDA is part of the Executive branch of the US government, and it is the country's regulatory agency responsible for the governance of new drug development. The FDA is housed within the Public Health Service, part of the Department of Health and Human Services. When a sponsor has generated sufficient discovery, formulation, and nonclinical data to justify (in their opinion) initiation of studies in humans, they prepare an investigational new drug application (IND). Generally, an IND includes data and information in four broad areas:

1. Animal pharmacology, pharmacokinetic, and toxicology studies.
2. Manufacturing information: These data address the composition, manufacture, stability, and controls used for manufacturing the drug.
3. Clinical study protocol: When originally submitted the general investigational plan should outline the overall plan, but it need articulate only the studies to be conducted during the first year of clinical development. The clinical study protocol submitted includes precise accounts of the design, methodology, and analysis considerations necessary to conduct the proposed study and analyze their results (see Section 4.8). A clinical investigator brochure is also typically included.
4. Investigator information: Information on the qualifications of clinical investigators is provided to allow assessment of whether they are qualified to fulfill their duties at the investigational sites used during the clinical trials.

As the IND progresses further clinical study protocols and the results of completed studies (manufacturing, nonclinical, and clinical) are submitted, and the IND grows accordingly.

When the clinical development program is complete and all nonclinical studies being conducted contemporaneously are complete, the sponsor submits a new drug application (NDA) (in the case of a biologic product, a biologics license application [BLA] is submitted). Typically, sponsors meet with the FDA to discuss the content and format of an NDA before its preparation, because this "pre-NDA meeting" can be crucial for the sponsor to understand the content and format that will best facilitate the FDA's review (see Regulatory Affairs Professionals Society or RAPS, 2007, for more details). Marketing approval by the FDA means that a drug can be marketed in all 50 states within the USA.

While the ICH publishes an extensive list of guidances, the FDA also publishes guidances for industry that can be very helpful and can be located via the FDA's website (www.fda.gov).

2.3.2 The European Medicines Agency

The European Medicines Agency (EMEA: the second E is correct here) has its headquarters in London and is responsible for the evaluation and supervision of medicines for human (and veterinary) use in Europe. The EMEA coordinates the evaluation and supervision of medicinal products throughout the European Union, bringing together the scientific resources of the 27 (at the time of writing) European Union member states. It cooperates closely with international partners in ICH activities.

At the point where an IND would be submitted to the FDA, a clinical trial application (CTA) is submitted by the sponsor. We noted earlier that an IND grows in size as additional clinical study protocols in a clinical development program are submitted to the FDA, each being incorporated into the overall IND. In contrast, CTAs are protocol specific and one CTA must be filed for each clinical study protocol. Hence, in this case, the number of individual CTAs increases during a clinical development program. CTAs are based on summary information only; no full study reports are submitted.

At the completion of the sponsor's clinical development program a marketing authorization application (MAA) is submitted. An MAA is used for both small molecule drugs and biologics. There are two submission routes for the sponsor to choose from:

1. the centralized procedure
2. the decentralized procedure.

The centralized procedure has been in place since 1995. The review of the MAA is coordinated by nominees from the Committee for Medicinal Products for Human Use (CHMP) called the rapporteur and co-rapporteur. This procedure leads to a single EU scientific opinion, which is then translated into a pan-EU decision by the European Commission. The centralized procedure is mandatory in some cases (for example, for biotech drugs, and drugs intended for oncology, HIV, diabetes, and neurodegenerative disease indications) and it is also gaining popularity for all new NCEs.

The decentralized procedure has been in place since 2006. The review of the MAA is conducted by a single agency, called the Reference Member State (RMS). However, other EU countries in which the sponsor wishes to market the drug receive a copy of the MAA and are involved in confirming the assessment made by the RMS. These additional agencies are called concerned member states (CMSs). The decentralized procedure has its roots in the earlier "mutual recognition" procedure that was put in place in 1995. The mutual recognition procedure operated in a similar way except that the CMSs did not receive the whole MAA until after the RMS had approved the product. In both the decentralized and the mutual recognition procedure, the EMEA and CHMP do not get involved unless the RMSs and CMSs cannot reach a consensus decision.

Choice between centralized and decentralized procedures in the case of many NCEs (those for which the centralized procedure is not mandatory) involves many factors, and the decision is a strategic milestone involving medical practice, manufacturing plans, the nature of product, market forces, and the size, resources, and strengths of the sponsor in the EU (see Harman, 2004, for more details).

Similarly to the FDA, CHMP and its Expert Working Parties provide scientific and regulatory guidelines that apply across the EU to complement ICH guidance. (Regulatory agencies in other countries and regions may develop guidelines as needed.) Thus, while considerable progress towards harmonization has been made, it is still important for those seeking global regulatory approvals to consider regional and national regulatory guidance. (For further

information see www.emea.europa.eu/htms/
human/humanguidelines/efficacy.htm and www.
emea.europa.eu/htms/general/contacts/CHMP/
CHMP_WPs.html).

2.3.3 GMP, GLP, and GCP

These three acronyms refer to good manufacturing practice (GMP), good laboratory practice
(GLP), and good clinical practice (GCP). The
various stages of new drug development should
be conducted according to the appropriate regulations and guidance. The initial "c" can precede
each of these acronyms, in each case standing
for the word current. The implication here is
that, in the years between rewrites of regulations
and guidance, certain modifications in the generally accepted best way of performing a certain
activity (best practices) may occur. Therefore,
while the guidance as written in the most recent
version reflects the "official" stance, it is considered wise to conform to modified ideologies as
appropriate.

2.3.4 Statistical aspects in the preparation of regulatory documentation

The discipline of Statistics plays a major role in
the preparation of all regulatory submissions,
including the INDs, NDAs, CTAs, and MAAs that
we have already mentioned. It also includes
other important documents such as study protocols, statistical analysis plans, clinical investigator brochures, and the prescribing information
and promotional materials that will be used by
the sponsor to inform clinicians (and, in countries such as the USA where direct-to-consumer
marketing is permitted, patients) about the drug.
Prespecification of the statistical analysis plan is
necessary to establish the credibility of study
results. The accurate (and concise) presentation
of the design of studies and their results is vital
to ensuring a favorable marketing decision and
approval of related documents.

2.3.5 Statistical aspects in the preparation of clinical communications

Sponsors typically publish the results of
important clinical trials in clinical communications in medical journals, and present the
results at scientific conferences. As for the preparation of regulatory documentation, scientific
communications depend heavily on the discipline of Statistics. Piantadosi (2005) made the
following comment about publishing clinical
communications:

> Reporting the results of a clinical trial is one
> of the most important aspects of clinical
> research. Investigators have an obligation to
> each other, the study participants, and the scien-
> tific community to disseminate results in a
> competent and timely manner (p. 479).

While the format of clinical communications
is different from the format of clinical study
reports that are submitted to regulatory agencies,
the discipline of Statistics provides the basis for
the approach taken. A typical format for a
clinical communication is:

- Abstract: A concise overview of the entire article
- Introduction: The rationale for the study
- Methods: The study design, study sample, methodology used, statistical analyses employed
- Results: The findings from the study
- Conclusions: The main findings and their interpretation
- Discussion: How the conclusions fit in with previous literature, and what the implications are for future research. Any limitations of the study are also a legitimate (and useful) aspect of this section.

The purpose of clinical research is to provide
information that guides clinical practice. Clinical communications are read by physicians who
use the information provided when deciding
whether a particular treatment might be appropriate for an individual patient. These articles are

therefore extremely important, and the information must be presented accurately, meaningfully, and ethically. The term "ethically" emphasizes that authors must tell "the truth, the whole truth, and nothing but the truth" about their study in these communications (see Turner, 2007, for further discussion).

Guidelines for reporting clinical trials in clinical communications are provided by the Consolidated Standards of Reporting Trials (CONSORT) group. We recommend that you read the CONSORT statements (see www.consort-statement.org). We also refer you to Bowers et al. (2006) and Stuart (2007) for extensive coverage of this topic.

2.4 Pharmaceutical manufacturing

Once it has been decided to progress an identified drug molecule to nonclinical testing, the molecule will be tested in various ways, both *in vitro* and *in vivo*. Initial testing may require extremely small amounts of the candidate drug molecule. However, as testing progresses, larger amounts are needed. In addition, when the molecule is ready to be given to animals, it needs to be administered in a certain manner – that is, a drug molecule delivery system needs to be manufactured. Once a certain stage of nonclinical research has been reached, the drug delivery system must be manufactured according to cGMP standards as detailed by regulatory agencies. GMP regulations also apply to drug delivery systems used in clinical trials.

When an investigational drug is tested in early preapproval clinical trials relatively small amounts of drug product supplies are needed. However, if and when later stage preapproval clinical trials are conducted, considerably larger drug product supplies are needed. If the investigational drug is then approved for marketing the amount of drug that needs to be manufactured increases again. The manufacturing facilities that are needed to make the drug on a postapproval marketing scale are likely to be very different in their operation (not just bigger) from the various manufacturing facilities used during the drug development process (see Turner, 2007).

Manufacturing is a critical topic that frequently does not get the recognition and attention that it deserves. Imagine discovering a new drug molecule that could do wonders, but you cannot find a way to manufacture a drug delivery system that will get the drug safely into a patient who needs it. The drug delivery system needs to be able to be manufactured and then be readily transported from the manufacturing plant to the pharmacy in a form that demonstrates stability, and therefore has a suitably long shelf life. If you cannot do all this, the wonder drug would, for all intents and purposes, be useless (recall that the definition of a useful drug in Section 2.1 included manufacturing considerations).

There are various methods of introducing a drug molecule into the body: Tablets and injections are just two examples. In this chapter we focus on the manufacture of drugs that are given orally in tablets, because the largest percentage of drugs are administered in this manner. A tablet is a complex, manufactured, drug delivery system that gets the drug molecule, the active pharmaceutical ingredient (API) that exerts the drug's pharmacodynamic effect, into the systemic (whole body) blood supply, which carries it round the body to its target receptors.

The API is likely to be a small component of the tablet. Various other nonpharmacologically active ingredients, called excipients, are also constituents of the tablet. Each of these excipients has a specific characteristic that enables it to perform a useful function in getting the API to its target receptor. Some of the excipients protect the API from various chemical attacks in the mouth and on its way to the gastrointestinal tract. Others help it to travel through the gastrointestinal tract. Eventually the API is released from its formulation so that it can be absorbed in the small intestine and be transported around the body in the blood supply.

2.4.1 Manufacturing drug products for clinical trials

An additional consideration when manufacturing the drug products that are used in preapproval clinical trials is that they need to be "disguised." As we see later in the book, the safety and efficacy of an investigational drug are compared with those of another compound, called a control compound. In the types of trials on which we focus this control compound is typically (but not always) a placebo. The experimental methodology employed in these trials (discussed in Chapter 4) requires that neither the participants in the trials nor the investigators who are conducting them know whether the participants are being given the investigational drug or the placebo. Therefore, both clinical drug products need to look, smell, and taste the same – that is, they need to be blinded. Trials in which neither the investigator nor the participant can identify the investigational drug are called double-blind trials.

The blinding of clinical drug products adds another degree of complexity to the manufacturing needed for these trials. It involves two steps: Making the investigational drug and the placebo the same in appearance, as noted, and then packaging them in such a way that they cannot be distinguished by the package in which they are supplied to investigators. This practice is, necessarily, contrary to the manner in which marketed drugs are supplied.

2.5 Nonclinical research

Nonclinical research (often called preclinical research, but we prefer the term "nonclinical") involves the *in vitro* and *in vivo* animal research that is conducted and reported to regulatory agencies before starting preapproval clinical trials. Once the drug molecule candidate identified in drug discovery has been optimized, it moves into the nonclinical development program. While human pharmacological therapy is the ultimate goal, an understanding of nonclinical drug safety and efficacy is critical to subsequent, rationally designed, ethical, human

trials. The term "efficacy" is used in drug development to refer to the desired therapeutic (biological) effect of the candidate drug. Nonclinical research gathers critical information about the best likely drug dose, frequency, and route of administration if and when research progresses to human trials. It also investigates pharmacokinetics, pharmacodynamics, and toxicology in animals.

Pharmacokinetics is the study of the effect that the body has on the drug. The pharmacokinetic phase can be regarded as the time from the drug's absorption into the body until it reaches its target receptor site. Dhillon and Gill (2006) noted that pharmacokinetics "provides a mathematical basis to assess the time course of drugs and their effects in the body." Pharmacokinetic processes that determine the concentration of a drug that has been administered include absorption, distribution, metabolism, and elimination (ADME). Pharmacodynamics is the study of the desired effect that a drug has on the body. For example, the pharmacodynamic effect of an antihypertensive drug is to lower blood pressure. The pharmacodynamic phase begins once the drug molecule reaches its target receptor. Toxicodynamics is the analogous study of the undesired effect(s) that a drug has on the body. The toxicodynamic phase begins once the drug molecule reaches a nontarget receptor(s).

Nonclinical safety pharmacology studies submitted to regulatory agencies are outlined in ICH Guidance S7A (2001), and the basic package includes evaluation of a drug candidate's effects on the central nervous system, respiration, and the cardiovascular system. Cardiovascular system evaluation includes assessment of cardiac function and cardiac electrophysiological activity.

Nonclinical toxicological testing is necessary because some compounds can be so toxic that they cause cell death, leading to loss of important organ function. Other toxicological effects are the result of interactions with various biochemical and physiological processes that do not affect the survival of the cells. ICH Guidance M3 (R1) (2000) addresses several topics related to toxicity, including single and repeat dose toxicity studies, genotoxicity, carcinogenicity, and reproductive toxicity. Relatively less evidence of toxicity is considered as relatively greater evidence of the safety of the drug. The route of administration of the drug compound in nonclinical research is typically the intended route in clinical settings and therefore the route that will be used in clinical trials.

Exploratory toxicology studies are conducted to provide an idea of the main organs and physiological systems involved, and to estimate the drug's toxicity when administered across a relatively short period of time. These studies do not need to be conducted according to cGLP guidelines and they are not typically conducted with a drug compound that has been manufactured to cGMP standards.

Regulatory toxicology studies are submitted to regulatory agencies and are conducted according to cGLP standards. Some regulatory toxicology studies need to be done before the first clinical trials are started. Other regulatory toxicology studies are typically conducted in parallel with clinical trials. These include toxicological studies in two or more animal species lasting up to 1 year, carcinogenicity tests and reproductive toxicology studies lasting up to 2 years, and interaction studies that examine possible drug–drug interactions with other drugs that may be prescribed concurrently in humans. These studies are expensive to conduct, and so they are typically not started unless and until the drug progresses into clinical studies.

Mutagenicity is the chemical alteration of DNA that is sufficient to cause abnormal gene expression. Mutagenicity, also known as genotoxicity, includes a comprehensive set of events, of which carcinogenicity and teratogenicity are important subsets. Carcinogenicity describes activity that leads to cancer, and teratogenicity describes activity that leads to the impairment of fetal development.

Nonclinical information can be useful in another arena once a drug has been approved. Prescribing information can include the results of nonclinical toxicology studies (carcinogenesis, mutagenesis, and impairment of fertility). In instances where no human (clinical) data are available, it is possible for a clinician to incorporate nonclinical evidence into his or her decision-making process when deciding whether the benefit:risk ratio of prescribing the

drug to a patient is favorable. The process of using clinical data to form such decisions can be challenging at times, and the process of using nonclinical data even more so. Nevertheless, in some instances nonclinical data may prove of assistance in this regard.

While a nonclinical development program is informative and important, no amount of nonclinical research can predict precisely what will happen once the candidate drug is given to humans. Therefore, a clinical development program is also necessary. The clinical development program builds in many meaningful ways on the results from the nonclinical development program.

2.6 Clinical trials

Clinical development programs consist of a variety of preapproval clinical trials, all designed for a specific purpose of revealing particular information concerning the investigational drug's safety and efficacy.

2.6.1 Categorization of clinical trials by phase

A common system of categorization for preapproval clinical trials includes Phase I, Phase II, and Phase III clinical trials (Phase IV clinical trials are conducted postapproval to collect additional information about a marketed drug). Phase I, II, and III clinical trials can be summarized as follows:

- Phase I: Pharmacologically oriented trials that typically look for the best range of doses to employ. These trials employ healthy adults, usually men. Comparison of the investigational drug's efficacy with other treatments (such as a placebo or a drug that is already marketed) is not a specific aim of these trials, because by definition healthy individuals do not have the disease or condition of interest. However, incorporation of an inactive control can be useful because some of the procedures employed in these trials may themselves give rise to physiological changes that could otherwise be perceived as adverse events (see Section 7.5 for additional discussion).

- Phase II: These trials are designed to look for evidence of activity and preliminary evidence of efficacy and safety at a number of doses. Relatively small numbers of individuals with the condition or disease of interest are used. To gain an understanding of efficacy a control treatment is typically used at this stage.

- Phase III: These trials employ larger numbers of individuals with the condition or disease of interest, and they are comparative in nature – comparison with another treatment (often a placebo, but possibly an active control) is a fundamental component of the design. These trials are undertaken if Phase I and II studies have provided preliminary evidence that the new treatment is safe and effective.

While this system of categorizing preapproval clinical trials is widespread, unfortunately it is not used consistently. As Turner (2007) noted, two studies with the same aims may be classified into different phases, and two studies classified into the same phase may have different aims. An alternative system has been suggested by the ICH.

2.6.2 ICH categorization of clinical trials

The ICH has published a series of Guidances on many aspects of conducting clinical trials (see www.ich.org). One of these, ICH Guidance E8 (1997), provides an alternative approach to categorizing clinical trials, classifying them according to their objective. This system is shown in Table 2.1.

Table 2.1 ICH classification of clinical trials

Objectives of study	Study examples
Human pharmacology Assess tolerance Describe or define pharmacokinetics (PK) and pharmacodynamics (PD) Explore drug metabolism and drug interactions Estimate (biological) activity	Dose–tolerance studies Single and multiple dose PK and/or PD studies Drug interaction studies
Therapeutic exploratory Explore use for the targeted indication Estimate dosage for subsequent studies Provide basis for confirmatory study design, endpoints, methodologies	Earliest trials of relatively short duration in well-defined narrow patient populations, using surrogates of pharmacological endpoints or clinical measures Dose–response exploration studies
Therapeutic confirmatory Demonstrate/confirm efficacy Establish safety profile Provide an adequate basis for assessing benefit:risk relationship to support licensing Establish dose–response relationship	Adequate and well-controlled studies to establish efficacy Randomized parallel dose–response studies Clinical safety studies Studies of mortality/morbidity outcomes Large simple trials Comparative studies
Therapeutic use Refine understanding of benefit:risk relationship in general or special populations and/or environments Identify less common adverse reactions Refine dosing recommendation	Comparative effectiveness studies Studies of mortality/morbidity outcomes Studies of additional endpoints Large simple trials Pharmacoeconomic studies

From ICH Guidance E8 (1997).

Trials that might otherwise be categorized as Phase I, II, III, and IV trials are referred to as human pharmacology, therapeutic exploratory, therapeutic confirmatory, and therapeutic use trials, respectively.

2.6.2.1 Human pharmacology trials

Human pharmacology or first-time-in-human (FTIH) clinical trials are undertaken in an extremely careful manner in tightly controlled settings, often in residential or inpatient medical centers. Typically, between 20 and 80 healthy adults participate in these relatively short studies, and are often recruited from university medical school settings where trials are being conducted. The main objectives are to assess the safety of the investigational drug, understand the drug's pharmacokinetic profile and any potential interactions with other drugs, and estimate pharmacodynamic activity. A range of doses and/or dosing intervals is typically investigated in a sequential manner.

Participants are given extensive physical examinations before they receive their first dose of the drug, at various intervals throughout the treatment, and once they have finished the drug regimen. The trials are designed to collect data that can be compared with similar types of data collected in nonclinical studies. As noted earlier, no animal model data can ensure that a drug will be safe when given to humans. However, it can be informative to see how similar the overall pictures of animal responses and human responses are. Single-dose trials in which the dose chosen is based on the nonclinical work are conducted first. Later, dose-finding studies are conducted to determine the maximum tolerated dose (MTD) of the drug, and to answer questions concerning the side-effects that are seen, their characteristics, and whether they are consistent across participants to any notable degree.

Although the data collected during human pharmacology trials are not in themselves enough to obtain marketing approval, they can certainly have the opposite effect: Unfavorable data can lead to a sponsor's decision not to pursue further development of the drug. While achieving marketing approval of an investiga-tional drug is the sponsor's goal, if the drug is unlikely to succeed it is financially attractive to discover this as early as possible in the drug development program. As we noted earlier, the sentiment here is "If you are going to fail, fail fast!" A well-conducted human pharmacology study can reduce the possibility of later failed trials by revealing unfavorable characteristics of the drug at this stage. This is preferable to the sponsor and, more importantly, in the best interests of individuals who may have been participants in later trials that failed.

From a statistical viewpoint the design of human pharmacology studies has certain impli-cations. These trials include a relatively small number of participants, but a lot of measure-ments are collected for each participant. This strategy has both advantages and limitations. The extensive array of measurements made allows the drug's effects to be characterized reasonably thoroughly. However, few participants in these studies makes generalization of results to the general population relatively harder than for studies with larger sample sizes.

2.6.2.2 Therapeutic exploratory trials

Therapeutic exploratory trials are conducted if the results of the human pharmacology trials are considered positive (someone has to decide that the results are positive). These trials involve the comprehensive assessment of the investigational drug's safety in perhaps 200–300 individuals with the disease or condition of interest. They are typically conducted by clinical pharmacolo-gists, and participants in these trials are often hospitalized and can therefore be closely moni-tored. Extensive data are collected, including self-report assessments by the participants and biochemical assessments.

Sometimes efficacy will be investigated in these trials. Participants are again typically hospitalized and can therefore be closely moni-tored. Assessments of efficacy are typically conducted by individuals specifically trained in clinical trial methodology.

2.6.2.3 Therapeutic confirmatory trials

If the therapeutic exploratory trials are successful (someone has to decide if this is the case), the drug development program will proceed to therapeutic confirmatory trials. By now, the earlier human pharmacology and therapeutic exploratory trials have defined the most likely safe and effective dosage regimen(s) for use in these therapeutic confirmatory trials. These trials may employ around 3000–5000 participants, each of whom has the disease or condition of interest, and they are typically conducted as randomized, double-blind, concurrently controlled trials (see Chapter 4).

Tight experimental control is an extremely important goal in all experimental trials. Consequently, we talk a lot about how to maximize such control in these trials. However, it is simply a realistic consequence of the way that therapeutic confirmatory trials have to be conducted that the experimental control cannot be quite as tight in these trials as it is in human pharmacology trials and therapeutic exploratory trials.

As we note many times in this book there are advantages and disadvantages associated with many occurrences in clinical trials, and with the last statement of the previous paragraph. The very high level of experimental control that is possible in therapeutic exploratory trials means that these trials are better at assessing the 'pure' biological effect of the drug, that is, the efficacy of the drug under near-ideal circumstances. However, if and when a drug is approved for marketing and is being used by many patients, the drug will not be taken in the same very highly controlled manner in which it was given to participants in therapeutic exploratory trials. The data from therapeutic confirmatory trials are therefore likely to be more indicative of how the drug will actually work in the general population if it receives marketing approval.

2.6.2.4 Therapeutic use trials

Therapeutic use trials are conducted once a drug has been approved to gain additional information about the safety and efficacy, or effectiveness, of the drug: The term "effectiveness" is used to describe how well the drug works in patients once the drug has been approved. One example of this type of trial is the simplified clinical trial (SCT). The intent of the word simplified

in the term "SCT" should be clarified here. It refers to the fact that the demands on participants and investigators are less than in preapproval trials. It is not meant to indicate that the implementation of these large trials is simple: On the contrary, their design and logistics are complex.

As in preapproval therapeutic confirmatory trials, participants in SCTs are randomly assigned to a treatment group. However, SCTs have several characteristics that distinguish them from therapeutic confirmatory trials. Probably the most immediately noticeable difference is the number of participants who participate in them. SCTs are designed to detect rare events by including sample sizes that are much larger than those employed in preapproval trials, and thus they are very important in safety monitoring. However, in order to facilitate the conduct of an SCT involving such a large number of participants, the amount of information collected per participant is much smaller than in therapeutic exploratory studies. The demands on both the participants and the investigators conducting the trial have to be reduced to make these studies viable. So, for example, instead of visiting the investigative site every week during a 12-week treatment period and having a large number of assessments made, participants may visit only twice (at the start and end of the treatment period) and have relatively few assessments made on those occasions. These assessments are those of most interest.

Participants in SCTs receive treatments in a more naturalistic setting than those in therapeutic confirmatory trials. Therefore, as well as more participants, the treatment settings are much more representative of how patients in general will be treated when the drug is approved. Advantages and disadvantages accompany many choices and occurrences in designing and conducting clinical trials.

2.7 Postmarketing surveillance

Postmarketing surveillance is conducted once the approved drug is in widespread use to examine safety in a more comprehensive manner. Postmarketing surveillance monitors all reports of adverse reactions and thus can be used to compile extended safety data. This pharmaco-surveillance is a critical component of the overall process of ensuring that all members of a target disease population receive the greatest protection from adverse reactions. As this book focuses on preapproval trials and their statistical methodology, postmarketing surveillance is not discussed. Readers are referred to Mann and Andrews (2007).

2.8 Ethical conduct during clinical trials

The ethical conduct of all clinical researchers is of supreme importance. Participants in all clinical trials are volunteers: while the word "volunteers" is typically exclusively used to describe participants in human pharmacology studies, all participants in all clinical trials are, by definition, volunteers (see Turner, 2007). Individuals participate in clinical trials for the greater good, not specifically to benefit themselves. Everyone involved in clinical research has an obligation to conduct all aspects of this research to the highest ethical standards.

2.8.1 Ethical principles

Several fundamental ethical principles guide drug development research in clinical trials (see Turner, 2007):

- Clinical equipoise: This requires that a comparative clinical trial must be started in the good faith that the investigational drug and the control treatment are of equal merit. The aim is to discover whether or not the investigational drug is of greater merit. Once there is compelling evidence that the investigational drug is of greater merit, it becomes unethical to give the control drug to participants.
- Respect for individuals: Investigators must give potential trial participants all pertinent information about the study, and answer all of their questions. If a potential participant then agrees to participate voluntarily (that is,

he or she is not coerced in any real or implied manner), informed consent is obtained.
- Beneficence: The study design employed in the trial must be scientifically sound, and any known risks of the research must be acceptable in relation to the likely beneficial knowledge that will be obtained.
- Justice: The burdens and the benefits of participation in clinical trials must be distributed evenly and fairly. Vulnerable populations (for example, prisoners, residents in nursing homes) should not be deliberately chosen for participation in clinical trials when nonvulnerable populations are also appropriate participants. The benefits of participation, such as access to potentially life-saving new therapies, should be available to all, including those not historically well represented such as women, children, and members of ethnic minorities.

The topic of ethics in clinical trials is addressed again in Section 3.16.1, where we talk about ethical considerations in choosing the nature of the control treatment used in trials involving investigational antihypertensive drugs.

2.8.2 Ethical considerations in statistical methodology

It is appropriate here to highlight the additional ethical responsibilities that are shouldered by those involved in statistical aspects of clinical trials, as outlined in the operational definition of Statistics presented in Chapter 1. Derenzo and Moss (2006) addressed the importance of ethical considerations in scientific and statistical aspects of clinical studies:

Each study component has an ethical aspect. The ethical aspects of a clinical trial cannot be separated from the scientific objectives. Segregation of ethical issues from the full range of study design components demonstrates a flaw in understanding the fundamental nature of research involving humans. Compartmentalization of ethical issues is inconsistent with a well-run trial. Ethical and scientific considerations are intertwined.

Derenzo and Moss (2006, p 4)

Ethical awareness and ethical responsibility are key aspects of statistical methodology in clinical trials. Areas where ethical and scientific considerations are inextricably linked include:

- Study design and experimental methodology: It is unethical to include people in a study where poor design and/or poor methodology will lead to less-than-optimum quality data and therefore less-than-optimum quality answers to the study's research question.
- Sample-size estimation: A trial requires sufficient participants to answer the research question without exposing them unnecessarily to the risks of the experimental therapy.
- Early termination of trials: Data monitoring committees (DMCs), independent groups charged with reviewing interim data from clinical trials, face difficult ethical challenges when deciding whether a clinical trial should be terminated early. In a recent guidance document the FDA described the roles and responsibilities of DMCs and when such committees may be useful or required (US Department of Health and Human Services, FDA, 2006).
- Communicating trial results: Researchers have an ethical responsibility to report information accurately and fully in clinical communications, as these directly impact patient care.

Correct study design is absolutely essential from both scientific and ethical perspectives when conducting clinical trials. If a study's design cannot lead to the collection of data that can be analyzed meaningfully, no meaningful information about the investigational drug can be gained. Participants in clinical trials have the legitimate expectation that their participation in the trial will help advance our knowledge of the investigational drug, and if the study's design cannot possibly provide additional knowledge about the drug their expectation is not fulfilled (Turner, 2007).

2.9   Review

1. What are the characteristics of a useful new drug?

2. Describe the ethical considerations in preparing clinical communications.

3. What is the role of pharmaceutical manufacturing in new drug development?

4. What is the role of nonclinical research in new drug development?

5. Consider the ICH classification of clinical trials: Human pharmacology, therapeutic exploratory, therapeutic confirmatory, and therapeutic use:

   (a) What is the role of each type of trial in the development of a new drug from a molecule to a new therapy?

   (b) How do results from these types of trials pertain to the use of the new drug in medical practice?

2.10 References

Bowers D, House A, Owens D (2006). *Understanding Clinical Papers*, 2nd edn. Chichester: John Wiley & Sons.

Derenzo E, Moss J (2006). *Writing Research Protocols: Ethical considerations*. Oxford: Elsevier.

Dhillon S, Gill K (2006). Basic pharmacokinetics. In: Dhillon S, Kostrzewski A (eds), *Clinical Pharmacokinetics*. London: Pharmaceutical Press, 1–44.

Harman RJ (2004). *Development and Control of Medicines and Medical Devices*. London: Pharmaceutical Press.

ICH Guidance E8 (1997). *General Consideration of Clinical Trials*. Available at: www.ich.org (accessed July 1 2007).

ICH Guidance M3 (R1) (2000). *Nonclinical Safety Studies for the Conduct of Human Clinical Trials for Pharmaceuticals*. Available at: www.ich.org (accessed July 1 2007).

ICH Guidance S7A (2001). *Safety Pharmacology Studies for Human Pharmaceuticals*. Available at: www.ich.org (accessed July 1 2007).

Mann, R. and Andrews, E. (2007) *Pharmacovigilance*. Hoboken, NJ: John Wiley & Sons.

Norgrady T, Weaver DF (2005). *Medicinal Chemistry: A molecular and biochemical approach*, 3rd edn. Oxford: Oxford University Press.

Piantadosi S (2005). *Clinical Trials: A methodologic perspective*, 2nd edn. Chichester: John Wiley & Sons.

Regulatory Affairs Professionals Society (2007). *Fundamentals of US Regulatory Affairs*. Rockville, MD: RAPS.

Stuart MC (2007). *The Complete Guide to Medical Writing*. London: Pharmaceutical Press.

Turner JR (2007). *New Drug Development: Design, methodology, and analysis*. Hoboken, NJ: John Wiley & Sons.

US Department of Health and Human Services, Food and Drug Administration (2006). *Establishment and Operation of Clinical Trial Data Monitoring Committees*. Available from www.fda.gov (accessed July 1 2007).

3

Research questions and research hypotheses

3.1 Introduction

One of the most efficient ways to acquire new knowledge about any topic is to devise questions that guide our investigations. These questions can focus our thinking and keep us on track as we gather information that contributes to our knowledge base. Devising more specific questions as we progress is typically a good strategy. While relatively loosely formed questions can be very helpful early on in the knowledge acquisition process, refining our knowledge is facilitated by asking more specific questions, and, in turn, acquiring more specific information and knowledge.

The scientific method is one particular method of acquiring new knowledge. In scientific research, including drug development, our questions need to be asked in a particular manner. These questions are called research questions, and they lead to the development of research hypotheses. The scientific method requires that these research hypotheses be structured in a certain way, and then tested in a scientific manner. As noted earlier, a fundamental characteristic of these research hypotheses is that they can be disproved. The word "disproved" is not a typo: These hypotheses need to be able to be disproved, not "proved."

3.2 The concept of scientific research questions

In our operational definition, Statistics is regarded as a multifaceted scientific discipline that comprises several activities. The first of these is identifying a research question that needs to be answered. We noted in Chapter 2 that the reason for the development of a new drug is usually the identification of an unmet medical need. The development of a drug that will meet this need requires a series of nonclinical studies that comprise the nonclinical development program, followed by a series of clinical studies that comprise the clinical program. In each case, the study will be designed to answer a specific research question or questions. (From a statistical perspective, it is a good idea to have a small number of research questions that will be answered by an individual study, despite the real temptation to try to collect data that will answer many research questions.)

3.3 Useful research questions

In Section 2.1 we cited Norgrady and Weaver's (2005) definition of a useful drug in the context of drug development. That definition is a good illustration of how the term "useful" is used in scientific research. A precise, operational definition is needed, rather than a vague statement such as "it looks pretty useful to me."

Turner (2007) provided an operational definition of a useful research question:

- It needs to be specific (precise).
- It needs to be testable.

If a candidate drug successfully makes it through the nonclinical development program, the safety and efficacy of the investigational drug will be tested in humans in a series of clinical trials that comprise the clinical development program. Each study that is conducted will test a particular aspect or facet of the drug, and the overall development program will employ these trials in a systematic fashion. We noted in Section 2.6 that three kinds of trials are typically conducted before a new drug is approved for marketing: human pharmacology trials, therapeutic exploratory trials, and therapeutic confirmatory trials. The information that is collected during human pharmacology trials forms the basis for the testing that is done in therapeutic exploratory trials, and the information from both categories of trials forms the basis for the testing that is done in therapeutic confirmatory trials – that is, a body of information and knowledge about the investigational drug is gained in an incremental manner, a hallmark of scientific investigation.

Information is gathered by conducting studies each of which asks a specific, testable research question. A general and vague question such as "Is this investigational drug good for people's blood pressure?" is simply not useful in this context, because it does not facilitate the acquisition of useful information. The same is true in nonclinical studies: the question "Do you think that the drug is pretty safe when given to a bunch of animals?" will not facilitate the acquisition of useful nonclinical information.

3.4 Useful information

You may have noticed that we used the term "useful information" twice in the previous paragraph. Accordingly, it is helpful to provide an operational definition of useful information in the context of drug development. Useful information has the following characteristics:

- It needs to be specific (this is the same as the first characteristic of a useful research question – see Section 3.3).
- It provides a solid basis for further studies that will acquire more useful information.
- It provides the rational basis for decision-making during the drug development process.
- It will be acceptable to regulatory agencies, which will eventually review the reports that provide the information to them.

3.5 Moving from the research question to the research hypotheses

Before discussing the connection between the research question and the associated research hypotheses, it should be noted that the word "hypotheses" here is not a typo: We meant to write the plural form "hypotheses" and not the singular form "hypothesis." As discussed shortly, each research question has two associated research hypotheses.

We noted in Section 3.3 that a research question needs to be useful. We also noted that the question "Is this investigational drug good for people's blood pressure?" is not useful, because it does not provide a precise definition of "good" – that is, the research question is not specific, or precise. A better research question might be "Does the investigational drug alter blood pressure?" At the outset of any scientific inquiry about the potential effects of an investigational hypertensive drug, we must entertain the notion that the drug may, contrary to our expectations, actually increase blood pressure. For reasons that we explain in Chapter 6, this potential is expressed in the statement of the statistical hypotheses. For now, this improved research question addresses the intention of our experiment and drug development program. However, we can do better.

3.6 The placebo effect

An interesting phenomenon in pharmacotherapy is called the "placebo effect." The dictionary currently sitting in our office (*The American Heritage College Dictionary*, 3rd edn) provides several definitions of the word placebo, including:

> A substance containing no medication and given to reinforce a patient's expectation to get well
>
> An inactive substance used as a control in an experiment to determine the effectiveness of a medicinal drug

Both of these definitions are helpful in the present context. The first is a more general one, and relates to the observation that, if a person is given a substance containing no medication, but that person believes that the substance will have a beneficial therapeutic effect, it is not unusual that improvement may be seen in the person's condition. The second definition is a particularly relevant definition in the context of this book, and the term "placebo" will be used extensively in later chapters.

3.7 The drug treatment group and the placebo treatment group

The terms "drug treatment group" and "placebo treatment group" will become very familiar to you as you work your way through this book. Chapter 4 provides more detail, but it is helpful at this point to comment briefly on the following aspect of certain preapproval clinical trials.

It is very common in therapeutic confirmatory trials (and in some therapeutic exploratory trials) to compare the effects of the investigational drug with the effects of a placebo (see also the discussions in Section 3.16.1) – that is, these trials are comparative in nature. One common study design involves giving the investigational drug to one group of individuals, the drug treatment group, and the placebo to a second group of individuals, the placebo treatment group. In addition, and extremely importantly, these individuals do not know whether they are receiving the investigational drug or the placebo. All individuals are treated identically throughout the trial, with the one exception of the treatment that they receive.

A key point to note is that individuals receiving the placebo treatment often show a small improvement in the condition that is the focus of the trial. In some instances, such as studies of antidepressants and analgesics, improvement is self-reported by the individuals themselves and can often be marked. In addition, improvement among individuals can be

accounted for by a phenomenon called "regression to the mean." Imagine a clinical therapeutic trial involving an investigational antihypertensive drug where individuals are eligible for enrollment only if they have a documented systolic blood pressure (SBP) of a specified level (say at least 140 mmHg). It is a simple fact that, as a result of expected and naturally occurring random variation, some individuals may initially show this level of SBP even though it does not accurately reflect their true SBP. On subsequent observations the level of the characteristic will return closer to its expected level, resulting in an "improvement" caused simply by the fact that the individual was enrolled at a time when his or her SBP was higher than normal. In trials involving investigational antihypertensive drugs, it is not unusual for individuals in the placebo treatment group to show small decreases in BP during the trial. Therefore, it becomes important to determine whether the investigational drug has a larger effect on BP than the placebo – that is, the trial is comparative in nature and the placebo is the control against which the investigational drug is compared.

3.8 Characteristics of a useful research question

In Section 3.4 we formulated some initial versions of a research question. We decided that the question "Is this investigational drug good for people's blood pressure?" is not useful. We noted that an improved research question might be "Does the investigational drug alter blood pressure?" This is certainly moving in the right direction. However, as noted at the end of that section, we can do better.

A good clue as to how we can devise a better research question comes from the discussions that we have just had about the comparative nature of these trials, in which the effect of the investigational drug is compared with the effect of the placebo. Based on these discussions an improved research question can be phrased as

"Does the new drug alter SBP more than placebo?" This version of the research question has several useful characteristics:

- It involves both of the treatments received by individuals in the trial: The investigational drug and the placebo.
- It is comparative. The goal is to compare the effects of the two treatments.
- It is precise. There will be a precise answer – yes it does, or no it doesn't. We will have to define the term "more" in more detail shortly, but in the meantime please trust us that this can indeed be done in a precise manner by using the discipline of Statistics.

3.9 The reason why there are two research hypotheses

In this book all research questions are addressed and then answered via the construction of two research hypotheses, commonly called the null hypothesis and the alternate hypothesis. (Although another name for the alternate hypothesis, the research hypothesis, has its own appeal, we employ the commonly used term "alternate hypothesis" in this book.) Both of these hypotheses are key components of the procedure of hypothesis testing. This procedure is a statistical way of doing business. It is described and discussed in detail in Chapter 6, but it is beneficial to introduce the main concept here.

3.9.1 The null hypothesis

The null hypothesis is the crux of hypothesis testing. (It is important to note that the form of the null hypothesis varies in different statistical approaches. As the main type of clinical trial discussed in this book is the therapeutic confirmatory trial, we talk about this first. We then talk briefly about the forms of the null hypothesis that are used in other types of trials in Section 3.10.) As noted earlier, therapeutic confirmatory trials are comparative in nature. We want to evaluate the efficacy of the investi-

gational drug, and the way that we do this is to compare its efficacy with the efficacy of a control treatment, typically a placebo. The key question, expressed in our research question, is "Does the new drug alter SBP more than placebo?" As noted earlier, we need to provide a precise definition of "more," and we will do this in due course. In this type of trial, called a superiority trial, the null hypothesis takes the following form:

> The average effect of the investigational drug on SBP is equivalent to the average effect of the placebo on SBP.

3.9.2 The alternate hypothesis

The alternate hypothesis reflects the alternate possible outcome of the trial, and therefore the alternate possible answer to the research question: The trial was conducted with the specific goal of providing an answer to the research question. In a superiority trial the alternate hypothesis takes the following form:

> The average effect of the investigational drug on SBP is *not* equivalent to the average effect of the placebo on SBP.

Note that the research question "Does the new drug alter SBP more than placebo?" allows for the fact that the investigational drug could actually *increase* SBP more than placebo, as does the alternate hypothesis, which includes the possibility that the drug could increase SBP. The reason for this is that the statistical information used to decide which hypothesis is more plausible must include the possibility, however remote we believe it to be, that the drug has the opposite effect of what we hope for. Another way of stating this is that exclusion of one side of the alternate hypothesis – that is, that the drug is worse than the placebo – is presumptive and contrary to the scientific process of collecting data to search for the true state of nature. It is certainly true that, if we find ourselves in a position to claim that the alternate hypothesis should be accepted because the drug did more harm than good (that is, increased SBP), we will have answered the research question. For now, we must accept that, despite its seeming incongruence with our preferred research question, the use of a two-sided alternate hypothesis is the norm in the regulated world of drug development.

3.9.3 Facts about the null and alternate hypotheses

It is important to note that, whatever the outcome of the trial, both of these hypotheses cannot be correct. It is also true that one of them will always be correct. Again, we operationally define the term "correct" in this context in due course, but the point to note here is that:

- It is never the case that neither hypothesis is correct.
- It is never the case that both hypotheses are correct.
- It is always the case that one of them is correct and the other is not correct.

The procedure of hypothesis testing allows us to determine which hypothesis is correct.

A helpful way of remembering which hypothesis is which – that is, which form the null hypothesis takes and which the alternate hypothesis takes – is to conceptualize that the alternate hypothesis states what you are "hoping" to find and the null hypothesis states what you are not hoping to find. It must be emphasized here, however, that, although helpful, this conceptualization skates on very thin scientific ice: As Turner (2007, p 101) noted:

> In strict scientific terms, hope has no place in experimental research. The goal is to discover the truth, whatever it may be, and one should not start out hoping to find one particular outcome. In the real world, this ideologically pure stance is not common for many reasons (financial reasons being not the least of them).

When a pharmaceutical or biotechnology company has spent many years and huge sums of money developing an investigational drug, and the drug has made it to the point where a therapeutic confirmatory trial is being conducted, the company hopes that the drug will indeed be more effective than placebo, and

in due course be approved for marketing by a regulatory agency. One reason for this hope is that patients will (relatively) soon have the opportunity to receive a new drug that is therapeutically beneficial for them. Another reason, as noted in the previous quote, is that the drug will be approved and make money for the company. Drug companies are for-profit businesses, and this is not a negative judgmental comment. The only way that they can develop future drugs is to sell present drugs for a profit: The costs in pharmaceutical research and development (R&D) are enormous. In this pragmatic sense, the alternate hypothesis (at least one side of it) can meaningfully be conceptualized as stating the outcome that you are hoping for.

3.10 Other forms of the null and alternate hypotheses

The forms of the null and alternate hypotheses are dictated by the goal of the trial. In the therapeutic confirmatory trial discussed so far the goal of the trial is to demonstrate that the investigational drug shows greater efficacy than the control treatment – that is, we are hoping to demonstrate that the investigational drug shows superior efficacy, hence the name superiority trial. Following our earlier memory tip, you can conceptualize the alternate hypothesis as stating what you are hoping to find and the null hypothesis as stating what you are not hoping to find. As we have seen, this leads to the following forms of these hypotheses:

- Null hypothesis: The average effect of the investigational drug on SBP is equivalent to the average effect of the placebo on SBP.
- Alternate hypothesis: The average effect of the investigational drug on SBP is *not* equivalent to the average effect of the placebo on SBP.

When we are hoping to demonstrate something different, however, these hypotheses take different forms. Consider the example of a trial called an equivalence trial. Equivalence trials are conducted to demonstrate that an investigational drug has therapeutic equivalence compared with a control treatment. Equivalence trials are also comparative in nature, but in this case the control treatment is not a placebo but a marketed drug. Here, the control treatment is referred to as an active comparator drug. This active comparator drug is typically the drug that is currently the best, or perhaps the only, treatment available for the disease or condition of interest, and is referred to as the gold standard treatment. The intent in an equivalence trial is to provide compelling evidence that the efficacy of the investigational drug is "equivalent" to that of the active comparator drug. (The term "equivalent" requires a precise statistical definition, and this is provided in Chapter 12.)

Why are equivalence trials important? That is, why would we be interested in a new drug that is only as effective as an existing drug? This is a good question, but one that has an equally good answer. One reason would be that we believe (hope) that the investigational drug is equally effective and also has the considerable advantage that its safety profile is better. This would lead to the same efficacy with less likelihood of side-effects. If the side-effects of the current gold standard drug are particularly unpleasant, this would be a considerable advantage. Other advantages that may justify the use of equivalence trials include convenience of the dosing regimen, and the inability to use an inactive control for ethical reasons.

In an equivalence trial the research question is: Does the new drug demonstrate equivalent efficacy compared with the reference drug? The resultant accompanying research and alternate hypotheses take the following forms:

- Null hypothesis: The investigational drug does not show equivalent efficacy to the comparator drug (the reference drug).
- Alternate hypothesis: The investigational drug does show equivalent efficacy to the comparator drug (the reference drug).

Following the logic of our memory tip, you will see that the alternate hypothesis in this case, just like in the case of a superiority trial, expresses what we are hoping to find, while the null hypothesis states what we are hoping not to find. The actual natures of the null and alternate hypotheses in an equivalence trial are different from those in a superiority trial, but this sentiment is the same. This is equally true in the case of various other types of trials, including noninferiority trials.

Noninferiority trials are similar to equivalence trials, but require that the investigational drug be in the worst case only trivially worse than the reference to be considered noninferior. A precise statistical definition of "trivially worse" must be agreed upon before the start of the trial. For noninferiority trials the research question is: Does the new drug demonstrate efficacy that is not unacceptably worse (Fleming 2007) than the reference drug? The null and alternate hypotheses corresponding to this research question take the form of:

- Null hypothesis: The efficacy of the investigational drug is unacceptably worse than the efficacy of the comparator drug (the reference drug).
- Alternate hypothesis: The efficacy of the investigational drug is not unacceptably worse than the efficacy of the comparator drug (the reference drug).

As for equivalence trials, additional details about noninferiority designs are provided in Chapter 12.

3.11 Deciding between the null and alternate hypothesis

A research question of interest, then, leads to the null hypothesis and the alternate hypothesis. As noted in Section 3.9.3:

- It is never the case that neither hypothesis is correct.
- It is never the case that both hypotheses are correct.
- It is always the case that one of them is correct and the other is not correct.

(We also noted in that section that we would address the precise operational definition of correct in due course, and we have not forgotten this.) Therefore, statistical analysis of the data acquired in the trial enables us to decide between these two mutually exclusive hypotheses. An ongoing theme in this book is that many decisions have to be made in drug development, and the discipline of Statistics provides numerical representations of information that provide the rational basis for decision-making. At the end of every trial, a decision needs to be made: Which of these two mutually exclusive hypotheses is correct – the null hypothesis or the alternate hypothesis? For the rest of this chapter we talk about superiority trials, but the points made apply equally to equivalence trials and noninferiority trials.

3.12 An operational statistical definition of "more"

Imagine the following results from a superiority trial:

- The average decrease in SBP for the individuals in the drug treatment group was 3 mmHg – that is, on average, the investigational drug lowered SBP by 3 mmHg in this trial.
- The average decrease in SBP for the individuals in the placebo treatment group was 2 mmHg – that is, on average, the placebo lowered SBP by 2 mmHg in this trial.

In this superiority trial we are interested to find out whether the investigational drug is more effective than the comparator treatment, the placebo. As the number "3" is numerically greater than the number "2," the simple mathematical answer is clear: Yes, the investigational drug lowered BP more than the placebo. However, you may well feel that this simple mathematical answer, although true, does not capture the spirit of the findings from the trial. The investigational drug managed to lower blood pressure only 1 mmHg more than the placebo, a substance that has no pharmacotherapeutic capability.

The term "treatment effect" is an important one in drug development, and is defined as the difference between the average response to the investigational drug and the average response to the comparator being used in the trial. In this case of the development of a new antihyperten-sive drug it is defined as the difference between the average decrease in BP shown by the individuals in the drug treatment group and the average decrease in BP shown by the individuals in the placebo treatment group. The logic here is that, as the placebo resulted in a small decrease, even though it has no pharmacotherapeutic capability, the pharmacotherapeutic capability of the investigational drug should be regarded as the decrease in BP over and above that caused by the placebo. Another interpretation of the treatment effect is that it is the amount of change in SBP attributed to the drug over and above that which would have been observed had the drug not been given. Therefore, the treatment effect here is 1 mmHg. This is > 0, and so the investigational drug is mathematically more effective than the comparator treatment, but, as noted earlier, you may be left feeling that the term "more" is not quite appropriate.

3.12.1 A very important aside: The concept of clinical significance

We are about to introduce you to the concept of a statistically significant difference between the means of two sets of numbers. These numbers can be any kind of data, not just the clinical data that are the focus of this book. No matter how large or how small the difference found between the means of two sets of numbers, it is possible for that difference to be declared statistically significantly different after appropriate analysis of those data. In some circumstances and for some data, a difference of just one unit between the means of the two groups of data may indeed be found to be statistically significantly different, and in such a case the use of the term "more" would be statistically appropriate.

However, in the context of clinical data, another extremely important concept is clinical significance. The clinical significance of a treatment effect is a completely separate assessment from the treatment effect's statistical significance. This is a clinical judgment, not the result of a single numerical calculation. It is perfectly possible for a treatment effect to be found to be statistically significant after an appropriate statistical analysis and yet judged by clinicians to be not clinically significant. As you will see, both statistical significance and clinical significance must be addressed in drug development – an observation that highlights that statisticians and clinicians must work very closely together during this process. Later discussions address the topic of clinical significance in detail.

3.12.2 An operational statistical definition of the term "more"

The discipline of Statistics provides us with methodology that tells us whether or not the use of the word "more" is appropriate from a statistical point of view. The formulation of a scientifically meaningful research question and its two associated hypotheses, the null hypothesis and the alternate hypothesis, allows us to reach an answer in an objective manner by following a prescribed methodology. Moreover, the regulatory and clinical communities acknowledge this methodology. Therefore, for a given set of data that have been collected in a trial, statistical testing provides a precise answer that is couched in statistical terms and that has effectively been agreed upon as objective by all interested parties (see Turner, 2007). This leads us to the concept of a statistically significant difference.

3.13 The concept of statistically significant differences

The concept of statistical significance and its practical implementation are discussed in more detail in Chapter 6, but it is appropriate here to set the scene for those discussions. The words "significant," "significance," and "significantly" are used differently in Statistics than they are in everyday language. In the language of Statistics they have precise quantitative meanings. We focus here on the meaning of the term "significantly" in the discipline of Statistics. The discipline of Statistics facilitates a single, quantitative

answer to questions concerning assessments of "more." For a given set of data collected in a superiority trial, the employment of the appropriate statistical analysis will reveal whether the treatment effect attained statistical significance – that is, it will reveal whether or not the investigational drug was statistically significantly more effective than the placebo. In this manner it provides a precise definition of the term "more." If there is a statistically significant difference between the average decrease in blood pressure in the drug treatment group and the placebo treatment group – that is, if there is a statistically significant treatment effect – the use of the term "more" is warranted.

3.14 Putting these thoughts into more precise language

The following are the research question and the two associated research hypotheses that we have formulated so far:

- Research question: Does the new drug alter SBP more than the placebo?
- Null hypothesis: The average effect of the investigational drug on SBP is equivalent to the average effect of the placebo on SBP.
- Alternate hypothesis: The average effect of the investigational drug on SBP is *not* equivalent to the average effect of the placebo on SBP.

The concept of statistical significance allows all three of these to be reframed as follows:

- Research question: Does the new drug alter SBP statistically significantly more than the placebo?
- Null hypothesis: The average effect of the investigational drug on SBP is *not* statistically significantly different from the average effect of the placebo on SBP.
- Alternate hypothesis: The average effect of the investigational drug on SBP is statistically significantly different from the average effect of the placebo on SBP.

Each of these is now expressed in a more precise manner. In addition, the null hypothesis now allows for the treatment groups to differ to a certain extent. In any trial involving any treatments, the group averages will almost certainly differ to some extent: The probability of a treatment effect of zero is extremely small.

3.15 Hypothesis testing

We have now formulated our research question, null hypothesis, and alternate hypothesis in precise statistical language. This facilitates the strategy of hypothesis testing. Hypothesis testing revolves around two actions after an appropriate statistical analysis: Rejecting the null hypothesis or failing to reject the null hypothesis. The language used to express these two actions is very important. After thinking about these two actions for a few minutes, you might think that these actions could be expressed as "accepting the alternate hypothesis" and "accepting the null hypothesis," respectively. In everyday thinking this might be thought very reasonable. However, in the discipline and the language of Statistics, the terminology of rejecting the null hypothesis or failing to reject the null hypothesis is deliberately employed. While data from two groups (for example, means) may suggest that the alternate is more plausible than the null hypothesis, the sample size of the study also has a direct bearing on our ability to reject the null hypothesis. If there is at least a small difference between groups in a study (which will almost certainly be the case), it is possible that a null hypothesis that is not rejected in a study of a certain size would be rejected if the study had been larger. The relationship between sample size and the probability of rejecting the null hypothesis or failing to reject the null hypothesis is explored in Chapter 12.

The statistical convention of using the expression "failing to reject the null hypothesis" reflects the position that null hypotheses of no difference can always be rejected if enough observations are studied. Statistical methodology necessitates making a choice here. One of these two actions, rejecting or failing to reject the null hypothesis, has to be taken at the end of all hypothesis testing. The action taken is precisely determined by the result obtained from the statistical technique used to analyze the data.

3.16 The relationship between hypothesis testing and ethics in clinical trials

The issue of ethical considerations in clinical trials was introduced in Section 2.8. The procedure of hypothesis testing illustrates one important ethical consideration, clinical equipoise, particularly well. The fact that we have two research hypotheses that express two opposing possible occurrences makes it clear that we do not know which best represents the actual state of affairs. The bottom line is that, at the point in time when the study is planned and started, we do not know whether or not the investigational drug will be more effective than placebo. This uncertainty is a necessary prerequisite of conducting a trial: If it were known that the investigational drug were more effective it would be unethical for people with the disease or condition of interest to be given a placebo.

The philosophy that makes it acceptable that some individuals receive a placebo in a clinical trial is that a comparative clinical trial in which some receive a placebo while others receive the investigational drug is the best way to find out if that drug is indeed effective. If it is, the individuals who received the placebo would not themselves have benefited on this occasion, but their participation in the trial was a crucial component contributing to the later treatment of patients with the approved drug. As noted earlier individuals take part in clinical trials for the greater good, not for their own immediate benefit.

Uncertainty is therefore a fundamental prerequisite to conducting a therapeutic exploratory or therapeutic confirmatory trial. The results of the trial will be used in a decision-making process at the end of the trial: In the light of the prevailing uncertainty, we need to decide whether the results of the trial have provided compelling evidence that the investigational drug is indeed effective. If the statistical results show that the drug is indeed effective – that is, the treatment is statistically significant – the next step is for clinicians to decide if the treatment is also clinically significant (as noted in Section 3.12.1 we discuss clinical significance later in the book). If the treatment effect is deemed to be both statistically and clinically significant, the study team is likely to decide to move forward to the next study in their clinical development program.

3.16.1 Ethics and the use of placebo controls

At this point, it is appropriate to point out diverging views on the use of placebo control treatment in any clinical trial. Some authors have expressed the view that the comparator should always be an active control if possible – that is, in cases where there is already at least one drug on the market that has been demonstrated to be effective for treating the disease or condition of concern, the comparator should be one of these drugs. This issue is reviewed very effectively by Temple and Ellenberg (2000), and we strongly recommend that you read their paper. We agree with the arguments that they present supporting the use of placebo controls in appropriate circumstances. In addition, ICH Guidance E12A (2000) comments on this issue specifically in the context of the evaluation of efficacy in clinical trials for an investigational antihypertensive drug. It states that, for several important reasons, short-term (defined as 4–12 weeks in duration), blinded, placebo-controlled studies are "essential." It also states that long-term studies (defined as 6 months or more) should also be conducted to demonstrate maintenance of efficacy and to assess long-term safety, and that these trials would typically use an active control.

In this book we have chosen to focus on teaching the computational aspects of statistical analyses by using examples involving designs in which the investigational drug is compared with a placebo in short-term trials. In Section 4.7, we describe two potential measurement scenarios that are possible during a 12-week trial: Taking measurements at baseline and at the end of every 2-week period, and simply taking measurements at baseline and at the end of week 12, the end-of-treatment measure. In this book we use the latter design for the sake of simplicity. We have therefore chosen this form of example because it is ethical as discussed in ICH Guidance E12A, and, as noted in the previous section, a comparative trial using both an investigational drug and a placebo treatment group is the best way to find out if the former is indeed effective.

3.17 The relationship between research questions and study design

Having introduced and discussed research questions in this chapter, the following quotes from authoritative sources emphasize their importance:

> The most critical and difficult prerequisite for a good study is to select an important feasible question to answer. Accomplishing this is primarily a consequence of biological knowledge. (Piantadosi, 2005)
>
> The essence of rational drug development is to ask important questions and answer them with appropriate studies. (ICH Guidance E8, 1997)

Between them, these quotes capture the notion that, once an important research question has been formulated, a "good" and "appropriate" study must be conducted to answer the question. As you have seen already, we provide operational definitions of terms that are used in statistical contexts. Accordingly, Chapter 4 provides operational definitions of the terms "good" and "appropriate" in the context of deciding how best to answer an important research question.

Before that, however, it is informative to consider the second sentence in the quote from Piantadosi (2005) – "Accomplishing this [selecting an important feasible question to answer] is primarily a consequence of biological knowledge." This book discusses the employment of the discipline of Statistics in a particular context, the development of a new drug. It is certainly true that the individual statistical analyses that we teach you can be informatively applied in other areas of investigation, but in this book their application is in the development of a biologically active drug that will influence patients' biology for the better (see Turner, 2007).

3.18   Review

1. What are characteristics of a useful research question?

2. Why is a placebo control used in many clinical trials?

3. When would a placebo control not be used?

4. How do the null and alternate hypotheses relate to the objective of a clinical trial?

5. What form do the null and alternate hypotheses take for a superiority trial with a placebo control?

6. What form do the null and alternate hypotheses take for an equivalence trial with an active control?

3.19   References

Fleming TR, DeMets DL (1996). Surrogate endpoints in clinical trials: are we being misled? *Ann Intern Med* **125**:605–613.

ICH Guidance E8 (1997). *General Consideration of Clinical Trials*. Available at: www.ich.org (accessed July 1 2007).

ICH Guidance E12A (2000). *Principles for Clinical Evaluation of New Antihypertensive Drugs*. Available at: www.ich.org (accessed July 1 2007).

Norgrady T, Weaver DF (2005). *Medicinal Chemistry: A molecular and biochemical approach*, 3rd edn. Oxford: Oxford University Press.

Piantadosi S (2005). *Clinical Trials: A methodologic perspective*, 2nd edn. Chichester: John Wiley & Sons.

Temple R, Ellenberg S (2000). Placebo-controlled trials and active-control trials in the evaluation of new treatments. *Ann Intern Med* **133**:455–463.

Turner JR (2007). *New Drug Development: Design, methodology, and analysis*. Hoboken, NJ: John Wiley & Sons.

4

Study design and experimental methodology

4.1 Introduction

Chapter 3 introduced the central topic of research questions in clinical trials. It also introduced the null and alternate hypotheses. This chapter discusses the relationship between research questions and study design, and shows how optimum experimental methodology is critical to the successful implementation of studies conducted to answer research questions.

Each study in a clinical development program addresses one or more research questions (we noted in the previous chapter that it is a good idea to limit the number of research questions in any given trial). In Chapter 3 we also noted two characteristics that a research question must possess to be considered useful:

- It needs to be specific (precise).
- It needs to be testable.

We can now take this thinking one step further. Formulating a good research question and then fine-tuning it is critical to the potential success of a trial. The research question is the driving force behind the way that the trial will be designed and implemented, because certain trial designs, or study designs, are needed to permit the acquisition of data that can be used successfully to answer the research question. The best research question in the world cannot be answered by the acquisition of inappropriate data via the conduct of an inappropriately designed trial, no matter how well the data are collected.

A useful research question suggests how a study needs to be designed to provide the appropriate information to answer the question. Choosing the best study design to answer the research question is therefore critical. The word "best" in the previous sentence is meaningful because there may be more than one study design that is capable of providing data that enable the question to be addressed and answered, but one of these designs may be more appropriate than the other possibilities.

This occurrence illustrates an important point. It is certainly true that the discipline of Statistics contains precise aspects that provide definite answers in situations where that answer is the only possible correct answer. However, it is also true that the successful practice and implementation of the discipline of Statistics require a considerable amount of well-informed judgment. It is therefore vital that professional statisticians are involved in all aspects of clinical trials. This comment may initially come as somewhat of a surprise: This is because there is a widespread tendency to think of statisticians being involved only at the end of a trial when all the data have been collected. This misperception is as unfortunate as it is widespread. The conduct of a successful trial requires that statisticians are involved from Day 1, which can be thought of as the time when a research team first decides that knowledge about a certain characteristic of the investigational drug is needed, to the end of the entire process of acquiring and disseminating the trial's results. This includes submitting the results from the trial to a regulatory agency (multiple agencies if marketing permission is desired in multiple countries) and publishing the results in a clinical communication for other research scientists and clinicians to read.

This chapter also discusses experimental methodology. As well as employing the best study design to facilitate the collection of data to answer a research question most appropriately and successfully the data acquired for this purpose must be of optimum quality. For example, each and every individual's blood pressure must be measured as accurately as possible every single time that a measurement needs to be made. The appropriate choice of the best study design and the implementation of optimum quality methodology work hand in hand to facilitate the acquisition of optimum quality data with which to answer the research question that led to the clinical trial being conducted.

4.2 Basic principles of study design

At the end of Chapter 3 we noted that we would provide operational definitions of the terms "good" and "appropriate study design" in the context of answering an important research question of biological (clinical) importance. Two more quotes from Piantadosi (2005) and ICH Guidance E8 (1997) are illuminating:

> Conceptual simplicity in design and analysis is a very important feature of good trials . . . . Good trials are usually simple to analyze correctly.

> Piantadosi (2005, p 130)

> Clinical trials should be designed, conducted, and analyzed according to sound scientific principles to achieve their objectives.

> ICH Guidance E8 (1997, p 2)

The first quote provides an excellent operational definition of the term "good" in the context of the design of clinical trials. It also captures a sentiment to which we return time and time again in this book. Study design and statistical analysis "are intimately and inextricably linked: the design of a study determines the analysis that will be used once the data have been collected" (Turner, 2007, p 5). Conceptual simplicity, as Piantadosi (2005) noted, is very important when designing a trial. As design and analysis are intimately linked, conceptual simplicity in design leads to conceptual simplicity in the associated statistical analyses.

Our operational definition of the term "appropriate" in the context of the design of clinical

trials has two aspects, one of which comes from ICH Guidance E8 (1997) as cited earlier: Trials need to be designed, conducted, and analyzed according to sound scientific principles. This chapter discusses the scientific experimental methodology that is appropriate for the design and conduct of trials. The second aspect of our operational definition of the term "appropriate" is that the design employed must be capable of providing the data needed to answer the research question of interest. There are many study designs, each of which is appropriate for providing the data necessary for specifically formulated research questions. A design that cannot possibly provide the data to answer the research question of interest is not appropriate, and the decision not to use that design is therefore clear cut. In some circumstances more than one study design is capable of providing the data needed to answer the research question. In this case the decision as to which one is the most appropriate requires a decision based on an informed judgment, and statisticians must be involved in this decision.

Clinical trials embody several fundamental principles of experimental design (Piantadosi, 2005). Three of these are:

1. replication
2. randomization
3. local control.

4.2.1 Replication

Replication refers to the fact that clinical trials employ more than one individual in each treatment group. The reason for this is that there is considerable variation in how individuals respond to the administration of the same drug, so it is not appropriate to choose only one individual to receive the investigational drug and another to receive the placebo: There is no way of knowing how representative the individuals' responses are of the typical responses of people in general.

Replication allows two important features of individuals' responses to the investigational drug to be assessed. One is just how different their responses are from each other. It might be that all individuals show responses that are pretty close to each other, or that there is a considerable difference between individuals' responses. The second is to evaluate the "typical" response of all the individuals. Both of these features are important assessments in the discipline of Statistics. Chapter 5 talks about these assessments and puts these ideas into statistical language. It also provides operational definitions of the term "typical": We use the plural term "definitions" because the typical response can be operationally defined in several ways, each of which is appropriate in certain circumstances.

4.2.2 Randomization

The goal of randomization is to eliminate bias or, in practical terms, to reduce bias to the greatest extent possible. Bias is the difference between the true value of a particular quantity and an estimate of the quantity obtained from scientific investigation. Various influences can introduce error into our assessment of treatment effects, and these are discussed at various points in the following chapters. At this point we discuss an example of systematic error, or bias.

Randomization involves randomly assigning experimental individuals to one of the treatment groups, the drug treatment group or the placebo treatment group. The premise of randomization is simple: Many potential influences on the drug response of individuals participating in the trial (for example, differences in the heights and weights of participants, differences in metabolic pathways involved in the metabolism of the investigational drug) cannot readily be controlled for. It is therefore important that, to the best of our ability, we take steps to ensure that these characteristics are likely to be equally represented in both treatment groups. If all of the individuals in one treatment group share a characteristic that is not present in any of the individuals in the other treatment group, it is not possible to ascribe differences between the groups to the one influence of central interest, that is, the different treatments received by the two groups. Putting all relatively tall individuals into one treatment group and all relatively short individuals into the other treatment group would be an example of systematic bias. In this

scenario, height would have a direct impact on the formation of the treatment groups and, therefore, if height were to be a source of influence on the blood pressure change demonstrated by individuals, height could be a cause of systematic bias in the results obtained.

The preapproval clinical trials discussed in this book are experimental studies: The data collected comprise a series of observations made under conditions in which the influence of interest, the type of treatment received, is controlled by the research scientist. (The term "experimental" is used here as defined by Piantadosi [2005]. The converse of an experimental study is a nonexperimental study. Nonexperimental studies are often called observational studies, but this term is inadequate, because it does not definitively distinguish between nonexperimental studies and experimental studies, for example, preapproval clinical trials, in which observations are also made. The methodology employed in preapproval clinical trials is experimental: It comprises a series of observations made under conditions in which the influences of interest are controlled by the research scientist. The methodology employed in other types of study can be nonexperimental; the research scientist collects observations but does not exert control over the influences of interest. The term "nonexperimental" is not a relative quality judgment compared with experimental; the nomenclature simply distinguishes different methodological approaches [Turner, 2007].)

There are various types of randomization strategies. The strategy employed in the trials discussed in this book is called simple randomization, which involves assigning treatments to individuals in a completely random way. Other more complex randomization techniques include block randomization, stratified randomization, and cluster randomization: These are not addressed in this book in any detail (see Turner, 2007, for a brief review). Randomization techniques have an important role in clinical research in general and in drug development in particular because they allow for balanced assignment of treatments within strata of interest (stratified randomization), minimize the possibility of a long run of assignments to the same treatment (block randomization), and facilitate the assignment of large groups of individuals to the same treatment (cluster randomization).

4.2.3 Local control

Another important feature of conducting, or running, clinical trials is local control. This topic takes us into the realm of methodology. Tight control on all aspects of methodology – for example, the manner in which the treatments are administered, the manner in which blood pressure measurements are made, and the apparatus used to make these measurements – must be exercised at all investigative sites. As an example, it is not appropriate that blood pressures for all individuals in one treatment group be measured using one strategy and measuring device whereas blood pressures for all individuals in the other treatment group are measured differently. This naïve strategy could bias the results of the study. As noted in Section 4.2.2, an important objective of control in clinical trials is to remove as much error from the results as possible, that is, to reduce potential bias.

Environmental conditions should also be controlled as much as possible. Taking measurements and evaluating some individuals in relatively cold conditions and others in a relatively warmer environment is not recommended. Taking this example further, and considering factors such as ease of access to the investigative site and the general atmosphere (relaxed, frenetic) of the site and its investigators, it is not appropriate to have all individuals in one treatment group enrolled at one investigative site and all individuals in the other treatment group enrolled at a different site.

4.3 A common design in therapeutic exploratory and confirmatory trials

As noted in Section 4.2, there are many study designs that are employed during a clinical

development program. Some of these are typically used in early human pharmacology trials, whereas others are typically used in later therapeutic exploratory and therapeutic confirmatory trials. We discuss one particular study design more than any others, but it must be emphasized that this does not mean that it is more important than other designs. Rather, its employment as our central example allows us to introduce you to statistical methodology and statistical analysis in our chosen way.

The design that is predominantly discussed in this book is the randomized, concurrently controlled, double-blind, parallel group design. The four descriptors in this title – randomized, double-blind, concurrently controlled, and parallel group – identify different aspects of this design. We start with the last two descriptors, parallel group and concurrently controlled, because these capture the fundamental nature of the design. We then discuss the first two descriptors, randomized and double blind.

4.3.1 The concurrently controlled, parallel group design

Individuals participating in a parallel group trial are randomly assigned to one of two or more distinct treatments. Those who are assigned to the same treatment are frequently referred to as a treatment group. While the treatments that these groups receive differ, all groups are treated equally in every other regard, and they complete exactly the same procedures. This parallel activity on the part of the groups of individuals is captured in the term "parallel group design."

The term "concurrently controlled" captures two aspects of this study design. We have already come across the concept that to quantify meaningfully the effect of the investigational drug (that is, the treatment effect), it is necessary to compare the average blood pressure reduction of the group of individuals receiving the investigational drug with the average of those receiving the placebo. The two parallel groups here are the drug treatment group and the placebo treatment group, and the latter functions as the control group. Sometimes this design is called a placebo-controlled parallel group design, because the control employed is a placebo and not another active, marketed drug. This is perfectly valid.

The term "concurrently" refers to the fact that the individuals in the placebo treatment group are participating in the trial at the same time as those in the drug treatment group. This is an important aspect of the study design. If all the individuals in the drug treatment group participated first, followed at some later time by all those in the placebo treatment group, several potential influences could impact the results of the trial. For example, the staff at the investigational sites at which individuals participate in the trial might have changed considerably, and aspects of the overall operation of these sites may have changed. The goal of experimental methodology is to control for all influences other than the type of treatment (drug or placebo) received by individuals, and so having all the individuals in one group participate at one time under one set of conditions and all those in the other group(s) participate at a later time under a potentially different set of conditions is not desirable. (The goal of study protocols is to detail the experimental procedures to be employed during the trial in sufficient detail that they will be executed identically by all research staff at all times. This should therefore minimize the differences just described. However, practical reality sets in here and, in the extreme example employed in the text, the study protocol probably would not be 100% successful.) This point links well with the discussion of local control in Section 4.2.3.

This last point is well acknowledged, and it is unlikely that a trial would not be "concurrently" controlled. Therefore, if the term "placebo controlled" is seen in a published report of a trial, it is almost certainly fair to assume that the trial is concurrently controlled. However, assumption is a dangerous thing, and you should check the details of the trial presented in the report to confirm this.

4.3.2 The crossover design

In contrast to the parallel design, individuals in a crossover design are assigned to receive two or more treatments in a particular sequence. For example, an individual in a crossover study may receive the drug treatment in the first period. Then, after a suitably long washout period during which the individual is off drug, he or she will receive placebo. Other individuals will receive placebo in the first period and then cross over to the drug treatment in the second period. Such a study would be considered a two-period, two-treatment, two-sequence crossover design. Crossover designs may involve a number of treatments, sequences, and periods. In a crossover design, individuals are randomized to treatment sequences, not treatment groups.

The greatest advantage of the crossover design is that individuals receive more than one treatment so that they act as their own controls. This results in more statistical efficiency and therefore smaller sample sizes. Crossover designs can, for this reason, be particularly useful in early pharmacology studies. Another advantage of crossover designs is that they can aid in recruitment of study participants when a serious condition is being treated and they would like to have access to a potentially helpful investigational drug.

Crossover designs also have some disadvantages – one is that their results can be difficult to interpret. As all individuals receive more than one treatment there can be a carryover effect from one or more early periods to subsequent periods, leading to a biased estimate of the treatment effect. When an individual does not contribute data to one of the periods, none of the data can be used in the most straightforward analyses – attributing adverse events or other untoward effects to a single treatment can be difficult. Another disadvantage is that they are not applicable to all therapeutic indications. Crossover trials are ideally suited for indications that are chronic in nature and do not vary in severity over time. For example, studying a new analgesic for migraines may not be feasible because, thankfully, migraines do not occur as frequently or predictably as would be required to evaluate a number of treatments over the course of two or more periods. Crossover designs would be better suited for chronic conditions such as hypercholesterolemia or hypertension. However, having two or more observations from the same individual under different experimental conditions introduces additional complexities (that is, dependence) for statistical analyses. These methods are beyond the scope of this book.

4.3.3 Randomization and the descriptor "randomized"

The topic of randomization was discussed in Section 4.2.2. Any trial that has employed a randomization strategy in its design is called a randomized trial.

4.3.4 Blinding and double-blind trials

We discussed blinding earlier. As a brief recap, making a drug and a placebo look, taste, and smell the same ensures one part of the double blind: It means that individuals do not know which treatment they are receiving. A second component of the blinding process is needed to ensure that the investigators – that is, those administering the treatments – do not know which treatment individuals are receiving. This component necessitates packaging the drug and placebo products at their site of manufacture so that investigators receiving them at the investigational sites cannot tell which is which. A system of codes guarantees that, when the blind is eventually broken once all the data have been acquired, it will be known which treatment each and every individual received.

The importance of double-blind trials can be expressed in both scientific and regulatory terms, with the second being a consequence of the first. These trials are the scientific gold standard, and the results from a trial that is run in a double-blind manner are afforded particular weight by regulatory agencies and clinicians.

4.4 Experimental methodology

Experimental methodology is concerned with all the aspects of implementation and conduct of a study. Experimental methodology and study design work hand in hand to ensure that optimum quality data are collected from which optimum quality answers to the research question can be provided. As we have seen, an appropriate study design must be used to allow the collection of optimum quality data, and we can think of study design as providing the opportunity to collect such data. To take advantage of this opportunity, optimum experimental methodology must be used in the acquisition of the data. Optimum quality methodology is no use if the wrong study design has been employed, and the appropriate study design can lead to optimum quality data only if optimum experimental methodology is employed.

Consider also the data analysis and interpretation that occur once data have been acquired in a trial. First, the appropriate analysis has to be employed as determined by the study design. However, the employment of this analysis alone is not enough to ensure optimum quality answers to the research question. A computationally perfect execution of the appropriate analysis, and the most meaningful interpretation of the results obtained, will not yield optimal answers if the data being analyzed are of less than optimal quality. Therefore, experimental methodology is also of critical importance.

At this point it is worth considering the length of time it takes to run a therapeutic confirmatory clinical trial. Such trials are often conducted as multicenter trials. Although the total numbers of individuals who participate in trials vary, we noted earlier that a typical number for a therapeutic confirmatory trial is 3000–5000 individuals. Each of these individuals needs to have the disease or condition of interest. It may be that 50 investigational sites are needed to enroll the total number of individuals needed for the trial. Imagine a hypothetical scenario where 5000 individuals are recruited at 50 sites, with the typical number of individuals per site at around 100 (in reality, the number of individuals recruited at each of the sites might differ considerably). Imagine also that the treatment length employed in this trial is 12 weeks. That is, investigational site 01 recruits a total of 100 individuals, and each individual receives either the investigational drug or the placebo for a period of 12 weeks.

The question of interest is: How long does it take to complete the trial? Although the answer "12 weeks" tends to come to mind when first thinking about this, the answer is that it will almost certainly take much longer than that because not all of the 100 individuals will start their participation in the trial on the same day. They will be recruited into the trial, and hence start participation in the trial, in a staggered manner. It is therefore quite possible that the last of the 100 individuals might start his or her 12-week participation months (and possibly years) after the first. This will likely be true at all the investigational sites. The expression "first participant first visit to last participant last visit" is often used to describe the length of the entire trial.

In addition to giving you a feeling for how long it takes to run real-life trials, we mention this point because it emphasizes that it is essential that methodological considerations receive constant vigilance in all studies because some trials can last several years.

4.5 Why are we interested in blood pressure?

The domain of experimental methodology embraces many aspects of conducting a trial, and we do not discuss the vast majority in this book. However, it is important to make you aware of the need for optimum quality methodology, and you can learn more about this from other sources: In particular we recommend Piantadosi (2005). Our discussions focus on one aspect of methodology that is directly relevant to a central theme of this book, namely the measurement of blood pressure. Before discussing this topic, however, it is worth considering why we want to develop drugs that lower blood pressure in the first place, and why optimum quality blood pressure measurements are therefore critical.

4.5.1 Clinically relevant observations

It is possible to make all sorts of observations about people. For example, some are tall, some are short, some have blonde hair, some have dark hair, some love dogs, some love cats, some have relatively high blood pressure, and some have relatively low blood pressure. In drug development we are interested in clinically relevant observations and in making these observations during a trial. (Recall the definition of experimental studies presented earlier: In experimental studies, observations are made when the influence of interest is under the control of the researcher.) In the trials discussed in this book, we are interested in observing (measuring) blood pressure for the duration of individuals' participation in the trial with the ultimate goal of assessing the investigational drug's treatment effect, that is, how much more the investigational drug lowers blood pressure than a placebo. Therefore, the question of interest here is: Why is blood pressure a clinically relevant observation? This takes us into the realm of surrogate endpoints.

4.5.2 Surrogate endpoints

Two clinical endpoints of particular relevance are morbidity and mortality: Morbidity can lessen quality of life and make mortality more likely, and mortality speaks for itself. Not surprisingly, pharmacotherapy (along with other medical interventions) is concerned with reducing both these clinical endpoints. However, the development of morbidity can be prolonged, and the impact of drug therapy on mortality during a clinical trial can be very difficult to evaluate. As it is very unlikely that many individuals will die during (most) clinical trials, the difference in death rates between the drug treatment group and the placebo treatment group is likely to be very small, and quite possibly zero. (Mortality is unfortunately not uncommon in clinical trials in some therapeutic areas and in trials involving very ill or terminally ill patients. On these occasions, it may well be possible to detect the beneficial influence of an investigational drug by focusing on the clinical endpoint of mortality.)

It therefore becomes important in clinical trials to evaluate the influence of the investigational drug on other endpoints of relevance. These can be termed "clinically relevant endpoints" or "surrogate endpoints." Surrogate endpoints are biomarkers or other indicators that substitute for the clinical endpoint by predicting its likely behavior. Justification for the choice of these endpoints is of fundamental importance: The endpoint chosen as the surrogate needs to represent the clinical endpoint in a meaningful manner. How can this be demonstrated? The following are characteristics of meaningful and useful surrogate endpoints (see Oliver and Webb, 2003; Machin and Campbell, 2005):

- Biological plausibility: A detailed knowledge of the pathophysiology of the disease or condition of interest is helpful, as is demonstration that the surrogate endpoint of interest in the clinical trial is on the causal pathway to the clinical endpoint of primary interest.
- A detailed knowledge of the drug's mechanism of action: Coupled with similar knowledge of the pathophysiology of the disease or condition of interest, this can provide a solid basis for believing that the drug will be beneficial. (A drug can certainly be clinically beneficial even if we do not know its mechanism of action, but this does not mitigate the point made here in the context of good surrogate endpoints.)

- The surrogate endpoint predicts the clinical endpoint consistently and independently.
- They are particularly useful in cases where the clinical endpoints occur after long periods.

The choice of endpoints used in studies of new therapies may evolve over time as knowledge is gained about the natural history of the disease or the reliability of surrogate endpoints. Endpoints used to evaluate the benefits of new drugs are provided in Table 4.1 for a number of diseases. Many diseases are associated with numerous medical conditions of consequence to the patient (for example, pain and disability resulting from rheumatoid arthritis), which may be the target for a particular new therapy.

Fleming and DeMets (1996) suggested that the use of surrogate endpoints is most helpful in early therapeutic exploratory studies to study activity and decide if larger, more definitive studies are warranted. Establishing the acceptability of a surrogate endpoint is a difficult undertaking. Fleming and DeMets (1996) cautioned about the use of surrogate endpoints in Phase III confirmatory trials. One frequently cited example (CAST Investigators 1989, 1992) of a misleading surrogate endpoint is from the Cardiac Arrhythmia Suppression Trial (CAST). Ventricular arrhythmia has been established as a risk factor for sudden death. In this study, three drugs that had been approved for the control of arrhythmias (encainide, flecainide, and moricizine) were evaluated for their effect on mortality among individuals with myocardial infarction and ventricular arrhythmia. The results from this study were surprising. All three drugs were associated with higher risks of death than placebo. Hence the benefit of these drugs with respect to arrhythmia did not extend to the underlying clinical endpoint.

We are interested in high blood pressure (hypertension) because of our interest in cardiovascular disease, a leading cause of morbidity and mortality. High blood pressure is a meaningful and useful cardiovascular surrogate endpoint because it is well established that chronic high blood pressure causes cardiovascular and cerebrovascular events.

Table 4.1   Examples of endpoints used in clinical trials of experimental drugs

Disease	Example endpoints
Cancer[a]	Survival
	Objective response (reduction in tumor size for a minimum amount of time)
	Time to progression of cancer symptoms
Rheumatoid arthritis[b]	Improvement in signs and symptoms
	Radiological progression of disease
Uncomplicated urinary tract infection[c]	Eradication of bacterial pathogen
Hypertension[d]	Change from baseline SBP
Postmenopausal osteoporosis[e]	Bone mineral density
	Bone fractures

[a]Food and Drug Administration (US Department of Health and Human Services or DHHS, FDA, 2007).
[b]Food and Drug Administration (DHHS, FDA, 1999).
[c]Food and Drug Administration (DHHS, FDA, 1998).
[d]ICH Guidance E12A (2000).
[e]Food and Drug Administration (DHHS, FDA, 1994).

4.6 Uniformity of blood pressure measurement

One method of measuring blood pressure is to use a stethoscope and a sphygmomanometer; you may have experienced this in your doctor's clinic/office. Other methods include the use of various automated devices. Although we do not go into these in detail here, the important point is that considerable attention must be paid to methodological considerations. It is important that the same measurement technique be used at all the investigational sites in a trial, and that time is taken before the trial starts to train every site in the correct use of whichever measuring device is chosen. This might happen at an investigators' meeting or a central meeting of all principal investigators held before the start of the trial to address procedural consistency across sites. It is also important that every measurement at each site be made correctly, and that any routine calibration of the measurement device is conducted as mandated.

4.7 Measuring change in blood pressure over time

As antihypertensive drugs are intended to lower blood pressure, their evaluation in clinical trials requires at least two measurements. One of these is an initial measurement, typically called a baseline measurement, and the other is a measurement some time later, such as at the end of the treatment phase (the end-of-treatment measurement). These two measurements allow us to calculate a change score that represents the change in blood pressure from the start to the end of the treatment phase. Change scores can be calculated in several ways. One of these, and the method that is used in all of the examples in this book, is simply to calculate the arithmetic difference between each individual's baseline measurement and his or her end-of-treatment measurement.

It is also possible that blood pressure may be measured more than twice in a trial. If the treatment period is 12 weeks long, measurements might be taken, for example, at baseline, week 2, week 4, week 6, week 8, week 10, and week 12 (end of treatment). By taking several measurements, the change across the treatment phase can be examined in more detail. Suppose that an individual's SBP decreases by 20 mmHg from baseline to end of treatment. There are many possible patterns of change across time here. For example, most of the individual's decrease in blood pressure could happen in the first few weeks, it could decrease steadily across the 12 weeks, or most of the decrease could occur during the last few weeks. Although this level of analysis is of interest in some trials, we focus on change scores calculated by using two measurements, the baseline measurement and the end-of-treatment measurement.

4.8 The clinical study protocol

When the clinical research team has decided on their research question, and the appropriate study design and methodology to acquire optimum quality data with which to answer this question, all this information needs to be documented. The clinical study protocol is the document that is written for this purpose. Chow and Chang (2007, p 1) noted that the study protocol is "the most important document in clinical trials, since it ensures the quality and integrity of the clinical investigation in terms of its planning, execution, conduct, and the analysis of the data."

The study protocol is a comprehensive plan of action that contains information concerning the goals of the study, details of individual recruitment, details of safety monitoring, and all aspects of design, methodology, and analysis. Input is therefore required, for example, from clinical scientists, medical safety officers, study managers, data managers, and statisticians. Consequently, although one clinical scientist or medical writer may take primary responsibility for its preparation, many members of the study team make critical contributions to it.

The following are some of the fundamental components in a study protocol for a therapeutic confirmatory trial for an investigational antihypertensive drug:

- How the disease or condition of interest will be diagnosed, that is, participating individuals need to be diagnosed as hypertensive. The protocol will state the precise criteria that constitute high blood pressure in this particular study, and how and by whom determining measurements will be taken.

- Inclusion and exclusion criteria: These provide detailed criteria for individual eligibility for participation in the trial. These eligibility criteria can often represent a compromise among several perspectives, such as regulatory, medical, and logistical. For example, the most valuable information about the benefits of the new treatment will be obtained from a group of study individuals who are most representative of the patients to whom the drug will be prescribed. On the other hand, "real world" patients may be taking a number of medications or have concurrent illnesses that may confound the ability to evaluate the investigational treatment. It may be logistically impossible to study individuals with poor reading abilities because they will not comply with study procedures. Eligibility criteria define the study population, a term that is discussed in greater detail in Chapter 5.

- The primary objective and any secondary objectives (it is a very good idea to limit the number of objectives): These must be stated precisely.

- Measures of safety: The criteria to be used to evaluate safety are provided. These will typically include adverse events, clinical laboratory assays, electrocardiograms (ECGs), vital signs, and physical examinations.

- Measures of efficacy: The criteria to be used to determine efficacy are provided. Decrease in blood pressure will be the primary measurement of interest. Also, it may be the case that average decreases of a certain magnitude are required for the investigational drug to be deemed effective.

- Drug treatment schedule: Route of administration, dosage, and dosing regimen are detailed. This information is also provided for the control treatment.

- The statistical analyses that will be used once the data have been acquired. The precise analytical strategy needs to be detailed, here and/or in an associated statistical analysis plan.

A study protocol is often supplemented with another very important document called the statistical analysis plan (sometimes referred to by similar names such as a data analysis plan or reporting analysis plan). The statistical analysis plan often supplements a study protocol by providing a very detailed account of the analyses that will be conducted at the completion of data acquisition. The statistical analysis plan should be written in conjunction with (and at the same time as) the protocol, but in reality this does not always happen. At the very least it should be finalized before the statistical analysis and breaking of the blind. In many instances (for example, confirmatory trials) it may be helpful to submit the final statistical analysis plan to the appropriate regulatory authorities for their input.

4.9   Review

1. What is the importance of replication, randomization, and local control in experimental design?

2. Define the following aspects of clinical trial study design:

   (a) double blind

   (b) concurrent control

   (c) parallel group.

3. What is the difference between a clinical endpoint and a surrogate endpoint?

4. What information is included in a study protocol?

4.10   References

Cardiac Arrhythmia Suppression Trial Investigators (1989). Preliminary report: Effect of encainide and fleicanide on mortality in a randomized trial of arrhythmia suppression after myocardial infarction. *N Engl J Med* **321**:406–412.

Cardiac Arrhythmia Suppression Trial Investigators (1992). Effect of the antiarrhythmic agent moricizine on survival after myocardial infarction. *N Engl J Med* **327**:227–233.

Chow S-C, Chang M (2007). *Adaptive Design Methods in Clinical Trials*. Boca Raton, FL: Chapman & Hall/CRC.

Fleming TR, DeMets DL (1996). Surrogate end points in clinical trials: are we being misled? *Ann Intern Med* **125**:605–613.

ICH Guidance E8 (1997). *General Consideration of Clinical Trials*. Available at: www.ich.org (accessed July 1 2007).

ICH Guidance E12A (2000). *Principles for Clinical Evaluation of New Antihypertensive Drugs*. Available at: www.ich.org (accessed July 1 2007).

Machin D, Campbell MJ (2005). *Design of Studies for Medical Research*. Chichester: John Wiley & Sons.

Oliver JJ, Webb DJ (2003). Surrogate endpoints. In: Wilkins MR (ed.), *Experimental Therapeutics*. Boca Raton, FL: Taylor & Francis Group, 145–165.

Piantadosi S (2005). *Clinical Trials: A methodologic perspective*, 2nd edn. Chichester: John Wiley & Sons.

Turner JR (2007). *New Drug Development: Design, methodology, and analysis*. Hoboken, NJ: John Wiley & Sons.

US Department of Health and Human Services, Food and Drug Administration (1998). *Providing Clinical Evidence of Effectiveness for Human Drug and Biological Products*. Available from www.fda.gov (accessed July 1 2007).

US Department of Health and Human Services, Food and Drug Administration (2007). *Challenge and Opportunity on the Critical Path to New Medical Products*. Available from www.fda.gov (accessed July 1 2007).

5

Data, central tendency, and variation

5.1 Introduction

Selecting an appropriate study design to best address the study objectives is just the first step towards answering the questions of interest. When most people think about Statistics they are probably thinking about data. Unfortunately, statisticians are not infrequently assigned the nickname "number crunchers," a name that accentuates the numerical aspects of the use of statistics but completely ignores the design, methodology, and interpretation aspects of the discipline of Statistics. Number crunching (and computational accuracy) is certainly a necessary component of Statistics, but it is important to bear in mind that it is far from sufficient.

Having reviewed the concepts of study design we now turn our attention to data. We are interested in various questions relating to data, such as: What are data? How might we classify different types of data? How are data used to answer questions arising during clinical trials? This last question is, perhaps, the most important one for this book. We start to answer it first in conceptual terms before turning our attention to more specific points.

5.2 Populations and samples

It is of considerable interest in new drug development to assess the effects of a drug in a particular population, the population containing individuals who may be prescribed the drug if and when it is approved. This population is known as the target population. Not all the adults in the USA and the UK would be ideal candidates for a therapeutic confirmatory trial because of the presence of other conditions or the use of other drugs, or for logistical reasons because they do not live close enough to a center that participates in clinical studies. Therefore, another population of interest is all adults in the USA and the UK who meet the specific eligibility criteria (including a precise definition of hypertensive) of a study. This group of individuals is considered the study population.

As study populations are often very large, however, it is not possible to administer the drug to every member of the population, so a sample from the study population is chosen and the effects of the drug in that sample are determined in a clinical study. In clinical trials, samples are typically considered or assumed to be simple random samples from the study population. A simple random sample is a sample in which each observational unit (for example, study participant) has the same probability of selection from the population. In other fields in which Statistics are used (most notably population surveys) samples need not be selected in this manner.

A clinical trial provides numerical statements of the drug's effects in the specific sample employed, but the investigator and the regulatory agency are really interested in the drug's (likely) effect in the whole population. Therefore, statistical procedures have been developed to allow numerical assessments of the likely effects in the study population based on the evidence collected from the sample that participated in the trial.

There are important limitations to the usefulness of generalizing the effects from a series of clinical trials to the patient population as a whole. The population from which clinical trial participants are sampled, the study population, may not truly be representative of the population (the target population) about which we would like to make conclusions. The target population may be sicker, have greater needs for concomitant medications, and have more chronic illnesses than the relatively homogeneous population from which the study sample arose. This point is well expressed by Senn (1997, p 28):

> In a clinical trial the primary formal objective is to assess what effects the treatments *did* have on the patients studied in order to say what effects they *may* have. To say what effects the treatments *will* have or even *will probably* have, requires arguments which go well beyond any formal examination of the data.

The following discussions address statistical methods that are applied to data from a sample of study participants with the objective of making an inference about the study population. By including relevant populations in studies and carefully documenting the methodology that gave rise to the study sample in regulatory documents and clinical communications, reviewers and physicians can judge for themselves the extent to which the results from the study can be inferred to the clinical situation.

5.3 Measurement scales

Data are anything that is measured. Examples of data encountered in clinical studies include height, weight, plasma concentration of a drug in a sample, days from the start of a study to a particular adverse event, the presence or absence of a characteristic of interest, and the gender of a study participant. Some of these examples may be surprising because we often think of data as numbers, but data may also be non-numeric.

Data can generally be classified into one of the following scales of measurement: nominal, ordinal, interval, or ratio.

5.3.1 Nominal scale

Nominal measurement scales involve names of characteristics. Characteristics frequently encountered in clinical studies that are measured on the nominal scale include gender (female or male), occurrence or not of an adverse event, a coded adverse event (for example, headache, asthenia, nausea), and race or ethnicity. Data measured on a nominal scale cannot be operated on arithmetically. We could not, for example, compare the values of females and males and come up with a meaningful result. An important caution is worth noting at this point. It is not uncommon to encounter data measured on the nominal scale to be represented as numbers or codes in electronic databases. An example would be when, in a database of a clinical study, the presence or absence of an adverse event (for example, headache) is represented as 0 (absent) or 1 (present). Before we undertake a statistical analysis of any sort it is necessary to understand fully the nature of the data.

5.3.2 Ordinal scale

This scale is best defined as one in which an ordering of values can be assigned. Examples of data from clinical studies measured on an ordinal scale include: severity of an adverse event classified as mild, moderate, or severe; age categorized as < 65, 65–70, 71–75, and > 75 years. The ordinal nature of the measurement scales means that we can say that a mild headache is less severe than a moderate headache, which is less severe than a severe headache. However, we cannot say that the difference between mild and moderate is the same as the difference between moderate and severe.

5.3.3 Interval scale

In contrast, differences between any two values measured on the interval scale do have meaning. Temperature measured on the Celsius or Fahrenheit scale is an example of an interval scale. For example, the difference between 32°F and 64°F is the same as the difference between 64°F and 96°F. On the interval scale, a value of zero is not a true zero (meaning absence of heat) because a value of $-1°F$ is colder still. We can perform addition and subtraction on interval scaled data but, because the value of zero is meaningless, we cannot perform multiplication or division and obtain a meaningful result.

5.3.4 Ratio scale

Data measured on the ratio scale have all of the characteristics of interval scaled data with the exception that, in this case, a value of zero does represent a true zero. Height, which is measured on the ratio scale, has a true zero. A height of zero centimeters or inches means that there is no height. Likewise, a weight of zero kilograms or pounds means that there is no weight. An important characteristic of ratio scaled data is that the ratio of two values can be computed. For example, a study participant who weighs 220 pounds weighs twice as much as one who weighs 110 pounds.

The importance of identifying these scales of measurement is that not all statistical analysis approaches are appropriate for each of them. It is important to note that, although a particular characteristic may be measured on one scale, it may be reported using another. For example, age at the time of study entry may be measured on a ratio scale, but reported using an ordinal scale (for example, < 25, 25–64, > 64 years).

5.4 Random variables

Many individuals are involved in clinical trials and a number of characteristics of these participants are recorded. As characteristics such as age, systolic blood pressure, and gender can vary from individual to individual, they are generally classified as random variables (or, simply, variables). A common convention in statistics is to represent a particular random variable as a letter, such as x. A particular realization, or value, of a random variable for a particular individual (participant i in this case) is often denoted using a subscript such as x_i. We use these conventions in this chapter and throughout the text.

5.5 Displaying the frequency of values of a random variable

Since a random variable such as age can take on a number of values for a group of study participants it is of interest to know something about the relative frequency of each value. The relative frequency is the count of the number of observations with a specific value (for example, the number of 30-year-old participants) divided by the total number in the sample. An informative first step in a statistical analysis is to examine characteristics of the relative frequency of values of the random variable of interest, which can also be called the empirical distribution of the random variable. This knowledge is an essential part of selecting the most appropriate statistical analysis. Statistical software packages offer a number of methods to describe the relative frequency of values including tabular frequency displays, dot plots, relative frequency histograms, and stem-and-leaf plots.

An example of a frequency table is provided in Table 5.1, in which the frequency of age values in a sample of 100 study participants is displayed. The left-hand column is the value of age for which frequency information is provided. The column labeled "Frequency" is the count of the number of participants with the particular value of age. The column "Percentage" is the count of the number of participants with the particular value of age divided by the total number of observations in the sample and multiplied by 100 to express this figure as a percentage of the total. The next column "Cumulative frequency" represents the total count of age values less than or equal to the age value on a certain row. Similarly, "Cumulative percentage" is the cumulative frequency count of age values as a percentage of the total. As seen in Table 5.1 there is one 40-year-old individual (1% of the total) and there are five who are 40 and younger (5% of the total). A frequency table allows us to see how common all values are, but it can be difficult to see whether or not certain values tend to cluster together.

Another helpful way of displaying the relative frequency of observed values is to group values into equally spaced intervals and display the

Table 5.1   Frequency table of age values

Age (years)	Frequency	Percentage	Cumulative frequency	Cumulative percentage
31	1	1.00	1	1.00
35	1	1.00	2	2.00
39	2	2.00	4	4.00
40	1	1.00	5	5.00
43	3	3.00	8	8.00
45	1	1.00	9	9.00
48	2	2.00	11	11.00
49	4	4.00	15	15.00
50	4	4.00	19	19.00
51	2	2.00	21	21.00
52	2	2.00	23	23.00
53	2	2.00	25	25.00
55	3	3.00	28	28.00
57	3	3.00	31	31.00
58	3	3.00	34	34.00
59	5	5.00	39	39.00
60	2	2.00	41	41.00
61	6	6.00	47	47.00
62	4	4.00	51	51.00
63	2	2.00	53	53.00
64	1	1.00	54	54.00
65	1	1.00	55	55.00
66	3	3.00	58	58.00
67	4	4.00	62	62.00
68	3	3.00	65	65.00
69	2	2.00	67	67.00
70	3	3.00	70	70.00
71	4	4.00	74	74.00
72	3	3.00	77	77.00
73	4	4.00	81	81.00
74	1	1.00	82	82.00
75	3	3.00	85	85.00
76	1	1.00	86	86.00
77	3	3.00	89	89.00
78	3	3.00	92	92.00
79	1	1.00	93	93.00
80	2	2.00	95	95.00
81	2	2.00	97	97.00
82	1	1.00	98	98.00
83	1	1.00	99	99.00
88	1	1.00	100	100.00

resulting frequency in a histogram. There is no single width of each interval, or bin, that can be recommended. However, one might consider the quantity W as a starting point for the width:

$$W = \frac{\text{Maximum value} - \text{Minimum value}}{n}$$

It is typically desirable to have at least 5 bins and no more than 10, although less or more may be informative. Once the number and width of the bins have been determined the next step is to count the number of observations that fall into each interval and display the frequency of each grouping with contiguous bars. It is important that the intervals or bins are defined such that each observation can be assigned to only one interval. Using the 100 age values in the previous example, a histogram, displayed in Figure 5.1, has been constructed from the following categories: 30–39, 40–49, 50–59, 60–69, 70–79, 80–89. Note that each bar is centered over the interval midpoint. For example, the bar centered at 54.5 represents the relative frequency of age values in the interval 50–59.

By grouping the 100 age values (that is, the 100 participants in the indicated age groups) into categories, much of the detail evident in Table 5.1 has been lost. A display that retains the graphical nature of the histogram and the detail of the tabular frequency is a stem-and-leaf plot. A stem-and-leaf plot displays the first significant digit of the value of random variable as a "stem" and the subsequent significant digit as a "leaf." The stems are ordered from lowest to highest so that the relative frequency of each value can be

surmised in one concise display. A stem-and-leaf plot of 100 individuals' age values is provided in Figure 5.2. To assist in your interpretation of this display, the youngest participant in this study was 31, the oldest was 88, and there were four 50 year olds.

The shape of the overall distribution in this case could be called somewhat bell shaped, as characterized by relatively fewer observations at either extreme than in the middle. Some distributions are symmetric, whereas others are asymmetric. Those that are asymmetric are said to be skewed. If fewer observations are at the upper end of the distribution (that is, the long tail is toward the right or higher values) the distribution's shape is called positively skewed. If the long tail is pointing toward the left, or lower values, the distribution is called negatively skewed. In the case of this particular example, turning Figure 5.2 on its side so it has lower values on the left reveals that the distribution of age values is somewhat negatively skewed. Although the stem-and-leaf display in Figure 5.2 has more detail (that is, more bins) than the histogram in Figure 5.1, the histogram retains the basic shape elements of the stem-and-leaf display.

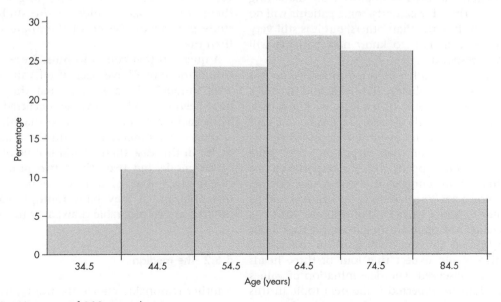

Figure 5.1   Histogram of 100 age values

3	1
3	599
4	0333
4	5889999
5	0000112233
5	55577788899999
6	001111112222334
6	5666777788899
7	000111122233334
7	55567778889
8	001123
8	8

Figure 5.2   Stem-and-leaf display of 100 age values

5.6 Central tendency

One fundamental idea in the development of new pharmaceutical products is that pharmaceutical companies (sponsors) would like to demonstrate that participants who receive a test treatment tend to fare better than those who receive some alternate therapy. This alternate therapy could be an inactive control (a placebo) or some other approved therapy (an active control). We said "tend to fare better" because participants will not all respond in the same way to the same test treatment. It is also true that, if and when the drug is approved for marketing and prescribed for patients, some patients will do better on the drug than others, but it is still very useful to clinicians to know how patients will tend to respond.

When we flip a fair coin ten times, we do not always expect to observe five heads and five tails. If we do several series of ten flips, we know that, by chance, we will observe six heads and four tails sometimes, and even more lopsided results would not be all that surprising. The same phenomenon happens with the response to test treatments in clinical studies. When doctors prescribe a new medicine to a patient it would be helpful to know what kind of response could be expected. Although we might expect that a fair coin flipped ten times will result in five heads, we also would expect that four or three heads could be observed. The determination of values that might be expected is the next topic in this chapter, that is, measures of central tendency.

Once we have assembled individual observations in a sample from a clinical study, our ability to understand the nature of those observations as a whole is limited by our ability to synthesize several disparate pieces of observation into an overall impression. Imagine that you have observed the following 10 observations of age of study participants in an early exploratory therapeutic clinical trial: 45, 62, 32, 38, 77, 28, 25, 62, 41, and 50.

Regulatory authorities are concerned about how well study participants match those in the general population of patients with the condition. How might such a question be answered? There are several strategies here.

5.6.1 The mode

One possible way to answer this question is to report that the most common value of age is 62. There are two such observations with this value of age. This measure of central tendency is known as the mode. The mode is most commonly used with non-numeric data (for example, most of the study participants were female), but it may also be useful for numeric data if there are only a few unique values. Unfortunately, the choice of the mode as the typical value in this case is a little misleading. Although there are two 62-year-olds in the study, most study participants (seven of them) are younger than that.

A question that comes to mind here is: What would the mode have been if all values of age were unique? The answer is that there would have been no mode – all values occurred equally as frequently. Likewise, suppose that there had also been two observations with the value of age of 32: In this case there would not be one value of the mode, but two. These two properties of the mode – that is, it is undefined in some instances and it may have multiple values in others – are considerable drawbacks to its use.

5.6.2 The median

Another reasonable choice for the typical value of age would be the value of age that is right in the middle of all values. This middle value is called the median. Citing the median would ensure that there were as many participants younger than the typical value as there were participants older. In this case, as there are 10 values there is no single middle value because there are an even number of values. The fifth and sixth greatest values of age are 41 and 45. To obtain the median value with an even number of observations, we simply split the difference between the two middle values. In this case the median is calculated as:

$$\frac{(41 + 45)}{2} = 43.$$

A quick check to know that we got it right is to see that exactly 5 observations are less than 43 and exactly 5 observations are greater than 43. When there is an odd number of observations, the median is the value of the middle observation after ordering them from the smallest to the largest. Unlike the mode, the median for a set of observations is unique: There is only one value and it is always defined.

5.6.3 The arithmetic mean

The last measure of central tendency that we consider is the most commonly encountered. The arithmetic mean is the sum of the individual observations divided by the total number of observations. Using mathematical notation the mean is calculated as:

$$\bar{x} = \frac{\sum_{i=1}^{n} x_i}{n}$$

where Σ stands for the addition of the values of each observation in the sample (n of them), that is:

$$\sum_{i=1}^{n} x_i = x_1 + x_2 + \ldots + x_n.$$

For our sample of 10 values of age, the mean is 46 (verification of this calculation is left to you). The arithmetic mean, commonly called the average, is the value that balances the weight of the distribution.

Some noteworthy characteristics of the mean are that, like the median, it is unique and always defined for a set of observations. However, the mean is sensitive to extreme observations – that is, if there is a single observation that is much higher or lower than the rest, the mean will be heavily influenced by that single observation.

One of the primary goals of Statistics is to use data from a sample to estimate an unknown quantity from an underlying population, called a population parameter. In general, we typically use the arithmetic mean as the measure of central tendency of choice because the sample mean is an unbiased estimator of the population mean, typically represented by the symbol μ. The main conceptual point about unbiased estimators is that they come closer to estimating the true population parameter, in this case the population mean, than biased estimators. When extreme observations influence the value of the mean such that it really is not representative of a typical value, use of the median is recommended as a measure of central tendency.

Returning to the query posed by the regulatory authorities, we came up with the following responses. The typical value of age in our sample using the mode is 62, using the median is 43, and using the mean is 46. Suppose that the authorities are satisfied with that response initially and then pose the following question. "So was your study among middle-aged adults with the condition?" You refer once again to the list of 10 observations and realize that it is not that simple. There actually were some younger adults in your study and it would be ideal to quantify the extent to which the mean does not tell the whole story. It is no surprise that not all values of age in the study are the same. Fortunately there are ways to quantify the extent to which they vary from participant to participant.

5.7 Dispersion

Dispersion refers to the variety or "spread" of individual observations in a sample. As for central tendency there are various measures of dispersion.

5.7.1 The range

A quick way to reflect the variety of values in a sample is to cite the lowest and highest values, the minimum and maximum. Calculating the difference between these two (calculated as maximum minus minimum) yields a value called the range:

$$Range = x_{max} - x_{min}.$$

Although the range is informative in that it conveys the difference between the two most extreme values, it does have a deficiency: It really does not adequately reflect the extent to which observations are similar or dissimilar. Imagine a study in which 99 of the 100 participants are aged between 20 years and 29 years, and one is 60 years old. The range is quite large (40 years), but the value of this range does not give any indication about how close together most age values in the sample are to each other.

5.7.2 The variance

In contrast, the variance of a sample does indicate how close together most values in a sample are. The sample variance is calculated as the sum of squared deviations of each observation from the sample mean divided by the sample size minus 1:

$$s^2 = \frac{\sum_{i=1}^{n} (x_i - \bar{x})^2}{n - 1}.$$

A calculation of this sort ensures that the measure of dispersion is positive (squaring the deviations ensures that) and dividing by $(n - 1)$ results in a quantity that represents an average of sorts. The sample variance is the "typical" or "average" squared deviation of observations from the sample mean. The use of the $(n - 1)$ in the denominator may seem confusing, but the reason why this is done is that calculating the sample variance in this manner yields an unbiased estimator of the population variance, which is represented by the symbol σ^2. (The exact mathematical demonstration that s^2 is an unbiased estimator of σ^2 is beyond the scope of this text.)

5.7.3 The standard deviation

Although very useful in some ways, the sample variance has the unfortunate characteristic that it is expressed in terms of squared units that are typically nonsensical. From our earlier example of 10 ages, we would calculate the sample variance as 282 "squared years." To overcome the significant drawback of squared units we can take the square root of the sample variance to obtain the standard deviation (s):

$$s = \sqrt{s^2}.$$

The standard deviation represents an average (of sorts) deviation of each observation from the sample mean. Again, the only reason why we do not call this quantity the average deviation without qualification is that there really are n deviations from the sample mean, but the standard deviation is calculated using the denominator of $(n - 1)$ instead of n. The sample standard deviation is an unbiased estimator of the population standard deviation. For our previous example of 10 age values, the value of the sample standard deviation is 16.8 years (we leave confirmation of this to you).

The sample standard deviation captures a great deal of information about the spread of the data. The value of the standard deviation is helpful across a number of datasets because of the results of what is called Tchebysheff's theorem. A simple way of thinking of Tchebysheff's theorem is that most values lie close to the sample mean. According to this theorem, no matter what the shape of the distribution is:

- 25% ($\frac{1}{4} = \frac{1}{2^2}$) or less of observations lie outside of 2 standard deviations away from the mean
- 11% ($\frac{1}{9} = \frac{1}{3^2}$) or less of observations lie outside of 3 standard deviations away from the mean
- 6% ($\frac{1}{16} = \frac{1}{4^2}$) or less of observations lie outside of 4 standard deviations away from the mean.

Applying Tchebysheff's theorem to our sample of 10 ages, we can say to the regulatory agency that the study really is not just among middle-aged adults.

5.7.4 Variability and the coefficient of variation

A commonly asked question among investigators is: How do I know if I have a lot of or a little variability in my study results? There is no straightforward answer to this question: The magnitude of the variance (or synonymously the standard deviation) can be called a lot or a little only when it is compared with some other quantity – that is, it is relative.

In Chapter 11 we discuss an analytical strategy called analysis of variance (ANOVA) in which one variance is compared with another. For now, another useful measure of relative dispersion is the coefficient of variation (CV), calculated as the ratio of the sample standard deviation to the sample mean:

$$CV = \frac{s}{\bar{x}}.$$

The coefficient of variation is useful when comparing the magnitude of variability between two or more different random variables.

To illustrate the coefficient of variation, consider the following (extremely simple and artificial) example. Imagine that there are two random variables in an early therapeutic exploratory clinical trial. One random variable is pulse (ranging from 50 to 80) and the other is age, which in this case is pulse minus 20. We can see that, from this example, values of pulse and age are just as disperse, but what differs between them is the mean. Hence, when we calculate the standard deviation, one random variable will appear to have more or less dispersion, but, after re-scaling the standard deviation with the sample mean, the measure of dispersion is the same.

5.7.5 Percentiles

Another descriptive measure of variability or dispersion is the percentile. The Pth percentile is the value of the random variable, $X = X_{\frac{P}{100}}$, such that:

- $P\%$ of values of X are $\leq X_{\frac{P}{100}}$
- $100 - P\%$ of values of X are $> X_{\frac{P}{100}}$.

For example, the 75th percentile is the value of X below which 75% of the values lie and above which 25% lie. The 50th percentile is synonymous with the median. Likewise the 25th percentile is the value of X below which 25% of the values lie and above which 75% lie. The difference between the 75th and 25th percentiles is called the interquartile range, which can be a useful measure of dispersion when the distribution of the random variable is heavily skewed or asymmetric.

5.8 Tabular displays of summary statistics of central tendency and dispersion

As we discuss in more detail in Chapter 6, one of the primary goals of studies in a clinical development program is to describe the effect that the test treatment had on study participants so that some inference can be made about the drug's effects on patients who may receive the drug in the future. Summary descriptive statistics of central tendency and dispersion give us better understanding of the typical effect of the test treatment and how varied participants' responses were.

In our experience the mean and the standard deviation are the most commonly used summary statistics for these purposes. However, other measures can be useful to reviewers when interpreting data from clinical studies. We encourage researchers to present the following statistics: The sample size, the mean, the median, the standard deviation, and the minimum and the maximum. Presenting all these values for a given random variable provides a reviewer with two measures of central tendency and two measures of dispersion. For clinical studies that are comparative in nature, such as therapeutic confirmatory trials, it is our recommendation that summary statistics – for example, the mean and standard deviation – be formatted in a report so that the primary comparison of interest is read across columns (left to right). In clinical studies this is typically treatment groups or dose groups. Secondary comparisons of interest – for example, time points of observation – should be arranged as separate rows.

5.9   Review

1. What scale are each of the following participant characteristics measured on:

   (a) eye color
   (b) body mass index (kg/m^2)
   (c) number of cerebrovascular events diagnosed in the past 5 years
   (d) days from study entry to last follow-up visit
   (e) concentration of test drug in plasma (ng/mL)
   (f) blood pressure classification: Normal; prehypertension; stage 1 hypertension; stage 2 hypertension.

2. Using the histogram in Figure 5.1 and the stem-and-leaf plot in Figure 5.2, comment on the appropriateness of each of the following measures of central tendency:

   (a) mean
   (b) median
   (c) mode.

3. From the frequency table of age values in Table 5.1, calculate:

   (a) the median or 50th percentile
   (b) the 25th percentile
   (c) the 75th percentile.

5.10 Reference

Senn S (1997). *Statistical Issues in Drug Development.* Chichester: John Wiley & Sons.

6

Probability, hypothesis testing, and estimation

6.1 Introduction

A common goal of pharmaceutical clinical trials is to establish with some high degree of confidence that the test treatment is superior to a control with respect to some measurable effect. If we are able to say that the expected effect of the test treatment tends to be superior (by some amount) to the expected effect of the control, we could conclude that the test treatment was superior to the control.

To accomplish this objective, sponsors design studies that allow them to attribute any difference in the response of interest to the test treatment itself. This is accomplished through the use of randomization, a carefully selected study population, treatment blinding, careful data collection, and other measures that minimize the possibility that other factors may have influenced the outcome of the study. However, if too few study participants are studied any difference observed might have been caused by chance. A chance, or spurious, result is one that may not be repeatable or, to put it another way, a chance result is not reliable. Provision of a high degree of confidence that a new drug is beneficial requires sponsors to demonstrate that effects observed from a new treatment are reliable. This chapter discusses the statistical concepts that allow researchers to make the conclusion that the effect seen in a study was unlikely to be the result of chance.

6.2 Probability

The statements at the end of the previous section can be expressed differently, and more quantitatively, in the language of Statistics. We noted that provision of substantial evidence that a new drug is beneficial requires sponsors to demonstrate that effects observed from a new treatment are reliable. This chapter discusses the statistical concepts that allow researchers to make the conclusion that the effect seen in a study is reliable, that is, it is unlikely to be the result of chance.

The statistical techniques that can be used to rule out chance events require us first to consider some concepts of probability. Many outcomes in life are inherently uncertain, and others can be considered certain. If you play the lottery, it is uncertain whether you will win on any given occasion (it is also incredibly unlikely). If you drop an apple, it is certain that it will fall to the ground. Other outcomes fall in the middle of the range. It is useful to be able to quantify the degree of certainty, and conversely the degree of uncertainty, associated with a particular occurrence. This is the realm of probability.

Like the word significance, the concept of probability is used in everyday language as well as in the discipline of Statistics. As Turner (2007) noted, the statement "I'll probably be there on Saturday" involves a probabilistic statement, but there is no degree of quantification (if you know the individual making this statement, past experience may lead you to have an informed opinion concerning the relative meaning of "probably," but this is a subjective judgment).

As for many aspects of statistical analysis, there are axioms in probability that make it a very useful tool. In the context of Statistics, probability can be defined in quantifiable terms. A probability is a numerical quantity between zero and one that expresses the likely occurrence of a future event. A probability of 0 denotes that the event will not occur. A probability of 1 denotes that the event will undoubtedly occur. Any numerical value between 0 and 1 expresses a relative likelihood of an event occurring.

A probability value can be represented as a fraction or as a decimal value. In addition, it is common in some aspects of Statistics to multiply the decimal expression of a particular probability by 100 to create a percentage statement of likelihood. A probability of 0.5 would thus be expressed as a 50% chance that an event would occur. Percentage statements of likelihood are a central component of hypothesis testing, which is introduced later in the chapter.

The probability of an event (E) can be represented as $P(E)$ and we use this notational convention. In general, the probability of either of two events (A or B) occurring is calculated as:

$$P(A \text{ or } B) = P(A) + P(B) - P(A \text{ and } B).$$

In other words, the probability of either event occurring is the sum of the probabilities of each event minus the probability of both occurring together (or jointly).

Consider the cross-tabulation of the gender and age of participants in a clinical trial as presented in Table 6.1. As seen there were 200 participants, 100 of whom were male and 100 female. There were 65 participants aged 45 years or younger, 90 between 46 and 64 years, and 45 who were aged 65 years or older. We illustrate several of the axioms of probability using Table 6.1. For example, the probability of selecting at random a participant from this group who was male or aged 65 years or older:

$$P(\text{male or} \geq 65) = P(\text{male}) + P(\geq 65) - P(\text{male and} \geq 65) =$$

$$P(\text{male or} \geq 65) = \frac{100}{200} + \frac{45}{200} - \frac{15}{200} = \frac{130}{200} = 0.65.$$

In the special case that the events A and B cannot occur at the same time, they are said to be mutually exclusive, meaning that $P(A \text{ and } B) = 0$. Hence, for mutually exclusive events A and B:

$$P(A \text{ or } B) = P(A) + P(B).$$

A randomly selected participant cannot be both "≤ 45" and "≥ 65." The events of selecting a participant aged 45 years or younger and one

65 years or older are mutually exclusive. This result is generalizable to more than two events of interest.

Table 6.1   Cross-tabulation of age and gender

Age (years)	Male	Female	
≤ 45	35	30	65
46–64	50	40	90
≥ 65	15	30	45
	100	100	200

If one or more events, $E_1, E_2, \ldots E_n$, represent all unique and mutually exclusive outcomes in a particular circumstance, the probability of observing at least one of the events sums to one:

$$P(E_1 \text{ or } E_2 \text{ or } \ldots \text{ or } E_n) = P(E_1) + P(E_2) + \ldots + P(E_n) = 1.$$

This result can be used to calculate the probability of one or more events of interest. For any event E_1 among n mutually exclusive and exhaustive events:

$$P(E_1) = 1 - \{P(E_2) + \ldots + P(E_n)\}.$$

This expression is called the complement rule and will be referenced throughout this book.

The probability of selecting a male at random can be calculated by adding the probabilities for the events "male ≤ 45 years," "male 46–64 years," and "male ≥ 65 years," because these are all mutually exclusive events. The probability can be calculated as follows:

$$P(\text{male}) = P(\text{male} \leq 45 \text{ years}) +$$
$$P(\text{male } 46\text{–}64 \text{ years}) + P(\text{male} \geq 65 \text{ years})$$
$$= \frac{35}{200} + \frac{50}{200} + \frac{15}{200}$$
$$= \frac{100}{200} = \frac{1}{2}.$$

The probability of an event B given that A has been observed is called a conditional probability and is defined as:

$$P(B \mid A) = \frac{P(A \text{ and } B)}{P(A)},$$

where the vertical bar signifies "given."

The probability of selecting a participant ≤ 45 years of age, given that a male has been selected, is:

$$P(\leq 45 \text{ years} \mid \text{male}) = \frac{P(\leq 45 \text{ years and male})}{P(\text{male})}$$

$$\frac{P(\leq 45 \text{ years and male})}{P(\text{male})} = \frac{\dfrac{35}{200}}{\dfrac{100}{200}} = \frac{35}{100}.$$

It follows that the probability of two events occurring jointly is calculated as:

$$P(A \text{ and } B) = P(A)P(B|A).$$

One important use of conditional probabilities occurs in Bayes' theorem. The conditional probability of an event A given an event B is:

$$P(A \mid B) = \frac{P(B \mid A)P(A)}{P(B)}.$$

Note that throughout this book we have adopted a standard mathematical notation for the product of two or more terms. In the expression above the numerator is the product of the two terms, $P(B|A)$ and $P(A)$, that is, these two quantities are multiplied. Please keep this standard in mind when you encounter other mathematical expressions.

It is also possible to state the probability of an event, A, as a function of two or more conditional events. If the events B and C are mutually exclusive and exhaustive – for example, they represent male and female – the probability of event A can be expressed as:

$$P(A) = P(A \mid B)P(B) + P(A \mid C)P(C).$$

This expression can be extended to more than two conditional events.

A common application of Bayes' theorem is in estimating the probability of a participant having a disease, given a positive test for that disease. These concepts are important in their own right with regard to the development of diagnostic tests. As the clinical trials discussed in this book are for the purposes of developing new pharmaceutical interventions rather than testing for the existence of a disease or condition, this issue may not seem directly relevant. However,

these concepts are discussed in Chapter 12 in a different light, and we would therefore like to establish these concepts at this earlier stage.

For simplicity, in the notation used in this example we define the following events using the symbol "$\equiv$" which means "is equivalent to":

- $D+$ $\equiv$ participant has the disease of interest
- $D-$ $\equiv$ participant does not have the disease of interest
- $T+$ $\equiv$ participant tests positive for the disease
- $T-$ $\equiv$ participant tests negative for the disease.

When developing a diagnostic test, investigators identify two groups: One is known (by some gold standard testing procedure) to have the disease; the other is known (also by a gold standard testing procedure) not to have the disease. Then all participants in both these groups are given the new diagnostic test. The accuracy of a new diagnostic test is measured by two criteria:

1. Sensitivity is the probability that a new test will have a positive result among those who are known to have the disease. This is denoted by: $P(T+|D+)$.
2. Specificity is the probability that a new test will have a negative result among those who are known not to have the disease. This is denoted by: $P(T-|D-)$.

Once a new diagnostic test has been developed it may be considered for a public health screening program. Evaluating the utility of a proposed new diagnostic test in a population involves the following two criteria:

1. The true positive rate is the probability that a participant has the disease given that she or he has tested positive. This is denoted by $P(D+|T+)$ and is also referred to as predictive value positive. The complement, $1 - P(D+|T+)$ $= P(D-|T+)$, is the false-positive rate.
2. The true-negative rate is the probability that a participant does not have the disease given that she or he has tested negative. This is denoted by $P(D-|T-)$ and is also referred to as predictive value negative. The complement, $1 - P(D-|T-) = P(D+|T-)$, is the false-negative rate.

If the true-positive rate is low (or the false-positive rate high) a number of participants will needlessly incur the expense and anxiety of further medical investigations. If the true-negative rate is low (or the false-negative rate high) a number of them will carry on undiagnosed. The goal would be to adopt a screening tool that had high rates of true positives and true negatives. Bayes' theorem can be used to show that the rates of true positives and true negatives are a function of the sensitivity and specificity of the diagnostic test itself and the prevalence of the disease in the population of interest.

We illustrate this concept for the true-positive rate, which is:

$$= P(D+ \mid T+)$$

$$= \frac{P(T+ \mid D+)P(D+)}{P(T+)} \text{ by Bayes' theorem.}$$

Bayes's theorem is applied again to obtain:

$$= \frac{P(T+ \mid D+)P(D+)}{P(T+ \mid D+)P(D+) + P(T+ \mid D-)P(D-)}.$$

Noting that $P(T+ \mid D-) = 1 - P(T- \mid D-)$ we have the desired result.

$$= \frac{P(T+ \mid D+)P(D+)}{P(T+ \mid D+)P(D+) + [1 - P(T- \mid D-)]P(D-)}.$$

Note that $P(D+)$ is often called the prevalence of the disease in a population. Its complement is $P(D-) = 1 - P(D+)$. Prevalence of a disease is estimated through the use of epidemiologic studies and not clinical trials. Thus, to fully evaluate the utility of the new diagnostic test, we must have an estimate of the prevalence of the disease, the sensitivity of the test, and the specificity of the test.

Two events are said to be statistically independent if the probability of one occurring does not depend on the other. If A and B are independent events the joint probability is given by:

$$P(A \text{ and } B) = P(A)P(B).$$

If we sample from our 200 study participants "with replacement" – that is, after each selection the participant is available for selection again – the probability of selecting a male does not depend on previous selections. The probability of selecting two males in a row is given by:

$$P(\text{two males in a row}) = P(\text{male})P(\text{male})$$

$$= \left(\frac{1}{2}\right)\left(\frac{1}{2}\right)$$

$$= \frac{1}{4} = 0.25.$$

The probability of selecting four males in a row is:

$$P(\text{four males in a row}) = $$
$$P(\text{male})P(\text{male})P(\text{male})P(\text{male})$$

$$= \left(\frac{1}{2}\right)\left(\frac{1}{2}\right)\left(\frac{1}{2}\right)\left(\frac{1}{2}\right)$$

$$= \frac{1}{16} = 0.0625.$$

These basic principles and characteristics of probability are referred to throughout subsequent chapters.

6.3 Probability distributions

In Chapter 5 we described a number of ways to examine the relative frequency distribution of a random variable (for example, age). An important step in preparation for subsequent discussions is to extend the idea of relative frequency to probability distributions. A probability distribution is a mathematical expression or graphical representation that defines the probability with which all possible values of a random variable will occur. There are many probability distribution functions for both discrete random variables and continuous random variables. Discrete random variables are random variables for which the possible values have "gaps." A random variable that represents a count (for example, number of participants with a particular eye color) is considered discrete because the possible values are 0, 1, 2, 3, etc. A continuous random variable does not have gaps in the possible values. Whether the random variable is discrete or continuous, all probability distribution functions have these characteristics:

- All possible values of the random variable must be represented by the distribution function.
- The probability of each value of the random variable occurring is bounded by 0 and 1, inclusive.
- The probabilities of values of the random variable occurring must sum to 1 (in the case of a discrete random variable) or integrate to 1 (in the case of a continuous random variable).

A simple example of a discrete probability distribution is the process by which a single participant is assigned the active treatment when the event "active treatment" is equally likely as the event "placebo treatment." This random process is like a coin toss with a perfectly fair coin. If the random variable, X, takes the value of 1 if active treatment is randomly assigned and 0 if the placebo treatment is randomly assigned, the probability distribution function can be described as follows:

$$P(X = x) = \frac{1}{2}, \text{ where } x = 0 \text{ or } 1.$$

This probability distribution function has the characteristics defined previously:

- The random variable can take on only values of 0 or 1.
- The probability distribution function is defined for both values.
- The probability of each value is between 0 and 1, inclusive. It is, in fact, half for both values.
- Finally, the sum of the probability of all mutually exclusive outcomes is equal to one, that is, $P(X = 0) + P(X = 1) = 1$.

6.4 Binomial distribution

The first probability distribution function that we discuss in detail is the binomial distribution, which is used to calculate the probability of observing x number of successes out of n observations. As the random variable of interest, the

number of successes, is discrete (as are all counts), the binomial distribution is called a discrete random variable distribution. The binomial distribution is applicable when the following conditions apply:

- Each of n observations results in only one of two outcomes (one is typically called a success and the other failure).
- The probability of a success, p, is the same from observation to observation.
- Each observation is independent of the others.

The probability of observing x successes out of n observations under these conditions (called a Bernoulli process) can be expressed as:

$$P(X = x; p, n) = C_x^n p^x (1 - p)^{n-x}.$$

The left part of this expression can be read as "the probability of the random variable, X, taking on a particular value of x, given parameters p and n." The quantity $(1 - p)$ is the probability of failure for any trial. The notation C_x^n is shorthand to represent the number of combinations of taking x successes out of n observations when ordering is not important. This quantity can be calculated as:

$$C_x^n = \frac{n!}{x!(n - x)!}$$

The expression $n!$ is read as "n factorial" and is calculated as $n(n - 1)(n - 2) \ldots (1)$.

The mean of the binomial distribution function is:

Mean $= np$.

The variance of the binomial distribution is:

Variance $= np(1 - p)$.

A simple example of the use of the binomial distribution is the result of four random assignments to either the active or the placebo treatment group when each outcome is equally likely. What is the probability of observing 0, 1, 2, 3, or 4 assignments to the active treatment group out of 4 random treatment assignments when the probability of assigning to active or placebo is equally likely? We must assume that the outcome of one assignment does not impact the outcome on subsequent assignments, that is, they are independent. There are only two possible outcomes on any given trial: Assignment to active or placebo. The probability of each outcome, the number of "successes" or assignments to active, can then be calculated using the binomial probability distribution function.

The probability of each outcome of four random treatment assignments is displayed in Table 6.2. In some instances, we may be interested in knowing what the probability of observing x or fewer successes would be, that is, $P(X \leq x)$. This cumulative probability is also displayed for each outcome in Table 6.2. For a discrete random variable distribution, the sum of probabilities of each outcome must sum to 1, or unity.

As you might expect, the most probable outcome is 2 actives (probability 0.375) and the least probable outcomes are 0 and 4 actives (each with a probability of 0.0625). We can use the cumulative probability distribution to answer other probability questions of interest. For example, what is the probability of observing 3 or fewer actives? This probability is denoted as $P(X \leq 3) = 0.9375$. We can use the complement rule from Section 6.2 to calculate the probability of observing 2 or more actives, $P(X \geq 2)$, as:

$$1 - P(X \leq 1) = 1 - 0.3125 = 0.6875.$$

The binomial distribution is discussed later in the chapter to illustrate concepts of hypothesis testing.

6.5 Normal distribution

Similar probability models can be used for continuous random variables. The most common, and arguably the most important of these in Statistics, is the normal distribution. As it is encountered so frequently in this book, we spend some time describing its characteristics and uses.

The normal distribution is a particular form of a continuous random variable distribution. The relative frequency of values of the normal distribution is represented by a normal density curve. This curve is typically described as a bell-shaped curve, as displayed in Figure 6.1.

More precisely, it is one specific kind of symmetrical curve. The precise nature of this curve can be described mathematically by a formula that contains both the mean, μ, and the standard deviation, σ, of the population that is being represented graphically by the normal curve:

$$f(x; \mu, \sigma) = \frac{1}{\sigma\sqrt{2\pi}} e^{-\frac{(x-\mu)^2}{2\sigma^2}}.$$

The term "population" is defined in detail later in the chapter. Until then we can think of a population as the largest group of experimental units (for example, study participants) about which we would like to make a conclusion.

As we need to know two parameters – that is, the mean, μ, and the standard deviation, σ, to fully characterize this distribution – it is consid-

Table 6.2 Distribution of the number of assignments to active from four random assignments when the probability of assignment to active and placebo is equal ($p=0.5$)

Outcome (no. of actives, x)	Probability of the outcome $P(X = x)$	Cumulative probability $P(X \leq x)$
0	$C_0^4 0.5^0 (0.5)^4 = 0.0625$	0.0625
1	$C_1^4 0.5^1 (0.5)^3 = 0.2500$	0.3125
2	$C_2^4 0.5^2 (0.5)^2 = 0.3750$	0.6875
3	$C_3^4 0.5^3 (0.5)^1 = 0.2500$	0.9375
4	$C_4^4 0.5^4 (0.5)^0 = 0.0625$	1.0000

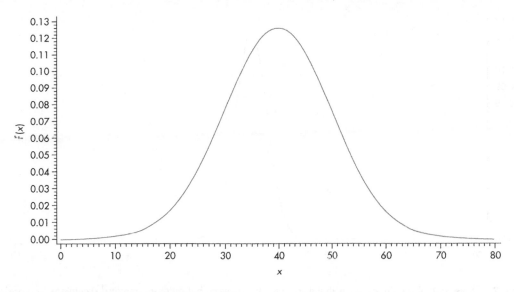

Figure 6.1   A normal density curve ($\mu = 40$, $\sigma = 10$)

ered to be a two-parameter distribution. This fact is also conveyed by the use of the symbols μ and σ on the left side of the expression. The mean specifies the distribution's location, whereas the standard deviation specifies the spread of the distribution. If a random variable X has a normal distribution with mean μ and variance σ^2, this is written as $X \sim N(\mu, \sigma^2)$. Note that most practical applications involve the use of σ rather than σ^2, but it is conventional to describe the normal distribution in terms of its mean and variance.

Figure 6.2 displays three normal density curves with the same mean (location) but different standard deviations (spread). Several characteristics of the normal distribution are very helpful in developing the statistical tests introduced in this book:

- The highest point of the normal curve occurs for the mean of the population, μ.
- The shape of the curve (relatively narrow or relatively broad) is influenced by the standard deviation, σ. The sides of the curve descend more gently as the standard deviation increases.
- At a distance of 2 standard deviations from the mean, the slope of the curve changes from a relatively smooth downward slope to a curve that technically extends out to infinity, that is, the curve technically never reaches (touches) the x axis of the graph. This concept

is analogous to starting a certain distance away from a fence and taking steps that always cover half the distance between you and the fence. As your next step always covers only half the remaining distance, theoretically you never reach the fence. However, after a certain number of steps, you are, to all practical purposes, at the fence. In the same manner, the curve is regarded as intercepting the axis at a distance of 4 standard deviations from the mean.

- The area under the curve is 1.0. This can be demonstrated formally using integral calculus, which is beyond the scope of this book: A simpler demonstration is provided by Turner (2007, pp 94–5). That the area under the curve is equal to 1 is analogous to the statement that the probability of all mutually exclusive events must sum to 1.

The precise mathematics of the normal distribution allows quantitative statements of the area under the curve between any two points on the x axis. Of most interest here is the area under the curve between two points that are equidistant from the mean.

These points, equidistant from the mean on either side, can be represented by statements of the form:

$\mu \pm$ distance.

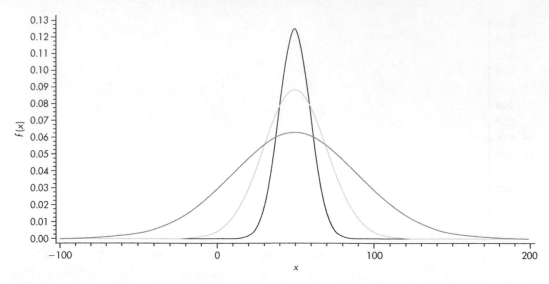

Figure 6.2   Three normal density curves with the same mean (location) but different standard deviations (spreads)

It can be shown for any normal distribution that:

- 68.3% of the area under the curve lies in the range $\mu \pm \sigma$
- 95.4% of the area under the curve lies in the range $\mu \pm 2\sigma$
- 99.73% of the area under the curve lies in the range $\mu \pm 3\sigma$.

As the area under the entire density curve equals 1 the statements above also imply by the complementary rule that:

- 31.7% of the area under the curve lies outside $\mu \pm \sigma$
- 4.6% of the area under the curve lies outside $\mu \pm 2\sigma$
- 0.27% of the area under the curve lies outside $\mu \pm 3\sigma$.

Expressing a similar concept in terms of pertinent "round number" percentages:

- The central 90% of the area lies in the range $\mu \pm 1.645\sigma$
- The central 95% of the area lies in the range $\mu \pm 1.960\sigma$
- The central 99% of the area lies in the range $\mu \pm 2.576\sigma$.

You may recall from Chapter 5 that by using Tchebysheff's theorem we could estimate the probability with which observations fall within k standard deviations for *any* distribution. You are encouraged to compare the results from Tchebysheff's theorem and those cited above for the normal distribution. Although values of any percentage of interest can be determined from statistical tables of normal distributions, the 95% and 99% values are of particular importance in the context of this book.

It is important to note here that the areas under the curve of a continuous random variable distribution can be thought of as probabilities. Assume that we know that age in a population of study participants is normally distributed with a mean of 40 and variance of 100 (standard deviation of 10). This normal distribution is displayed in Figure 6.3 with vertical lines marking 1, 2, and 3 standard deviations from the mean.

It is then possible, using the results above and similar ones from statistical tables, to estimate the probability that a participant randomly selected from the population of study participants would be aged > 50 or < 30. The answer is 0.32 or 32% – that is, the proportion or

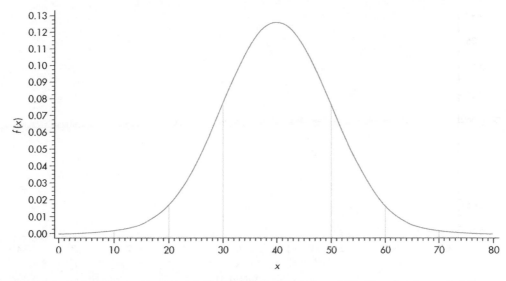

Figure 6.3   Normal distribution with mean of 40 and standard deviation of 10. Note that the vertical lines represent $\mu \pm \sigma$, $\mu \pm 2\sigma$, and $\mu \pm 3\sigma$

percentage of the area under the curve translates directly in to the percentage of participants (or other observational units) whose age values fall outside of the two identified points.

6.5.1 The standard normal (Z) distribution

One unique and important normal distribution is the standard normal distribution, or Z distribution, which has a mean of 0 and a variance of 1. If a random variable X is distributed as standard normal with mean 0 and variance 1, it is written as $X \sim N(0,1)$. To use some of the general results from normal distributions provided earlier, we can make the following statements for the standard normal distribution:

- The central 90% of the area lies between ± 1.645
- The central 95% of the area lies between ± 1.960
- The central 99% of the area lies between ± 2.576.

The standard normal or Z distribution is used extensively in Statistics and throughout this

book. For later reference, the standard normal distribution is provided in Figure 6.4. Note that the area under the curve to the left of the value -1.96 is 0.025 (or 2.5%). As the distribution is symmetric, the area under the curve to the right of the value 1.96 is also 0.025. Another way of stating this is that, if we were to randomly select a value from the distribution, there is a 95% chance that the value would be between -1.96 and $+1.96$. One can also think of the values -1.96 and $+1.96$ as the 2.5th and 97.5th percentiles, respectively.

Values of the Z that define areas under the standard normal curve in the left tail, the right tail, and the symmetric central region are provided in Appendix 1.

6.5.2 Transforming a normal distribution to the standard normal distribution

One helpful method possible with a random variable that has a normal distribution with mean, μ, and variance, σ^2, is to transform values of the random variable so that they have the scale of the standard normal distribution. This

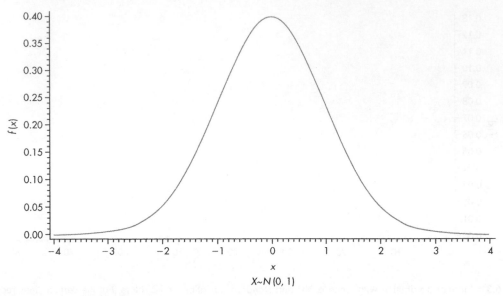

Figure 6.4   The standard normal (Z) distribution

makes it possible to answer a number of probability questions using statistical tables that provide the areas under the standard normal curve. In general, for a random variable $X \sim N(\mu, \sigma^2)$, the random variable:

$$Z = \frac{X - \mu}{\sigma}$$

is normally distributed with mean 0 and variance 1.

We can use the example from earlier in Section 6.5 to illustrate this method. If age in a population of study participants is normally distributed with a mean of 40 and variance of 100 (standard deviation of 10), what is the probability that a participant randomly selected from the population of study participants would be aged > 50 or < 30?

First we are interested in the probability that a randomly selected participant will be > 50 years of age. The transformed value for $X = 50$ is:

$$Z = \frac{50 - 40}{10} = 1.$$

As a result of this transformation, $P(X > 50)$ corresponds to $P(Z > 1)$. The probability, $P(Z > 1)$, can be obtained from Appendix 1, the look-up table for areas under the standard

normal distribution curve. As seen in Appendix 1, the area under the standard normal distribution curve for $Z > 1$ is 0.159.

Then we would like to know what the probability is that a randomly selected participant will be < 30 years of age. The transformed value for $X = 30$ is:

$$Z = \frac{30 - 40}{10} = -1.$$

As above, $P(X < 30)$ is equal to $P(Z < -1)$. Using Appendix 1 as a reference, the area under the standard normal distribution curve for $Z < -1$ is 0.159.

The probability of interest is obtained by summing the two probabilities associated with $P(Z > 1)$ and $P(Z < -1)$ because the two events are mutually exclusive. That is, a participant cannot be both < 30 and > 50, so the probability of interest is 0.159 + 0.159 or 0.318.

At first glance it may seem that this transformation method is useful only in a few instances (when the random variable is known to have a normal distribution) and contrived ones at that. However, it is actually useful in many instances. Many random variables can be shown to have approximately normal distributions. The reason for this is given shortly. It turns out that, if a random variable has an approximate normal distribution, for which the mean and variance are known, a transformation results in a random variable that has an approximate standard normal distribution.

6.6 Classical probability and relative frequency probability

Before concluding the first part of this chapter on the fundamentals of probability it is important to point out that there are two ways to estimate a probability. To contrast these two types of probability we consider the question: "What is the probability of observing a 'head' when tossing a coin?"

The first type of probability, termed by some "classical" probability, is based on an assumption about the state of the experiment and some basic mathematical expressions. For example, we would begin answering this question by assuming that the coin was fair. Further, we would note to ourselves that a fair coin has two sides, the only two outcomes of a coin toss are "heads" and "tails," and only one of these two outcomes is the one of interest. The probability of observing a head from a single toss of a fair coin is therefore ½ or 0.5. The most straightforward way to solve classical probability problems is to write out all of the unique possible outcomes, the sample space, and then identify the number of times that the outcome of interest would occur. In this case the sample space is "heads" or "tails." The event of interest, observing heads, is represented by just one of these events, so the probability of interest is ½. The use of the binomial distribution to calculate the probability distribution of observing the number of assignments to active is another example. In that case we knew (by design) that the probability of assignment to active was exactly half.

Many Statistics students have suffered immensely over the years by having to solve classical probability problems. Marilyn vos Savant (1997) stumped many readers with the following classical probability problem:

A woman and a man (unrelated) each have two children. At least one of the woman's children is a boy, and the man's older child is a boy. Do the chances that the woman has two boys equal the chances that the man has two boys?

vos Savant (1997, p 15)

What is your answer? We leave it to you to conduct an online search to investigate the controversy surrounding this problem. We do not dwell any further on this method of estimating probabilities because we also dislike them, and the second type is more useful for us anyway.

The second type of probability, relative frequency probability, is calculated by repeating an experiment a large number of times (say n) and counting the number of times out of n that the outcome of interest (say m) occurred. The probability of the event is then calculated as:

$$P(\text{event}) = \frac{m}{n}.$$

The calculated probability is simply an estimate of the true probability (which remains unknown).

Using a relative frequency approach to estimating the probability of observing a head we would toss the coin a number of times (for example, 10), count the number of times a head landed face up (for example, 4 times), and then calculate the probability as 4/10 or 0.4. It is perhaps not surprising that the estimated probability here is not exactly 0.5. We were only one head shy of 5/10, so the relatively small number of coin tosses may have had an impact. You can imagine tossing the coin 100 times and observing 46 heads for a probability of 0.46. That would be much closer to the classical probability solution. Another possible reason that only four heads came up could be that the coin really was not fair at all. For the classical probability solution to this problem we would need to assume that the coin was fair or be told that it was. The relative frequency solution has the advantage of not requiring the assumption of a fair coin, but has the disadvantage of possibly being limited by the number of experiments.

Our initial probability estimate of 0.4 from 10 coin tosses does not seem to be that far off because we might reason that observing 4, 5, or 6 heads would be expected from 10 tosses of a fair coin. You may be intuitively thinking that, if we were to repeat the 10 coin tosses, we would probably count 4–6 heads again. Your intuition would be correct, and there is a statistical concept that explains how results from experiments vary from sample to sample. The magnitude of expected differences from sample to sample enables us to estimate a quantity that we can never really know, one that represents the truth. In the case of the coin-tossing experiment, our goal would be to infer whether or not the true probability of observing a head was 0.5.

6.7 The law of large numbers

In clinical trials we do not know what the probability of observing a particular serious adverse event is, but we observe a large number of outcomes (for example, participants exposed to a new treatment) to estimate it. As the sample size increases the estimate becomes more precise (that is, closer to the truth). An illustration of the "law of large numbers" is provided in Figure 6.5. Suppose that a relatively uncommon adverse

event is represented by the chance event of two thrown dice landing with a total of two (or "snake eyes"). The classical probability solution to estimating the probability of this event is $(1/6)^2 = 0.02778$. The relative frequency solution can be obtained by rolling two dice a large number of times (n), counting the number of times "snake eyes" occurs (m), and estimating the probability as m/n. The most convenient means to conduct this experiment is using computer simulation. As seen in Figure 6.5, the estimates of the probability (denoted by the oscillating curve) vary quite a bit from the truth (represented by the horizontal reference line) until the sample size is around 10 000. The implication of the law of large numbers for clinical trials of new drugs is that the unknown quantities of interest are more precisely estimated with larger samples. These would include the mean change in SBP (systolic blood pressure) or the proportion of participants experiencing a serious adverse event. Given the limited size of most clinical development programs, the most precise estimates of risks of new therapies become evident only once a new drug has been marketed and used by many thousands of patients.

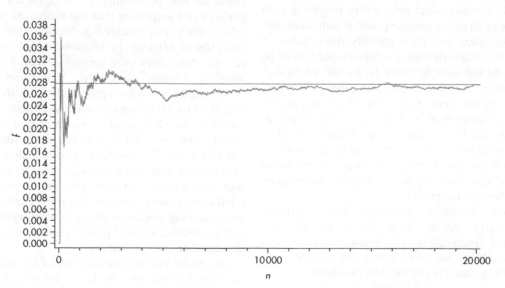

Figure 6.5   Illustration of the law of large numbers: Proportion of two dice coming up as "snake eyes" as a function of sample size (n)

6.8 Sample statistics and population parameters

The unknown quantities of interest described in the previous section are examples of parameters. A parameter is a numerical property of a population. One may be interested in measures of central tendency or dispersion in populations. Two parameters of interest for our purposes are the mean and standard deviation. The population mean and standard deviation are represented by μ and σ, respectively. The population mean, μ, could represent the average treatment effect in the population of individuals with a particular condition. The standard deviation, σ, could represent the typical variability of treatment responses about the population mean. The corresponding properties of a sample, the sample mean and the sample standard deviation, are typically represented by $\bar{x}$ and s, which were introduced in Chapter 5. Recall that the term "parameter" was encountered in Section 6.5 when describing the two quantities that define the normal distribution. In statistical applications, the values of the parameters of the normal distribution cannot be known, but are estimated by sample statistics. In this sense, the use of the word "parameter" is consistent between the earlier context and the present one. We have adhered to convention by using the term "parameter" in these two slightly different contexts.

An expression that defines how individual observations are used to derive a numerical estimate is called an estimator (much like a formula is used to calculate a number). The sample mean,

$$\bar{x} = \frac{\sum_{i=1}^{n} x_i}{n},$$

is considered an estimator for the population mean, μ. When individual observations are applied to the estimator, the result is a numeric value or estimate. When a single value is calculated, it represents a best guess of sorts, and is called a point estimate. No single estimate could be expected to be perfect so "interval estimates" are commonly used to reflect more accurately a range of plausible values.

Inferential statistics comprises two distinct, although closely related, procedures. In each case observations from a sample are used to:

- calculate an interval estimate that includes the unknown population parameter with some degree of confidence; in clinical trials, it is common practice to use a 95% confidence interval
- test whether or not a sample statistic is consistent with or contrary to a hypothesized value of the population parameter.

Inferences about a population are made on the basis of a sample taken from that population. The process of inferential statistics requires:

- identification of a representative sample of participants from a population of interest
- collection of individual observations
- calculation of sample statistics from the individual observations
- a statistical method to relate the sample statistic to the parameter of interest; this can be done in one of two ways:

  - estimation of plausible values of the parameter
  - testing a hypothesis of a proposed value of the parameter.

We discuss the former method, confidence intervals, first, after a necessary introduction to the concept of sampling variation. The latter method (hypothesis testing) is discussed later. First, however, it is useful to introduce a few other ideas.

6.9 Sampling variation

If we take a sample of 100 numbers from a population of 100 000 numbers, that sample's mean, which is precisely known, will provide an estimate of the population mean. The same is true for the standard deviation, that is:

- $\bar{x}$ is an estimate of μ
- s is an estimate of σ.

If we replaced the first sample of 100 numbers and then took another sample of 100 numbers, it is likely (effectively guaranteed) that the numbers would not be identical to those in the first sample, and that the calculated sample mean would be different from the first one. This logic applies to any number of means taken. Suppose that we were to repeat this process a number of times (in a simulated manner using computer software) and, at the end of each replication, tabulate the values of the sample mean or plot their relative frequencies. The shape of the resulting distribution of values would be recognizable. We would notice that a typical value would be apparent (the population mean μ), as would a symmetrical bell-shaped distribution. In short, the sample statistic from a sample of size n (in this case the sample mean) varies from sample to sample and its distribution has a mean and a standard deviation. Such a distribution is called a sampling distribution. An important general result for the sampling distribution of the sample mean is as follows:

- For any continuous random variable X which has a distribution with population mean, μ, and variance, σ^2, the sampling distribution of the mean for samples of size n has a distribution with population mean, μ, and variance, σ^2/n.

The square root of the variance,

$$\sqrt{\frac{\sigma^2}{n}} = \frac{\sigma}{\sqrt{n}},$$

is the population standard error of the mean, which describes the typical variability of sample means around the population mean. If we know, or can assume, that the random variable X has a normal distribution with population mean, μ, and variance, σ^2, the sampling distribution of the mean of samples of size n will also have a normal distribution with population mean, μ, and variance, σ^2/n. Using the notation described earlier, this result can be summarized in this manner:

If $X \sim N(\mu,\sigma^2)$ then $\bar{X}_n \sim N(\mu,\frac{\sigma^2}{n})$.

6.10 Estimation: General considerations

It is not possible to *know* whether any single sample estimate, like the sample mean, is a good estimate of the population parameter that it is intended to estimate. However, it is possible to use the fact that most estimates of the sample statistic (for example, sample mean) are not too far removed from the population parameter, as specified by the shape of the sampling distribution, to define a range of values of the population parameter (for example, population mean) that are best supported by the sample data.

As exact knowledge of the population parameter is not possible, we must settle for a range of values that, with some specified probability or confidence, are most plausible. In other words, we would like to know the lower limit (LL) and upper limit (UL) of the most probable range of values of the true population parameter. In the case of the population mean, we seek two values, LL and UL, such that:

$P(\text{LL} < \mu < \text{UL}) = 1 - \alpha.$

The quantity α is the probability that the interval estimate does not include the value of the parameter of interest – that is, μ in this case. In most cases small values of α are desirable (for example, 0.10 or 0.05). Depending on the importance of the decision to be made on the basis of the interval estimate defined by LL and UL, very small values of α may be desirable (for example, 0.01 or 0.001).

When conducting a clinical trial, we do not know if our sample was representative of the population or not. We have only data from a sample and the statistics calculated from the sample data. Yet, our ultimate interest is not in the sample but in the population. In this chapter we consider the sample statistics for the mean and the standard deviation, $\bar{x}$ and s. A clinical trial represents a situation in which we can take only one sample from a population. Given that, what degree of certainty can we have that the mean of that sample represents the mean of the population? Before we answer this question fully we define a confidence interval for the sample mean in a special case. This special case will serve as our starting point for more realistic and common cases.

6.10.1 Confidence interval for the population mean when the population variance is known

Assume that the random variable X has a normal distribution with an *unknown* population mean, μ, and with a *known* population variance, σ^2. For a sample size of n, the sampling distribution of the sample mean has a normal distribution with population mean, μ, and variance, σ^2/n. The implication of this result is that, for example:

- 90% of the sample mean values lie between $\mu \pm 1.645 \frac{\sigma}{\sqrt{n}}$

- 95% of the sample mean values lie between $\mu \pm 1.960 \frac{\sigma}{\sqrt{n}}$

- 99% of the sample mean values lie between $\mu \pm 2.576 \frac{\sigma}{\sqrt{n}}$.

In general, the following statement is true. For samples of size n, $(1 - \alpha)\%$ of sample means $\bar{x}$ lie in the range:

$$\mu \pm z_{1-\alpha/2} \frac{\sigma}{\sqrt{n}}$$

where $z_{1-\alpha/2}$ is the value from the standard normal distribution that defines the upper and lower tail areas of size $\alpha/2$. Note that $z_{1-\alpha/2}$ is a particular example of a reliability factor. As the Z distribution is symmetric it is also true that the Z value on the negative side that cuts off an area of size $\alpha/2$ in the lower tail is equal to the Z value on the positive side (change in sign) that cuts off an area of size $\alpha/2$ in the upper tail. Equivalently, in mathematical terms, this means:

$$|z_{\alpha/2}| = z_{1-\alpha/2}.$$

We can therefore express a two-sided $(1 - \alpha)\%$ confidence interval for the population mean as:

$$P(\bar{x} - z_{1-\alpha/2} \frac{\sigma}{\sqrt{n}} < \mu < \bar{x} + z_{1-\alpha/2} \frac{\sigma}{\sqrt{n}}) = 1 - \alpha.$$

This expression for a two-sided $(1 - \alpha)\%$ confidence interval can be shortened in the following manner:

$$\bar{x} \pm z_{1-\alpha/2} (\sigma/\sqrt{n}).$$

The assumption of a normal distribution for the random variable X is somewhat restrictive. However, for any random variable, as the sample size increases, the sampling distribution of the sample mean becomes approximately normally distributed according to a mathematical result called the central limit theorem. For a random variable X that has a population mean, μ, and variance, σ^2, the sampling distribution of the mean of samples of size n (where n is large, that is, > 200) will have an approximately normal distribution with population mean, μ, and variance, σ^2/n. Using the notation described earlier, this result can be summarized as:

$$\bar{X}_n \rightarrow N(\mu, \frac{\sigma^2}{n})$$

when n is large. This is an important result, because it holds no matter the shape of the original distribution of the random variable, X. The reader is encouraged to search for online references that illustrate, through animation, this important theorem.

Therefore, the expression written above for the confidence interval for the population mean also applies to any continuous random variable as long as the sample size is large (as just noted, of the order of 200 or more). The other rather restrictive assumption required for this confidence interval is that the population variance be known. Such a scenario is neither common nor realistic.

We now apply the fundamental concept of the confidence interval as developed here to the case where the population variance is not known, but there is interest in defining a confidence interval for the population mean.

6.10.2 Confidence interval for the population mean when the population variance is unknown

A reasonable suggestion for devising a confidence interval for the population mean would be to substitute the sample estimate, s, for the corresponding population parameter, α and proceed as described earlier in Section 6.10. However, when the sample size is small (particularly < 30) the use of the Z distribution is less appropriate. William S Gossett, writing anonymously as "Student" while employed at Guinness Brewery, proposed the following statistic as an alternative. When X is a normally distributed variable and the sample size is small, the statistic

$$t = \frac{\bar{x} - \mu}{s/\sqrt{n}}$$

follows a t distribution ("Student's t"). The single parameter defining its shape is $(n - 1)$ degrees of freedom (df), the sufficient number of observations needed to estimate the sample mean. The

t distribution is symmetric about its mean (zero) and looks like a normal distribution with, in cases of sample sizes > 200, heavier "tails."

Three density functions are plotted for t distributions with 5, 30, and 200 df in Figure 6.6. The greater the number of df, the "flatter" the tails. In the figure, the two curves that are closest together are associated with 30 and 200 df. It is interesting to note (and a convenient fact) that the area under the density curve between any two points for the case with 30 df is not appreciably different from the case with 200 df.

As was the case with the normal distribution, the shape of the t distribution can be used to find two values that define a central area under the density curve of size $(1 - \alpha)$. It can be shown that, once a value of t associated with an area of interest is determined, the difference between the sample mean $\bar{x}$ is within $t(s/\sqrt{n})$ of the population mean, μ. This enables us to calculate a confidence interval for the population mean when the sample size is small and the population variance unknown.

The interval estimate of the population mean, the two-sided $(1 - \alpha)\%$ confidence interval for the population mean, is:

$$\bar{x} \pm t_{1-\alpha/2,\,n-1}(s/\sqrt{n}).$$

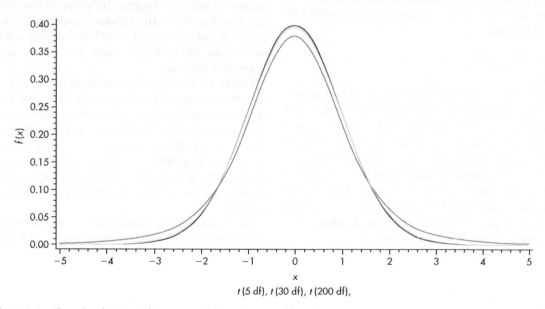

t (5 df), t (30 df), t (200 df),

Figure 6.6   The t distribution with 5, 30, and 200 degrees of freedom

As in Section 6.10, the confidence interval has three components:

1. point estimate
2. standard error
3. reliability factor.

The point estimate in this case is the sample mean, which represents the best estimate of the population mean.

The second component is the standard error of the mean, which quantifies the extent to which the process of sampling has mis-estimated the population mean. The standard error of the mean has the same meaning as in the case for normally distributed data – that is, the standard error describes the degree of uncertainty present in our assessment of the population mean on the basis of the sample mean. It is also the standard deviation of the sampling distribution of the mean for samples of size n. The smaller the standard error, the greater the certainty with which the sample mean estimates the population mean. When n is very large the standard error is very small, and therefore the sample mean is a very precise estimate of the population mean. As we know the standard deviation of the sample, s, we can make use of the following formula to determine the standard error of the mean, SE:

$$SE = \frac{s}{\sqrt{n}}.$$

At this point, it is worth emphasizing the difference between the terms "standard error" and "standard deviation," which, despite the same initial word, represent very different aspects of a data set. Standard error is a measure of how certain we are that the sample mean represents the population mean. Standard deviation is a measure of the dispersion of the original random variable. There is a standard error associated with any statistical estimator, including a sample proportion, the difference in two means, the difference in two proportions, and the ratio of two proportions. When presented with the term "standard error" in these applications the concept is the same. The standard error quantifies the extent to which an estimator varies over samples of the same size. As the sample size increases (for the same standard deviation) there

is greater precision in the estimate of the population mean because the standard error becomes smaller as a result of the division of the square root of the sample size.

The third component of the interval estimate is a reliability factor, which represents the number of standard deviations required to enclose $(1 - \alpha)\%$ of the sample means from the sampling distribution. It is used to quantify how close we would like our estimate to be to the real population mean or, in short, how reliable it is. The particular value of the reliability factor chosen above, $t_{1-\alpha/2,n-1}$, is the value of t with $(n - 1)$ df that "cuts off" an area of $\alpha/2$ in the upper tail. As the t distribution is symmetric it is also true that the t value on the negative side that cuts off an area of size $\alpha/2$ in the lower tail is equal to the same t value but with a change in sign that cuts off $\alpha/2$ in the upper tail. Equivalently, in mathematical terms, this means that $|t_{\alpha/2,n-1}| = t_{1-\alpha/2,n-1}$. Values of $t_{1-\alpha/2,n-1}$ are provided in Appendix 2 for various values of α.

For a sample size of 100 (99 df) the reliability factors for two-sided 90%, 95%, and 99% confidence intervals are 1.66, 1.98, and 2.63. The implication of these three values is that, all other things being equal (that is, $\bar{x}$, s, and n), requiring greater confidence in the interval estimate results in wider interval estimates. The more confidence that is required, the less reliable is the single sample estimate, and therefore greater numerical uncertainty is expressed in the interval estimate. This very important point is illustrated in the following example.

The following values of age ($n = 100$) were examined using a stem-and-leaf display in Chapter 5:

53, 69, 72, 48, 60, 61, 49, 71, 43, 31, 62, 51,
58, 61, 70, 66, 78, 39, 75, 63, 59, 53, 49, 61,
50, 88, 51, 80, 68, 75, 78, 81, 57, 70, 68, 66,
43, 60, 57, 35, 75, 61, 71, 45, 50, 82, 52, 65,
61, 77, 80, 58, 50, 59, 55, 59, 50, 39, 78, 72,
71, 79, 48, 55, 52, 55, 62, 59, 68, 63, 81, 69,
67, 67, 58, 57, 70, 73, 49, 43, 76, 73, 71, 77,
61, 62, 72, 73, 67, 62, 64, 40, 66, 74, 77, 67,
49, 83, 73, 59.

Assuming that these observations represent a simple random sample from the population of interest and that the age values in the population are normally distributed, the task is to calculate the two-sided 90%, 95%, and 99% confidence intervals for the population mean age.

The sample mean age is 62.6 and the standard deviation 12.01. The standard error of the mean is calculated as:

$$SE = 12.01/\sqrt{100} = 1.20.$$

With these numbers calculated, all that is left to compute the three confidence intervals are the reliability factors associated with each. For the 90% confidence interval, the value of the reliability factor will be the value of t that cuts off the upper 5% of the area (half the size of α) under the t distribution with 99 df. This value is 1.66 and can be verified from a table of values or from statistical software. Note that the t value of -1.66 is the value of t that cuts off the lower 5% of the area (half of the size of α) under the t distribution with 99 df. The reliability factors listed previously for the two-sided 95% and 99% confidence intervals can also be used to compute the following interval estimates:

- 90% CI = 62.6 ± (1.20)(1.66) = (60.6, 64.6)
- 95% CI = 62.6 ± (1.20)(1.98) = (60.2, 65.0)
- 99% CI = 62.6 ± (1.20)(2.63) = (59.4, 65.8).

Note that the two values that comprise the lower and upper limits of the confidence interval are typically placed in parentheses. The width of the confidence intervals (the difference between the upper and lower limits) increases because greater confidence (corresponding to smaller values of α) is required.

A statistical interpretation of these results is to say that we are 90% confident that the mean age of the population from which this sample was selected is enclosed in the interval 60.6–64.6 years. If greater confidence is required, we can say that with 99% confidence the mean age of the population is enclosed in the interval 59.4–65.8 years. Another interpretation of these confidence intervals is that they represent the most plausible values of the population mean. It is important to note that the lower and upper limits of the confidence interval are random variables. The population mean is considered to

be an unknown fixed quantity for which the confidence interval serves as an estimate.

To summarize, the computational aspects of confidence intervals involve a point estimate of the population parameter, some error attributed to sampling, and the amount of confidence (or reliability) required for interpretation. We have illustrated the general framework of the computation of confidence intervals using the case of the population mean. It is important to emphasize that interval estimates for other parameters of interest will require different reliability factors because these depend on the sampling distribution of the estimator itself and different calculations of standard errors. The calculated confidence interval has a statistical interpretation based on a probability statement.

Another useful interpretation of confidence intervals is that the values that are enclosed within the confidence interval are those that are considered the most plausible values of the unknown population parameter. Values outside the interval are considered less plausible. All other things being equal, the need for greater confidence in the estimate results in wider confidence intervals, and confidence intervals become narrower (that is, more precise) as the sample size increases. This last fact is explored in greater detail in Chapter 12 because it is directly relevant to the estimation of the required sample size for a clinical trial. The methods to use for the calculation of confidence intervals for other population parameters of interest are provided in subsequent chapters.

6.11 Hypothesis testing: General considerations

As this book focuses on clinical trials our primary interest is in providing you with relevant examples of hypothesis testing in that arena. However, it is useful initially to lay some conceptual foundations with simpler examples. As for many other examples in statistics and probability, we illustrate these concepts first with flips of a coin.

Imagine the following scenario. You are holding a half-dollar coin. Our question to you is: Do you think this coin is fair or not? You examine it and hold it and with no other information you decide that you really cannot tell without more information. You propose to flip the coin twice. Flipping it twice, you get the following results: Heads (H) and heads (H). If we forced you to answer our question at this time, you may guess, based on these two observations, that the coin is not fair. After all, if the coin were really fair you would "expect" one head (H) and one tail (T). However, you are not at all confident with your answer because you note that the probability of observing two heads is not that small. It is $(0.5)(0.5) = 0.25$. This means that an outcome like this results 25% of the time that you conduct such an experiment. Accordingly, you wisely recognize that it would be better to have additional data before making your guess, because with just two heads observed out of two flips there is a non-trivial chance that you have guessed incorrectly.

Suppose you then revise the experiment and request that the results from 10 flips of the coin be recorded. You reason that, if the coin were fair, you would expect five heads and five tails. If you were to observe that only one or as many as nine heads came up out of ten tosses, you would conclude that the coin was not fair. Your logic is that, by chance alone, a fair coin would not very likely yield such a lopsided result. If you were to observe an event with even more extreme result, that is, 0 or 10 heads out of 10 tosses, you would also have concluded, perhaps with even more confidence, that the coin was not fair.

The rule that you intuitively arrived at was that if you observed as few as 0 or 1 or as many as 9 or 10 heads out of 10 coin flips, you would conclude that the coin was not fair. How likely is it that such a result would happen? In other words, suppose you repeated this experiment a number of times with a truly fair coin. What proportion of experiments conducted in the same manner would result in an erroneous conclusion on your part because you followed the evidence in this way? This is the point where the rules of probability come into play. You can find the probability of making the wrong conclusion (calling the fair coin biased) by

following such a decision rule using the binomial distribution.

Using the binomial distribution, the probability of observing 9 heads out of 10 when the probability of observing a head with each trial is ½ is 0.00977. Likewise, the probability of observing 10 heads out of 10 is 0.00098. So the probability of observing either 9 or 10 heads is the sum of these two (we sum them because these are mutually exclusive outcomes). That probability is 0.01075 (around 1%). We note that the probability of observing 0 or 1 heads is the same as for observing 9 or 10. Therefore the probability of observing a result as extreme as 1 or fewer or 9 or more heads is around 0.02. If after 10 coin flips, we have observed 1 or fewer heads or 9 or more heads, we would conclude that the coin was biased because a fair coin would yield such a result only with probability around 2% (not very often). Put another way, if we conducted this experiment many times and used such a rule when we have observed such a result, we would be incorrect in 2% of the experiments. That seems like an acceptable risk to take. Besides, in this scenario, there seems to be no adverse consequence to being wrong except for a bit of damaged pride.

This rather simple example is an illustration of the conceptual components of hypothesis testing. The basis of hypothesis testing is "proof by contradiction." We use the word "proof" rather liberally here because the scientific standard for establishing proof is more rigorous than a single trial or set of trials could possibly provide. Hypothesis testing is a statistical method in which we use data (evidence) to choose between two decisions, each with their own course of action and related implications. The real world implication of making either decision depends on the field of study. In the world of new drug development, these decisions could be to decide that a drug is not efficacious at any dose studied, and is therefore not worth studying further. Another decision could be to select one particular dose (among many studied) for further development in confirmatory trials.

The process of testing a hypothesis usually begins with the statement of the hypothesis that we would like to conclude as a result of the research (we refer to this as the alternate hypothesis). There is another hypothesis that we need to define and it is referred to as the null hypothesis. The null hypothesis can be viewed as a "straw man" hypothesis, one that we would like to knock over by collecting evidence that contradicts it in favor of the alternate hypothesis. One important consideration in the statement of the two hypotheses is that they should represent all possible outcomes. In the context of our coin-tossing illustration, the alternate hypothesis would be that the coin is biased and the null hypothesis would be that the coin is fair. In that experiment, we counted the number of heads and were looking for evidence that would contradict the null hypothesis and compel us to conclude that the alternate hypothesis was true. Evidence that contradicted the null hypothesis would be a very high or very low proportion of heads because a fair coin would yield approximately the same number of heads as tails. Importantly, these two hypotheses cover the only two possible outcomes: The coin is either fair or biased.

The next part of the hypothesis-testing process is to decide on a numerical result (a test statistic) that, if observed, would sufficiently contradict the null hypothesis such that the null hypothesis would be rejected in favor of the alternate hypothesis. As we discovered with our coin-tossing example, some results would not be all that rare by chance alone. Therefore, our decision rule should be defined such that erroneous conclusions are not made more often than we are willing to tolerate.

You will recall that we might have chosen other results before we concluded that the coin was biased, but we chose results that would rarely be expected by chance alone. In fact, the decision rule is based on our chosen probability of rejecting the null hypothesis when it is really true. For the coin example, this is the probability of claiming that the coin is biased when it is really fair. When asked to take part in this experiment the fairness of the coin remains unknown to us, but we choose a decision rule that is consistent with results that would not be expected by chance very often.

6.11.1 Type I errors and type II errors

Rejecting the null hypothesis when it is true is called a type I error. The probability of making a type I error is called alpha (α). There is another kind of error that we might commit by using data from our sample (in this case, 10 coin tosses) to make an inference about the state of nature. This second kind of error is called a type II error and results from failing to reject the null hypothesis (suppose we observed seven heads) when, in fact, the alternate hypothesis is true (that is, the coin was biased). We would then act as if the coin were fair – perhaps taking part in a new challenge that involved wagering a lot of money.

When making decisions of any type, whether they are as inconsequential as our coin-tossing experiment or as important and costly as developing a new drug, we would like to minimize the chances that we make the wrong decision. In planning a new study or experiment, such as a clinical trial, it is worthwhile to consider minimizing the probability of committing each of these errors. The two types of errors are presented in Table 6.3. In clinical trials a type I error is committed when we claim that the new antihypertensive is superior to placebo but it really is similar. A type II error is committed when we fail to claim the new antihypertensive is superior to placebo but it really is. In reality we cannot know the truth, but the study design, including the sample size and the statistical analyses used to evaluate the trial, will enable us to limit the probability of committing each of these errors.

6.11.2 Probability of type I and II errors

An important aspect of study design is defining the probabilities of committing each of these two kinds of errors. A type I error could mean that a new drug is approved for marketing but really does not provide a benefit. Ideally, the probability of committing a type I error of this type would be fairly small. Committing a

Table 6.3 Two possible errors in hypothesis testing

Decision based on test statistic	Truth about null hypothesis	
	True	**False**
Fail to reject null hypothesis	Correct	Type II error
Reject null hypothesis	Type I error	Correct

type II error in a superiority trial of a new anti-hypertensive is not appealing for a study sponsor because it could lead to discontinuation of a development program for a new treatment that is actually efficacious. Therefore, it is desirable to limit the probability of committing a type II error as well. We have more to say about these two probabilities in subsequent chapters, but for now it is sufficient to identify them formally.

The probability of committing a type I error is the probability of rejecting the null hypothesis when it is true (for example, claiming that the new treatment is superior to placebo when they are equivalent in terms of the outcome). The probability of committing a type I error is called α, which is sometimes referred to as the size of the test. The probability of committing a type II error is the probability of failing to reject the null hypothesis when it is false. This probability is also called beta (β). The quantity $(1 - \beta)$ is referred to as the power of the statistical test. It is the probability of rejecting the null hypothesis (in favor of the alternate) when the alternate is true. As stated earlier it is desirable to have low error probabilities associated with a test. As we would like α and β to be as low as possible the quanti-

ties $(1 - \alpha)$ and $(1 - \beta)$ are typically fairly large. These probabilities are provided in Table 6.4.

6.11.3 Hypothesis testing and research questions

Statistical hypothesis testing represents a means to formulate and answer the research question in a quantitative manner. The null hypothesis is the hypothesis that is tested. If quantitative data are produced that are not consistent with the null hypothesis, it is rejected.

Before proceeding with this statistical approach, a research question must be posed, which will then prompt the design of a study that will lead to the collection of data and an appropriate statistical analysis. A simple research question from a drug development program, as stated in Chapter 3, is "Does the investigational drug lower blood pressure?" A way to answer this research question is to design a study to estimate the mean change from baseline in SBP. If the mean change from baseline is negative, the answer to the research question would be that the investigational drug does lower blood pressure. This example will be used to illustrate the concept of hypothesis testing.

Table 6.4 Probabilities of outcomes (conditional on the null hypothesis) in hypothesis testing

Decision based on test statistic	Truth about null hypothesis	
	True	**False**
Fail to reject null hypothesis	$1 - \alpha$	β
Reject null hypothesis	α	$1 - \beta$ (i.e., power)

6.12 Hypothesis test of a single population mean

Suppose our interest is in testing whether the population mean was equal to a particular hypothesized value, μ_0. A hypothesis testing process typically starts with a statement of the null and alternate hypotheses. The null hypothesis can be stated in the following manner:

$$H_0: \mu = \mu_0.$$

If data are found to contradict the null hypothesis, it will be rejected in favor of the alternate hypothesis:

$$H_A: \mu \neq \mu_0.$$

The alternate hypothesis is two sided in the sense that values clearly less than μ_0 would be consistent with it as would values that were clearly greater than μ_0. Rejection of the null hypothesis because $\mu_0 << \mu$ (μ is much greater than the hypothesized value μ_0) may lead to one decision (for example, continue with the development of the new drug with a larger study) whereas rejection of the null hypothesis because $\mu_0 >> \mu$ (μ is much less than the hypothesized value μ_0) may lead to a completely different decision (for example, to stop development of the new drug because it has no effect on SBP or actually increases SBP). What is important is that, *a priori*, either outcome is possible.

The next step of the hypothesis testing process is to identify a numeric criterion by which the plausibility of the null hypothesis is tested. This numeric criterion is called the test statistic, and we use it to decide if the value that resulted from the study contradicts the null hypothesis or not. The test statistic to be used in this case is:

$$t = \frac{\bar{x} - \mu_0}{s/\sqrt{n}}.$$

If the null hypothesis is true – that is, the population mean is the hypothesized value, μ_0 – the value of the test statistic will be close to 0. The further the test statistic value is from 0 (either negative or positive) the less plausible is the hypothesized value, μ_0 – that is, the null hypothesis should be rejected in favor of the alternate.

The next step of hypothesis testing is to determine those values of the test statistic that would lead to rejection of the null hypothesis, that is, to determine the critical region.

Assuming that the random variable is normally distributed (or approximately so if the sample size is > 30) and if the null hypothesis is true, the test statistic just defined has a t distribution with $(n-1)$ df. Referring to Figure 6.6 you will see that most values of a random variable that follow a t distribution fall in the range -1 to $+1$. A value in this range would be expected just by chance alone. However, values < -2 or $> +2$ occur much less frequently, that is, there is less area to the left of -2 and to the right of $+2$. We would like to define a critical region that is associated with small tail areas because values in the tail do not occur frequently, whereas values in the center of the distribution are very common. In other words, we would like to define the test so that we do not reject the null hypothesis very often when in fact it is true – that is, we would like to define a critical region so that the probability of committing a type I error, α, is small.

In most scientific endeavors the choice of α is 0.05. We are willing to accept a 1 in 20 chance that, at the end of the study, it is concluded that the population mean is not the hypothesized value when in fact it really is. It is important to remember that the choice of α is part of the study design, and not a result of a study. Also, it is important to note here that there is nothing special about the value of 0.05. Depending on the stage of development or the severity or importance of the disease for which we wish to develop the drug, we may choose a value of α that is higher or lower than 0.05. What is important in the choice of α are the implications (for sponsors, regulatory bodies, clinicians, and patients) of committing a type I error. Having alerted you to the possibility of choosing other values for α, and the fact that this choice has various implications, we adopt the conventional value of α of 0.05 in subsequent discussions.

Knowledge of the distribution of the test statistic enables us to define a critical region that would erroneously lead to rejection with probability of 0.05. In the case of the current test, the critical region will be any value of the test statistic such that:

$t < t_{\alpha/2,n-1}$ or $t > t_{1-\alpha/2,n-1}$.

Similarly to the case of the standard normal distribution, the critical values can be obtained from a series of tabulated values or from statistical software. A number of percentiles of various t distributions are provided in Appendix 2. It is important to note that there is not just one t distribution; there are many of them, and their shapes are determined by the number of degrees of freedom. As either low or high values of the test statistic could lead to rejection, the hypothesis test is considered a two-sided test. The probability of committing a type I error is 0.05, but, because the critical region is evenly split between low values and high values, the probability of committing a type I error in favor of one direction (for example, large values of t) is $\alpha/2$.

Once the critical region of the test has been defined, the next step of hypothesis testing is to calculate the value of the test statistic from the sample data. The test statistic is calculated as:

$$t = \frac{\bar{x} - \mu_0}{s/\sqrt{n}}$$

where $\bar{x}$ is the sample mean, μ_0 the hypothesized value of the population mean, s the sample standard deviation, and n the sample size.

If the value of the test statistic is in the critical region the null hypothesis is rejected and the conclusion is made that the population mean is not equal to μ_0. When the null hypothesis is rejected, such a result is considered "statistically significant" at the α level, meaning that the result was unlikely (with probability no greater than α) to have been observed by chance alone. If the value of the test statistic is not in the critical region we fail to reject the null hypothesis. It is important to emphasize the fact that we cannot claim that the population mean is equal to μ_0, but simply that the data were not sufficient to conclude that they were different.

The use of this method, the one-sample t test, is appropriate when:

- the observations represent a simple random sample from the population of interest
- the random variable is continuous
- the random variable is normally distributed or approximately normally distributed

(mound shaped) with a sample size of at least 30.

This hypothesis test is illustrated with the following simple example.

Imagine that, having identified a promising new investigational antihypertensive drug, a pharmaceutical company would like to administer it to a group of 10 hypertensive individuals to see if the drug has the desired effect. For simplicity we assume that there is no control group. The first study of the new antihypertensive will be a single-dose, nonrandomized, uncontrolled trial in 10 participants. SBP was recorded at the start of the study before initiation of treatment (baseline) and at the end of 4 weeks (end of study). The research question of interest is: Does the new drug lower SBP? The scientists designing the trial would like to maintain a type I error of 0.05, that is, $\alpha = 0.05$. As the test conducted is two sided, the probability of making a type I error in favor of the drug having a beneficial effect (one side of the critical region) is 0.025.

The null hypothesis is:

H_0: $\mu = 0$.

And the alternate hypothesis is:

H_A: $\mu \neq 0$.

The one-sample t test will be used to test the null hypothesis. As there are 10 observations and assuming the change scores (the random variable of interest) are normally distributed, the test statistic will follow a t distribution with 9 df. A table of critical values for the t distribution (Appendix 2) will inform us that the two-sided critical region is defined as $t < -2.26$ and $t > 2.26$ – that is, under the null hypothesis, the probability of observing a t value < -2.26 is 0.025 and the probability of observing a t value > 2.26 is 0.025.

Baseline and end-of-study values of SBP are presented for the 10 participants in Table 6.5, along with their respective change scores.

The mean change score is -7 and the standard deviation is 7.1. (We leave it to you to verify this.) The test statistic is therefore calculated as:

$$t = \frac{-7 - 0}{7.1/\sqrt{10}} = -3.10.$$

Table 6.5   Systolic blood pressure (SBP) values and change scores

Study participant	Baseline SBP (mmHg)	End-of-study SBP (mmHg)	Change in SBP (mmHg)
1	143	147	4
2	152	144	−8
3	162	159	−3
4	158	157	−1
5	147	131	−16
6	149	133	−16
7	150	145	−5
8	148	144	−4
9	154	150	−4
10	149	132	−17

As this calculated test statistic is in the critical region ($t = -3.10 < -2.26$) the null hypothesis is rejected. The result is considered statistically significant at the $\alpha = 0.05$ level because there was less than a 5% chance of such a result being observed by chance alone. The conclusion from the study is that the new drug did lower SBP by a mean of 7 mmHg. Scientists from the sponsor company may use this information as sufficient preliminary evidence to continue with the development of the new drug.

6.13 The *p* value

One shortcoming of the hypothesis testing approach is the arbitrary choice of a value for α. Depending upon our risk tolerance for committing a type I error, the conventional value of 0.05 may not be acceptable. Another way to convey the "extremeness" of the resulting test statistic is to report a *p* value.

A *p* value is the probability that the result obtained or one more extreme (in favor of the alternate) would be observed by chance alone. We know from the definition of the critical region that a value of the test statistic $t < -2.26$ or $t > 2.26$ would have occurred with probability ≤ 0.05 by chance alone. In fact, the test statistic value was -3.10 which lies to the left of -2.26. A value of -3.10 led to rejection, as would values < -3.10 or > 3.10. The *p* value in this case is the

area under the *t*-distribution density curve with 9 df associated with values of $t < -3.10$ or > 3.10 and is equal to 0.01. This means that there is only a 1% chance of observing a value of the test statistic as large as 3.10 (in absolute magnitude) or larger by chance alone. The difference between α (a design parameter) and the *p* value (a study result) can be seen in Figure 6.7, where the areas to the left and right of the dashed lines represent α and the areas to the left and right of the solid line represent the *p* value.

The *p* values can be estimated from a table of values from the appropriate *t* distribution (for example, by finding the tail areas associated with a particular value of the test statistic). More commonly, however, statistical software is used for all statistical analyses and *p* values are included in the results. The following is a helpful way to interpret *p* values:

- Hypothesis tests are rejected if the calculated *p* value $\leq \alpha$.
- Hypothesis tests are not rejected if the calculated *p* value $> \alpha$.

It is not uncommon for results of hypothesis tests to be represented simply by the *p* value. However, it is not a wise practice to rely solely on them. Recall that increasing the sample size reduces the standard error, which increases the size of the test statistic and therefore reduces the *p* value. This serves as a reminder that it is not just the statistical significance of the result (that is, the *p* value) that counts. The clinical relevance of the size of the effect (for example, the

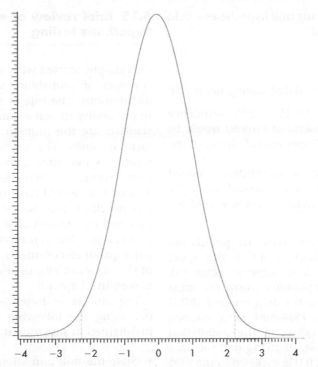

Figure 6.7 The *t* distribution with 9 degrees of freedom, critical region (dashed line) and *p* value (solid line). Note that the critical region is represented by the tail areas to the left and right of the dashed lines; the *p* value is represented by the tail areas to the left and right of the solid lines

confidence interval for the parameter of interest) is probably more important than the *p* value, as we argue in the following section.

6.14 Relationship between confidence intervals and hypothesis tests

Confidence intervals can be used to test a number of hypotheses. This is illustrated using the study data from the previous example in Section 6.12.

Scientists from the pharmaceutical company believe that reporting a 95% confidence interval for the population mean change in SBP may prove helpful. Following the confidence interval defined in Section 6.10, a 95% confidence interval for the population mean is:

$$-7 \pm 2.26(7.1/\sqrt{10}) = (-12.1, -1.9).$$

The scientists can report from this study that they are 95% confident that the true population mean change in SBP is within the interval $(-12.1, -1.9)$. One interpretation of this interval is that the scientists are 95% confident that the drug works by reducing SBP, as evidenced by an upper limit of the confidence interval that is less than 0. Another less favorable interpretation is that the drug does not work all that well – after all, the confidence interval does not rule out some very minor reductions in SBP (upper limit of -1.9 mmHg). It is true that, had the scientists hypothesized a value of the population mean outside of the values of this 95% confidence interval, the null hypothesis would have been rejected at the $\alpha = 0.05$ level. For example, the following null hypotheses would have been rejected:

$$H_0: \mu = 2$$
$$H_0: \mu = -15.$$

Conversely, the following null hypotheses would not have been rejected:

$H_0: \mu = -8$
$H_0: \mu = -2.$

This relationship can be stated more generally as:

- All values outside the $(1 - \alpha)\%$ confidence interval for a parameter of interest would be rejected by a hypothesis test (of size α) of the parameter.
- Values within the $(1 - \alpha)\%$ confidence interval for a parameter of interest would fail to be rejected by a hypothesis test (of size α) of the parameter.

In this example, μ represents the population mean change from baseline SBP. If the upper limit of the 95% confidence interval excludes 0, negative values of population mean are most plausible, implying that the drug lowered SBP. If the lower limit of the 95% confidence interval excludes 0, positive values of the population mean are most plausible, implying that the drug actually increased SBP. If 0 is enclosed in the 95% confidence interval, negative and positive values of the mean are most plausible, implying that we cannot rule out the possibility that the drug had no effect. These three scenarios are displayed in Figure 6.8.

As confidence intervals can be used to test a number of hypotheses simultaneously, they convey much more information than a single *p* value resulting from a hypothesis test. In addition to being able to test various hypotheses (the null hypothesis of zero change from baseline was rejected) the confidence interval allows regulatory agencies and physicians who review the data to interpret the clinical relevance of the magnitude of the values within the confidence interval.

6.15 Brief review of estimation and hypothesis testing

This chapter started with an introduction to the concepts of probability and random variable distributions. The role of probability is to assist in our ability to make statistical inferences. Test statistics are the numeric results of an experiment or study. The yardstick by which a test statistic is measured is how extreme it is. The term "extreme" in Statistics is used in relation to a value that would have been expected if there was no effect, that is, the value that would be expected by random chance alone. Confidence intervals provide an interval estimate for a population parameter of interest. Confidence intervals of $(1 - \alpha)\%$ can also be used to test hypotheses, as seen in Chapter 8.

The process of hypothesis testing is carried out using the following steps, which will be highlighted in subsequent chapters:

- State the null and alternate hypotheses. It is sometimes easier to state the alternate hypothesis first because that is what we would like to conclude at the end of the study. The null hypothesis then covers the remainder of values of the population parameter. The specific statements of the null and alternate hypotheses depend on the type of study and the analysis approach used. We cover many different examples in later chapters.
- Determine the test statistic appropriate for the method used. Choosing the appropriate test statistic depends on the analysis method and the assumptions that we must make.
- Select a value of α (as noted earlier, our standard for this book is 0.05).

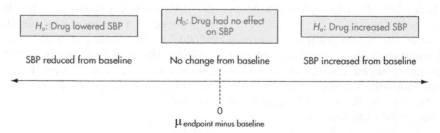

Figure 6.8   Conclusions to be drawn from the population mean change from baseline

- Calculate the value of the test statistic under the null hypothesis and the corresponding p value. Compare the p value with the value of α.
- State the statistical decision either to reject or to fail to reject the null hypothesis.

Statistical inference is one way to use data to make a decision in the presence of uncertainty. The resulting decisions are not perfect. The commission of either a type I or a type II error can have significant impacts on drug companies, study participants, patients, and public health. Therefore, minimizing the probability that each might occur is an important part of the study design, including the manner in which data are analyzed and interpreted.

6.16   Review

1. Using Table 6.1, calculate the probability of selecting a participant who is:

   (a) female
   (b) female and $\geq$ 65 years of age
   (c) $\geq$ 65 years of age
   (d) female given that the participant is $\geq$ 65 years of age.

2. Show that the true negative rate of a diagnostic test is a function of the sensitivity and specificity of the test and the prevalence of the disease.

3. Assume that SBP among all adults aged 30 years and older in the UK has a normal distribution with mean 120 mmHg and variance 100 mmHg. What proportion of participants in this population has:

   (a) SBP < 90 mmHg?
   (b) SBP < 120 mmHg?
   (c) SBP < 100 mmHg or SBP > 140 mmHg?
   (d) SBP > 160 mmHg?

4. What is the difference between standard deviation and standard error?

5. What is α? How does a researcher decide on a value for α?

6. What is β? How does a researcher decide on a value for β?

7. What are the three components of a confidence interval?

8. What is a two-sided hypothesis test?

9. The one-sample t test is being used for a two-sided test of the null hypothesis, $H_0: \mu = 0$. For each of the following scenarios, define the rejection region for the test:

   (a) $n = 10; \alpha = 0.10$
   (b) $n = 10; \alpha = 0.01$
   (c) $n = 30; \alpha = 0.05$
   (d) $n = 30; \alpha = 0.001$.

10. For each of the following 95% confidence intervals for the population mean, would a two-sided test of the null hypothesis, $H_0: \mu = 0$, be rejected or not rejected?

    (a) (−4.0, 4.0)
    (b) (−2.0, −1.0)
    (c) (22.3, 44.6)
    (d) (−12.7, 0.01).

6.17 References

Turner JR (2007). *New Drug Development: Design, methodology, and analysis.* Hoboken, NJ: John Wiley & Sons.

vos Savant M (1997). Ask Marilyn. *Parade Magazine* 30 March, p. 15.

7

Early phase clinical trials

7.1 Introduction

As we noted in Section 1.11, this book focuses on teaching you the statistical methodologies and analyses that are employed in the therapeutic confirmatory clinical trials conducted before a sponsor applies for marketing approval for the drug that they have been developing. We also noted that there are other clinical trials that precede therapeutic confirmatory trials. Two other categories of preapproval trials mentioned are Phase I (human pharmacology) trials and Phase II (therapeutic exploratory) trials. Therefore, before focusing on therapeutic confirmatory trials in Chapters 8–11, it is appropriate to provide an overview of human pharmacology and therapeutic exploratory trials.

The usefulness of numerical information from clinical trials in decision-making is an ongoing theme in this book. The first few clinical studies for new drugs are important because they provide information relevant to the critical decisions that must be made with regard to continued investment in the development program. Ideally, studies are designed to answer research questions, the answers to which provide sufficient information to inform the next step of development, that is, either to go forward (a "go" decision) or not to go forward (a "no-go" decision). The answer to these critical early questions must be "go" if we are to reach the later stages of clinical development. For example, we need to have reasonable confidence that the drug is safe enough to progress to therapeutic exploratory trials in which it will be administered for the first time to participants with the disease or condition of interest.

In addition, we need to have reasonable confidence that a particular selected route of adminis-

tration will prove successful for administering the drug to patients if and when the drug is approved. Although many other questions must be addressed during later-stage clinical development, these critical early phase questions have significant bearing on the ultimate safety and efficacy attributes of the product, as well as commercial implications (for example, route or schedule of administration).

Discussions in this chapter emphasize statistical considerations in early phase clinical trials. These include study designs employed, the types of data collected, and the usefulness and limitations of these data.

7.2 A quick recap of early phase studies

Human pharmacology studies are pharmacologically oriented trials that typically look for the best range of doses to employ. These trials typically involve healthy adults. Comparison with other treatments (such as a placebo or a drug that is already marketed) is not typically an aim of these trials, which are undertaken in an extremely careful manner in very controlled settings, often in residential or inpatient medical centers. Typically, between 20 and 80 healthy adults participate in these relatively short studies, and participants are often recruited from university medical school settings where trials are being conducted. The main objectives are to assess the safety of the investigational drug, understand the drug's pharmacokinetic profile and any potential interactions with other drugs, and estimate pharmacodynamic activity. A range of doses and/or dosing intervals is typically investigated in a sequential manner.

From a statistical viewpoint, the design of human pharmacology studies has certain implications. They include a relatively small number of participants, but a lot of measurements are collected for each participant. This strategy has both advantages and limitations. The extensive array of measurements made allows the drug's effects to be characterized reasonably thoroughly. However, as so few participants participate in these studies, generalizations to the general participant population are relatively more tenuous than for studies with larger sample sizes.

7.3 General comments on study designs in early phase clinical studies

A disappointing result in early clinical studies, as a result of either a real liability of the investigational drug or chance alone, can doom the prospects for the new drug ever entering the market. No-go decisions are a logical consequence of such disappointing results. To provide optimum quality data and the associated optimum quality information upon which to base go and no-go decisions, early clinical studies are very well controlled, thereby limiting extraneous sources of variation as much as possible. Early clinical studies, especially FTIH (first-time-in-human) studies, are typically conducted at a single investigative center. As a relatively small number of participants are studied in such early phase trials, a single center can feasibly accommodate the study by itself. It can recruit enough participants at that single location, and provide all the necessary resources for investigators at that site to conduct all the study procedures documented in the study protocol. Conducting a study at a single center ensures greater consistency with respect to participant management, study conduct, and assessment of adverse events, and provides for frequent and careful monitoring of study participants.

Participants in early clinical studies are usually healthy adults whose health status is carefully documented at the start of the study through physical examinations, clinical laboratory tests, and medical histories. Limiting early studies to healthy participants allows the sponsor to attribute any untoward findings to the drug, or to a particular dose of the drug, as significant background diseases are all but absent.

Early clinical studies frequently involve the use of a concurrent inactive control. This can be important because the study procedures can be somewhat invasive and associated with some adverse effects themselves – for example, frequent blood draws resulting in a lowering of hematocrit. Without a concurrent control arm (even in a study of healthy participants) study sponsors and investigators would not be able to rule out a drug effect when observing such occurrences, which are expected, easily explained, and non-drug related. In early studies that involve inpatient facilities for close monitoring, other controls may be instituted, for example, standardized meals and set times for study procedures.

7.4 Goals of early phase clinical trials

Early clinical trials used in new drug development typically have the following goals:

- characterize the pharmacokinetic profile of the investigational drug
- describe the safety and tolerability of the investigational drug in study participants who do not have significant medical conditions
- describe the extent to which a pharmacodynamic effect is affected by different doses of the new drug
- begin to identify a dose range that would likely provide adequate exposure to yield an important clinical effect.

Although somewhat overly simplistic (especially to readers who are students of pharmacy) we can consider pharmacokinetic effects as "what the body does to the drug" and pharmacodynamic effects as "what the drug does to the body." For those readers who are less familiar with pharmacokinetics and pharmacodynamics, Tozer and Roland (2006) provide an excellent and very readable introduction to these topics.

Patients with diseases or conditions of interest can have a number of attributes that, although very important in the context of the eventual use of the new drug, make accurate assessments of the safety and pharmacokinetics of the investigational drug difficult. For example, patients with the disease may have compromised kidney or liver function, which would confound the characterization of the metabolism of the new drug. Similarly, patients with the disease may take several other medications for the disease under study or for other related or unrelated diseases. It then becomes difficult to ascertain in early studies whether potential adverse effects or laboratory abnormalities are attributable to the investigational drug, to concomitant drugs, or to any potential interactions between the investigational drug and other drugs. (Drug interactions are not discussed in this book and readers are referred to Hansten [2004].)

The employment of healthy participants in early clinical studies provides essential information about the pharmacokinetics, pharmacodynamics, and safety of the new drug. This chapter focuses on the research questions relevant to early human studies, the designs used to address them, the data and analysis approaches commonly encountered, and the development decisions that are made as a result of these studies.

We should note here that there are some special cases for which the use of healthy participants is not justified in early studies. For particularly invasive therapies (for example, implantation of a medical device) or therapies with known toxicity (for example, oncologics) it is not ethical to study healthy participants. The use of healthy participants in early studies may also provide a misleading result for future studies of participants with disease. For example, the maximum tolerated dose of new antidepressants or anxiolytics may differ quite markedly between healthy participants and those with the disease.

7.5 Research questions in early phase clinical studies

In the early clinical development of a new drug, the following questions arise:

- How does the magnitude of systemic exposure to the new drug differ as a function of increasing concentrations of the drug?
- How does the magnitude of systemic exposure to the new drug differ as a function of different dosing schedules (for example, once, twice, or three times a day)?
- How do varying degrees of drug exposure modify measurable pharmacodynamic effects?
- How does the total amount of drug exposure from the route of administration being studied (for example, oral) compare with the total amount of drug exposure when administered parenterally (that is, intravenously or intra-arterially)? In other words, how bioavailable is the drug?
- How safe is the new drug? Evaluations include clinical laboratory tests, physical assessments, vital signs, adverse events, and cardiac effects through electrophysiological monitoring via an ECG.

To address the first four research questions listed above, pharmacokinetic data are typically collected at various time points in early clinical studies: These data are discussed in the next section. To evaluate the difference between background variation (influences that are not directly of interest) and changes brought about by the administration of drug (influences that are of interest), measurements are collected on several occasions before the start of the drug, at several times during drug administration, and at least once after the administration of the drug when its effect is likely to be minimal (for example, 24 hours later). Evaluation of the fifth question is discussed in Section 7.10.

7.6 Pharmacokinetic characteristics of interest

Investigations at this stage of a clinical development program focus primarily on a very careful evaluation of how well the drug reaches the bloodstream, and how its concentrations in the bloodstream change over time, that is, on pharmacokinetics. The extent and duration of a drug's presence in the bloodstream determine how good a chance it has ultimately to exert its intended clinical effect by reaching and interacting with its target receptors, the domain of pharmacodynamic investigation. Therefore, we need to study pharmacokinetic factors before studying the actual clinical effects of the drug in therapeutic exploratory trials, trials in which the relationship between drug concentrations and clinical response are typically addressed for the first time.

As mentioned in Section 2.5, the term "pharmacokinetics" generally refers to the absorption, distribution, metabolism, and excretion (ADME) of a drug. When developing a new drug a great deal of time and effort is devoted to formulating the drug so that it has the most desirable characteristics from the standpoint of safety, efficacy, and commercial concerns (for example, patient convenience and patient adherence to the prescribed regimen). There are several commonly used summary measures that are useful for quantifying absorption and excretion. In contrast, metabolism and distribution are not as easy to define in terms of quantifiable measures, although it is possible to characterize how a drug is metabolized through the identification of certain markers.

7.6.1 Total systemic exposure

Total systemic exposure to an administered drug is usually measured by the area under the drug concentration curve. For each participant the drug concentration (in nanograms/milliliter) can be plotted as a function of time, as displayed in Figure 7.1. The maximal drug concentration (C_{max}) and the time at which it is observed (t_{max}) are also shown. These two parameters are discussed in Section 7.6.2.

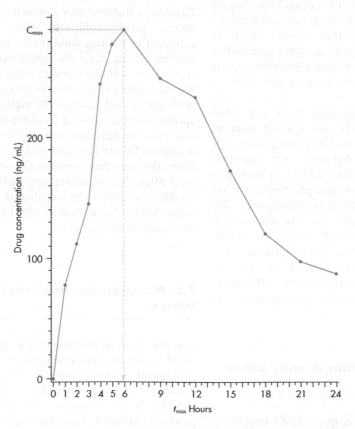

Figure 7.1 Sample drug–concentration time curve for a single participant (C_{max} of 290 ng/mL and t_{max} of 6 hours)

The estimated area under the curve from time point zero to infinity ($AUC_{(0-\infty)}$) is calculated using the trapezoidal rule. There are two steps in this process:

1. Calculate the trapezoidal area between all adjacent time points
2. Sum all areas calculated in the first step.

This calculation is an estimate of the real $AUC_{(0-\infty)}$, but a meaningful and useful estimate. By progressively increasing the sampling frequency we could obtain more and more precise measurements, but pragmatism dictates frequency, and a reasonable frequency produces a useful estimate of $AUC_{(0-\infty)}$. $AUC_{(0-t)}$ denotes the area under the curve from 0 to any time point t.

7.6.2 Maximum concentration

Another important measure of absorption is the peak or maximum concentration or maximum systemic exposure (C_{max}). It may be of interest to know the C_{max} associated with a beneficial effect. However, it is more common to use the value of C_{max} to provide assurance that, despite observing a specific C_{max} value, there was no unwanted toxicity. If the C_{max} is too high for a given dose of drug as measured by a clinical effect, such a finding could guide development of other formulations and treatment schedules. The C_{max} is calculated as the maximum value of the drug concentration during the period of monitoring. The time from administration to achieve the C_{max} is called t_{max}. Depending on the intended clinical use for the new drug, it may be more desirable to have shorter or longer values of t_{max}. For example, when in need of headache pain relief, we might be interested in a t_{max} that is as short as possible. As noted in the previous section, both C_{max} and t_{max} are shown in Figure 7.1, where C_{max} has a value of 290 ng/mL and t_{max} has a value of 6 hours.

7.6.3 Elimination

Elimination of a drug is measured using a quantity called a half-life ($t_{1/2}$). A half-life is the time required to reduce the plasma concentration to half its initial value. Longer half-lives can be associated with desirable characteristics (for example, longer activity requiring less frequent administration of the drug) or undesirable ones (for example, adverse effects).

7.6.4 Excretion

Excretion concerns the removal of a drug compound from the body. Both the original (parent) drug compound and its metabolites can be excreted. The primary mode of investigation here is excretion balance studies. A radiolabeled drug compound is administered and radioactivity is then measured from excretion sites (for example, urine, feces, expired air). These studies provide information on which organs are involved in excretion and the time course of excretion.

7.7 Analysis of pharmacokinetic and pharmacodynamic data

Statistical analyses of pharmacokinetic and pharmacodynamic effects are primarily descriptive in nature. As described in Chapter 6, inferential statistical methods such as hypothesis testing are used to make decisions in the presence of uncertainty, while limiting the likelihood of making decisions with unwanted consequences (for example, marketing an ineffective drug or not bringing to market an effective one). The decisions to be made in pharmacokinetic studies do not have such dire consequences nor are they directly applicable to the real world use of the new drug. Rather, the data acquired in pharmacokinetic studies are used as a starting point to identify doses, dosage forms, and dosage regimens for the new drug which, when studied in individuals with the disease, will allow a reasonable chance at evaluating the potential benefits and risks associated with its use.

Pharmacokinetic measures such as $AUC_{(0-24)}$, C_{max}, and t_{max} are analyzed as continuous measures. As seen in the example in Table 7.1, measures of central tendency and dispersion can be helpful to highlight differences among groups.

Table 7.1   Pharmacokinetic measures: Mean (SD) for three dosage regimens of a new investigational drug

	Dosage regimen		
	20 mg once a day ($n = 10$)	20 mg twice daily ($n = 10$)	20 mg three times daily ($n = 10$)
$AUC_{(0-24)}$ (ng h/mL)	812 (132)	1632 (264)	2237 (412)
C_{max} (ng/mL)	174 (61)	181 (74)	308 (94)
t_{max} (h)	2.4 (0.9)	2.6 (0.6)	7.4 (1.0)

Before discussing the interpretation of the data in Table 7.1, a couple of points about tabular displays like this one are worth pointing out. First, every study or analysis has a primary comparison of interest: In this case it is to compare AUC across groups. The ability of a regulatory reviewer to interpret data with respect to the primary comparison is aided by displaying data across columns for the comparison. In this case, a single summary measure of interest (AUC) represents a row and the groups may be compared by reading left to right. Secondary comparisons should then be placed as rows on a table.

A common example of a secondary comparison in pharmacokinetic studies is the concentration of drug at various time points during the study. It is important to know how the within-group average concentration changes over time, but it is more important to know how the mean concentration differs among groups at one time point. The fundamental nature of clinical trials is comparative, above all else. The second point about tabular displays such as this one is that the table itself is well labeled with titles and column headers. In the regulated world of drug development, presentation is extremely important. "Substance" is our first concern, but "style" is certainly important to convey the substance to a regulatory reviewer.

Descriptive analyses were discussed in Chapter 5, particularly measures of central tendency and dispersion. Those discussions now enable us to examine the pharmacokinetic data presented in Table 7.1. As can be seen, a total of 10 participants were studied in each group. The mean (SD) AUC values were 812 (132), 1632

(264), and 2237 (412), respectively. From these results we can conclude that the three times daily dosage regimen resulted in overall greater systemic exposure to the drug.

7.7.1 Decisions and inferences from FTIH studies

Having completed one or more pharmacokinetic and pharmacodynamic studies in early development, a multidisciplinary team, consisting of clinical scientists, regulatory specialists, pharmacologists, and statisticians, will examine these early clinical data to plan for studies of early efficacy and safety in individuals with the disease or condition of interest. They will interpret the data to decide which combinations of dosage forms, concentration, and regimen resulted in the optimal exposure to the drug with minimal apparent toxicities. In many instances the data may be too ambiguous to make clear decisions, especially as a degree of subjectivity is present in such decisions. For example, two regimens may have similar total exposure (as measured by AUC) but one may be associated with a greater C_{max}, which may lead to adverse effects in subsequent studies. These judgments and decisions are fairly imperfect anyway because the relationship between pharmacokinetics and clinical effects is more relevant.

For this reason alone, early clinical studies are not considered definitive and most sponsors are wise to interpret the data carefully. Ideally, certain combinations of dosage forms, drug concentrations, and regimens can be eliminated from future consideration as a result of early studies (for example, inadequate exposure, too much exposure). Pharmaceutical companies can then conduct future research on the drug in forms that may realistically provide a benefit. AUC and C_{max} are very useful measures in initial clinical development activities and, accordingly, we need statistical methods and analyses to assess them in a scientific and therefore informative manner. However, these are not the parameters that are of ultimate interest: It is the clinical benefits and risks of the new drug that are ultimately the characteristics of importance. The statistical evaluation clinical benefits (therapeutic efficacy) and risk (adverse events, etc.) are covered in Chapters 8–11.

7.8 Dose-finding trials

A drug's dosing regimen comprises the dose of the drug given and the schedule on which it is administered – that is, both concentration and timing are important characteristics. A variety of dosing regimens may be explored in these trials, and the specific regimens chosen in a specific trial depend on the objectives of the trial and the type of drug being studied.

Dose-finding studies are conducted to provide information that facilitates selection of a safe and efficient drug administration regimen. Chevret (2006a, p 5) defined dose-finding trials as "early phase clinical experiments in which different doses of a new drug are evaluated to determine the optimal dose that elicits a certain response to be recommended for the treatment of patients with a given medical condition." Chevret (2006a) also provided some related definitions that are helpful:

- Dose: The amount of active substance that is given in a single administration or repeated over a given period, as dictated by an administration schedule of equal or unequal single doses at equal or unequal intervals.
- Response: The outcome of interest in study participants. This can be defined in pharmacodynamic terms as the therapeutic points of interest, or in terms of pharmacotoxicity/ tolerability of the drug.

- Maximum tolerated dose (MTD): The highest dose that produces an "acceptable" risk for toxicity or, expressed differently, the dose that, if exceeded, would put individuals at "unacceptable" risk for toxicity.
- Minimally effective dose (MED): The dose that elicits a specified lowest therapeutic response.

Before continuing with our current discussions, the word "acceptable" in the third bullet point may initially seem somewhat incongruous here. All drugs lead to some side-effects, that is, some adverse events. Therefore, there is some degree of risk associated with taking any drug. To be useful, a drug needs to have an acceptable benefit–risk ratio – that is, the benefit must be larger than the risk, and it must be larger by a certain amount. Stating the precise amount by which a drug must provide more benefit than it may lead to harm is a difficult judgment call that must be made ultimately by physicians. However, we can make some observations. If a drug that is extremely beneficial to very sick patients shows relatively strong side-effects, a clinician may well decide that the benefit–risk ratio is still acceptable. In contrast, a drug taken for a relatively mild condition such as a headache would need to show relatively much less strong side-effects for the benefit–risk ratio to be acceptable.

Human pharmacology studies often involve dose-finding trials that focus on the evaluation of MTDs such as trials in oncology. It is important to note that studies that aim to define an MTD require clear and consistent definitions of toxicities and toxicity grades. In many disease areas outside cancer it is difficult to define the MTD in a clear manner because the drugs themselves may not be as apparently toxic as a new chemotherapeutic. Dose-finding trials that focus on the evaluation of MED are commonly referred to as early Phase II trials. (As noted in Chapter 2, the categorization of clinical trials into Phase I, II, or III, although very common, can result in confusing and less than definitive nomenclature. Here, the nomenclature "early Phase II trials" is used to distinguish these trials from therapeutic exploratory or "late Phase II trials.") One common design for FTIH studies is a dose-escalation cohort study. In this design the first cohort consists of participants administered the lowest dose of the drug or placebo. An assessment of the safety of the first dose is undertaken and, if the lowest dose is considered safe, a second cohort of participants is studied at the next highest dose. Additional cohorts are studied in this manner until a dose has been found to have unacceptable risks or the maximum dose has been studied in the final cohort. Chevret (2006b) provides a comprehensive discussion of dose-finding experiments.

7.9 Bioavailability trials

Another type of early clinical study may be conducted with the primary objective of establishing the bioavailability of a particular dosage form, concentration, and regimen. Bioavailability can be defined as the proportion of an administered dose that reaches the systemic circulation in an unchanged form. Maximum bioavailability results after an intravenous injection of the drug. In this case, the bioavailability is by definition 100%. When administered orally, however, a drug experiences first-pass metabolism, also called first-pass loss, before it reaches the systemic circulation.

Metabolism is a complex and tremendously beneficial process in most cases, but one that poses interesting challenges in pharmacological therapy. We are constantly exposed to xenobiotics, substances that are foreign to our bodies. For example, our modern environment is a constant source of xenobiotics that are toxicants. These can enter our bodies via our lungs as we breathe and our stomachs as we eat, and some can enter the body through our skin. In addition, animal and plant food contains many chemicals that have no nutritional value but do have potential toxicity. Fortunately, our bodies are very good at getting rid of bodily toxicants. The processes of metabolism and excretion are involved in this. As noted by Mulder (2006), metabolism can be divided into three phases:

1. Phase 1: The chemical structure of the compound is modified by oxidation, reduction, or hydrolysis. This process forms an acceptor group.
2. Phase 2: A chemical group is attached to the acceptor group. This typically generates metabolites that are more water soluble and therefore more readily excreted.
3. Phase 3: Transporters transport the drug or metabolites out of the cell in which Phase 1 and Phase 2 metabolism has occurred.

Along with all animals, humans have a wide variety of xenobiotic-metabolizing enzymes that convert a wide range of chemical structures to water-soluble metabolites, which can be excreted in urine. Humans have a high concentration of these enzymes in the gut mucosa and the liver. This arrangement ensures that systemic exposure to potentially toxic chemicals is limited. A high percentage of these may be caught in first-pass metabolism. Xenobiotics that are absorbed from the intestine travel via the hepatic portal vein to the liver, the major organ of metabolism, before being circulated systemically, and metabolism in the liver means that damage to the rest of the body is ameliorated. Under normal circumstances this is extremely advantageous.

From the point of view of pharmacological therapy, however, this protective system represents a considerable challenge. Orally administered drugs also travel via the hepatic portal vein to the liver before being circulated systemically. Therefore, before the drug gets a chance to exert any therapeutic activity in the body, it has to withstand this first attempt to degrade it. This first-pass metabolism is more or less effective depending on factors including the drug's chemical and physical properties, but almost certainly there will be some degree of degradation. This means that most orally administered drugs display less than 100% bioavailability.

The most rigorous quantitative way to assess the extent of bioavailability for an orally administered drug is to compare the areas under the respective plasma–concentration curves after oral and intravenous administration of the same dose of drug. The AUC is then calculated for both, and a ratio calculated by dividing the AUC for the oral administration by that for the intravenous administration. If the area ratio for the drug administered orally and intravenously is 0.5 (which can be expressed as 50%), only 50% of the oral dose was absorbed systemically.

Consider the development of a new drug that is going to be given orally. Assessing its bioavailability is important. An intravenous infusion of the new drug will result in a certain systemic exposure as measured by the AUC. This amount of systemic exposure will by definition be called 100% bioavailability. It is important to identify the dosage form and schedule that provide relatively high bioavailability. In this case, participants may be randomly assigned to receive one of the following drug administration regimens:

- intravenous infusion of the drug for 4 hours
- 10 mg tablet once a day
- 10 mg tablet twice a day
- 10 mg three times a day
- 20 mg tablet once a day
- 20 mg tablet twice a day
- 20 mg three times a day.

At the end of the study, the pharmacokinetic characteristics of the drug would be evaluated, and the systemic exposure for each dosage regimen compared with the intravenous route of administration.

7.10 Other data acquired in early phase clinical studies

As we saw in Section 7.5, one research question of interest in early phase trials is:

- How safe is the new drug? Evaluations include clinical laboratory tests, physical examinations, vital signs, adverse events, and cardiac effects through ECG monitoring.

More extensive discussion of these safety assessments is provided in the following chapters, but it is useful to introduce these topics at this point.

7.10.1 Clinical laboratory tests

There is a very wide range of clinical chemistry tests that can be conducted, including liver (hepatic) and kidney (renal) tests. These are discussed in Section 9.2.

7.10.2 Physical examinations

Although perhaps not as sensitive as other safety assessments, physical examinations are still very helpful, because a general exam may identify more pronounced effects to the drug such as allergic reactions or edema (fluid retention). Data collected from physical exams include a subjective assessment by the investigator as to whether the participant has "normal" or "abnormal" function for each body system (for example, respiratory, dermatologic) examined. If the body system is considered abnormal, additional descriptions of the particular abnormality are also recorded. Data recorded as normal or abnormal are measured on the nominal scale. These data are typically summarized by tabulating the number and percentage of individuals with each result.

7.10.3 Vital signs

Monitoring of vital signs, including heart rate, respiration rate, and blood pressure, is carried out on a regular basis, typically several times a day. Each of these is measured on the continuous scale. Analyses of these outcomes primarily focus on measures of central tendency and dispersion.

7.10.4 Adverse events

The collection of adverse events can be based on observation by either the investigator or participant self-report. Participant self-reports of adverse events can vary according to how the information is elicited from them. It is advisable to standardize the manner in which participants are asked about how they feel during the trial. Data collected from adverse events usually include text descriptions of several characteristics of the adverse event:

- the adverse event, for example, "rash on left forearm"

- the severity or intensity of the adverse event, for example, mild, moderate, severe
- the date and time of onset
- the outcome of the adverse event (resolved without sequelae, resolved with sequelae, or ongoing)
- any treatments administered for the adverse event
- any action taken with the study drug (for example, temporarily discontinued, stopped, none)
- whether or not the adverse event is considered serious.

To standardize the reporting of adverse events, the adverse event descriptions are coded using medical dictionaries such as MedDRA (*Medical Dictionary for Drug Regulatory Affairs* coding dictionary: See, for example, Chow and Liu, 2004, p. 563) or COSTART. The original description of the adverse event provides qualitative information about the finding that may not be captured in the coded event. Both aspects – that is, coded and uncoded – are retained in the scientific database for reporting and analysis.

7.11 Limitations of early phase trials

In this chapter we have discussed the importance, and the strengths, of early phase clinical trials. Before moving on to later phase clinical trials, it is also appropriate to consider their limitations. The word "limitations" should not be seen as a negative assessment in this context. As we will discuss in Chapter 12, later-phase preapproval clinical trials also have their limitations. Acknowledgment of the strength and the limitations of any method of inquiry is legitimate and helpful: As Katz (2001, p xi) noted, "to work skillfully with evidence is to acknowledge its limits."

7.11.1 Studying pharmacokinetics in healthy participants

Studying the pharmacokinetics of a new investigational drug in FTIH studies – that is, in individuals with healthy renal and hepatic systems – results in a pharmacokinetic assessment that is somewhat artificial. In later stages of development, it may be necessary to study the drug in individuals with impaired kidney or liver function, especially if these conditions are expected in the types of patients who will be prescribed the drug if and when it is approved for marketing. However, this initial FTIH assessment can serve as a useful starting point and provide guidance for such later studies.

7.11.2 Extremely tight experimental control

It may seem paradoxical to see tight experimental control listed in a section discussing the limitations of a clinical trial. After all, in Chapter 4 we extolled the merits of such control. The issue here is related to the issue addressed in Section 7.2. Since the investigational drug is administered in such a carefully controlled manner, the generalizability of the results from these studies becomes questionable. If and when the drug is approved for marketing, patients who are prescribed the medication will be unlikely to take the medication in such a precisely controlled manner. As in many places in drug development, there are advantages and disadvantages to this strategy. We have noted the disadvantages and now focus on the advantages.

The advantage of very tight control in early Phase II (therapeutic exploratory) trials is that the "pure" efficacy of the drug can be assessed as well as possible. The drug has every chance to demonstrate its efficacy in these circumstances.

In other words, we can assess how well the drug *can* work. It is not so easy to assess how the drug *will* work if and when approved and prescribed to a very large population of heterogeneous patients who take the drug in various states of adherence with the prescribed regimen, but that is another question for another stage of the clinical development program.

7.12 Review

1. What are some reasons that inferential statistics (that is, hypothesis testing) are not used very often in early phase studies?

2. What information from early phase trials may be used to inform the study designs of therapeutic exploratory and therapeutic confirmatory trials?

3. Name three advantages or strengths of early phase trials as they pertain to the overall development of a new drug.

4. Name three disadvantages of early phase trials as they pertain to the overall development of a new drug.

7.13 References

Chevret S (2006a). Basic concepts in dose-finding. In: Chevret S (ed.), *Statistical Methods for Dose-finding Experiments*. Chichester: John Wiley & Sons, 5–18.

Chevret S (ed.) (2006b). *Statistical Methods for Dose-finding Experiments*. Chichester: John Wiley & Sons.

Chow S-C, Liu J-P (2004). *Design and Analysis of Clinical Trials: Concepts and methodologies*. Chichester: John Wiley & Sons.

Hansten PD (2004). Important drug interactions and their mechanisms. In: Katzung BG (ed.), *Basic and Clinical Pharmacology*, 9th edn. New York: McGraw-Hill, 1110–1124.

Katz DL (2001). *Clinical Epidemiology and Evidence-based Medicine: Fundamental principles of clinical reasoning & research*. Thousand Oaks, CA: Sage Publications.

Mulder GJ (2006). Drug metabolism: inactivation and activation of xenobiotics. In: Mulder GJ, Dencker L (eds), *Pharmaceutical Pharmacology*. London: Pharmaceutical Press, 41–66.

Tozer TN, Roland M (2006). *Introduction to Pharmacokinetics and Pharmacodynamics: The quantitative basis of drug therapy*. Baltimore, MD: Lippincott, Williams & Wilkins.

8

Confirmatory clinical trials: Safety data I

8.1 Introduction

The regulatory standard for the approval of new drugs for marketing can be framed in the following manner: The benefits associated with the new treatment outweigh the risks associated with the new treatment. All pharmaceutical products carry the potential for side-effects, some of which are more serious than others. Therefore, for a given investigational drug to be approved for marketing the regulatory agency needs to be presented with compelling evidence that the likely benefits to the target population with the disease or condition of interest outweigh the likely risks. This requires conducting clinical trials that employ samples selected from the target population, and use of Statistics to design these trials appropriately, collect optimum quality data, analyze and interpret the data correctly, and make inferences about the population from which those samples were drawn.

Judgments about the benefit–risk profile of an investigational drug require, by definition, consideration of both benefit and risk. This means that the therapeutic benefit of the investigational drug needs to be assessed quantitatively, and considered together with quantitative assessments of risk. In this chapter we discuss the assessment of risk in terms of evaluating the drug's safety profile. Even though we typically use the nomenclature benefit–risk profile and not risk–benefit profile, we discuss safety evaluations first because the safety of patients must be our first concern.

Safety analyses in pharmaceutical clinical trials tend to be largely descriptive because there are so many adverse events (AEs) and other safety parameters evaluated, and analysis of them leads to issues of multiplicity (see Section 8.9). As described in Chapter 6, the appropriate use of inferential statistics requires a prespecified hypothesis of interest. As knowledge is gained about an experimental therapy during its development (for example, in therapeutic exploratory trials) a specific hypothesis about the drug's safety may emerge and can then be tested appropriately. In such instances there are inferential statistical analyses that can be used for safety data, and we present some of those applicable to AEs in this chapter. (See also Chow and Liu [2004b, Chapter 13] for additional discussions of safety assessment.)

8.2 The rationale for safety assessments in clinical trials

When a clinician prescribes a new treatment for a patient for the first time, the clinician and indeed the patient may be interested in the following questions about the safety of the drug:

- How likely is it that my patient will experience an adverse drug reaction? (The term "adverse drug reaction" refers to an unwanted occurrence caused by a drug. Hence, a prescribing clinician [and researchers conducting post-marketing surveillance studies] is concerned with adverse drug reactions. During preapproval clinical trials, we do not know which treatment an individual is receiving, so unwanted occurrences are called AEs. Formal definitions are provided shortly.)
- How likely is it that my patient will experience an adverse drug reaction that is so serious that it may be life threatening?
- How will the risk of an adverse drug reaction vary with different doses of the drug?

- How will the risk of an adverse drug reaction change with the length of treatment?
- Are the typical adverse drug reactions temporary or permanent in nature?
- Are there specific clinical parameters that should be monitored more closely in my patient while he or she is receiving this treatment because of increased risks from the newly marketed drug?

At the time that a new drug receives marketing approval, the best information available upon which the clinician can form an answer to these questions is the information gathered during the preapproval clinical trials. This information is provided to the clinician (and to all patients receiving an approved drug) in the package insert. (This situation changes in due course as additional [and more detailed] safety evaluation takes place during the process of postmarketing surveillance [see Mann and Andrews, 2007]. However, this process may take several years to acquire meaningful data, and so the statement in the text may remain true for quite a while.)

A number of clinical parameters are assessed during preapproval clinical trials. This information provides the basis upon which the clinician will formulate answers to these questions. The precise set of clinical parameters employed in a given trial may vary according to the disease and the type of drug under study. In general, the safety evaluation of new drugs is intended to detect quantifiable effects in as many organs and systems as possible. In other words, when looking for risks associated with a new drug, the strategy is to "cast a wide net."

8.3 A regulatory view on safety assessment

The view of the US Food and Drug Administration (FDA) concerning safety reviews is presented in their guidance document on the safety review of new drug applications (US FDA, 2005, p 5). As this guidance states, most therapeutic exploratory and therapeutic confirmatory trials are carefully designed to establish that a new drug is efficacious, while controlling the probability of committing a type I or II error. Unless safety concerns have arisen in earlier stages of the clinical development program, these trials typically do not involve assessments of safety that are as sensitive as those designed for establishing the efficacy of the investigational drug. Quoting from this guidance:

> In the usual case, however, any apparent finding emerges from an assessment of dozens of potential endpoints (adverse events) of interest, making description of the statistical uncertainty of the finding using conventional significance levels very difficult. The approach taken is therefore best described as one of exploration and estimation of event rates, with particular attention to comparing results of individual studies and pooled data. It should be appreciated that exploratory analyses (for example, subset analyses, to which a great caution is applied in a hypothesis testing setting) are a critical and essential part of a safety evaluation. These analyses can, of course, lead to false conclusions, but need to be carried out nonetheless, with attention to consistency across studies and prior knowledge. The approach typically followed is to screen broadly for adverse events and to expect that this will reveal the common adverse reaction profile of a new drug and will detect some of the less common and more serious adverse reactions associated with drug use.

US FDA (2005, p 5)

Safety evaluations of investigational drugs focus primarily on estimating the risk of unwanted events associated with the drug, and, more specifically, on the risk of those events relative to what would be expected in the patient population as a whole if the drug were to be approved. Although more specialized tests and assays may be evaluated in certain instances, in this chapter and in Chapter 9 we describe statistical approaches used for the most common clinical data used to assess the safety of new drugs: AEs, clinical laboratory data, vital signs, and changes in ECG parameters. This chapter focuses on discussions of AEs. Adverse events are nominal data, and therefore summaries of AEs are based on counts.

8.4 Adverse events

ICH Guidance E6 (R1) (1996, p 2) provides the following definition of the term adverse event:

> Any untoward medical occurrence in a patient or clinical investigation subject administered a pharmaceutical product and which does not necessarily have a causal relationship with the treatment. An adverse event (AE) can therefore be any unfavourable and unintended sign (including an abnormal laboratory finding), symptom, or disease temporally associated with the use of a medicinal (investigational) product, whether or not associated with the medicinal (investigational) product.

ICH Guidance E2A (1995, p 3) provides a definition of the term "adverse drug reaction" that is applicable during preapproval clinical experiences with a new medicinal product:

> All noxious and unintended responses to a medicinal product related to any dose should be considered adverse drug reactions.

There are various types of AEs, as shown in Table 8.1.

The length of observation for AEs is typically specified in the study protocol. In most instances, on-treatment AEs (also called treatment-emergent AEs) are considered to be those events with an onset from the time that study treatment has been initiated through the protocol-defined follow-up period. For example,

a protocol may specify that AEs occurring within 30 days of the last exposure to the study drug be reported. In some therapeutic areas it may be desirable to assess separately those AEs that occur once treatment has been discontinued, for example, to evaluate withdrawal or rebound effects during the follow-up period.

In the hypothetical data presented in Table 8.1, the numbers of participants in the drug and placebo groups are deliberately similar but not identical. This is why provision of both absolute numbers and percentages is so informative when making comparisons between the treatment groups.

8.5 Reporting adverse events

Adverse events are typically reported in one of two ways:

1. By study investigators on the basis of their own observations (for example, from a physical exam)
2. By the study participant as a self-reported event.

In the second case, it is advisable to elicit AEs from participants using a standardized script to ensure that they are collected as accurately as possible. For example, a question such as "Have you noticed anything different or had any health problems since you were last here?" is a

Table 8.1 Participant accountability (Safety Population: Study AB0001)

Adverse events (AEs)	Number (%) of participants	
	Placebo (*n* = 2603)	Drug (*n* = 2456)
Pre-treatment AEs	24 (1)	31 (1)
On-treatment AEs[a]	297 (11)	386 (16)
Drug-related AEs[b]	31 (1)	42 (2)
Serious AEs	20 (1)	27 (1)
AEs leading to withdrawal	12 (< 1)	17 (1)

[a]AEs that occur on any treatment, whether active or nonactive.

[b]"Drug-related" is a designation made by an investigator who decides that there is a reasonable chance that the AE was caused by the treatment being taken.

way of asking a participant about potential AEs without leading him or her to answer in a certain way.

Study personnel who interact with participants are trained to capture the essence of any self-reported AEs on a case report form (CRF), one of the most important documents in clinical trials. Examples of reported AEs include "shortness of breath," "rash on left wrist," "dry mouth," and "vomiting." In addition to the description of the nature of the AE, additional information such as the following is typically collected:

- the severity
- the date and time of onset
- the resolution date (if the event resolved), any action that was taken with the study drug (for example, stopped, dosage reduced)
- the presumed relationship to the study treatment
- whether or not the AE was considered "serious" according to a regulatory definition.

8.6 Using all reported AEs for all participants

The first question listed in Section 8.2 was: "How likely is it that my patient will experience an adverse drug reaction?" We turn this question around, and reframe it in terms of assessing how likely it is that a participant in a preapproval clinical trial will experience an AE. The data that are typically used to answer this question are all on-treatment AEs for all participants treated (or exposed) in each treatment group. The probability that a participant in a particular treatment group will report any AE is estimated by the proportion of participants in the group who reported any AE.

When describing proportions, it is important to note what event is being counted in the numerator and what event in the denominator. Many times it is clear what the appropriate numerator for a proportion should be, but not so clear what the appropriate denominator should be. The simplest starting point for determining which participants should be counted in the denominator is to identify all those who

are at risk of experiencing the event of interest. For example, the proportion of participants experiencing an AE in the first 90 days should be calculated by counting the number of participants who were treated for at least 90 days in the denominator and the number of participants who were treated for at least 90 days and reported an AE in the first 90 days in the numerator.

As described earlier, proportions are numbers between 0 and 1. We have also noted that it is common for proportions to be multiplied by 100 so that the quantity being assessed is expressed in percentage terms. In the present context, we are interested in the percentages of participants experiencing a certain event.

The probability of an individual reporting an AE in a trial is estimated by the following proportion:

$$\frac{[\text{Number of participants who were administered the treatment and reported any AE}]}{[\text{Number of participants who were administered the treatment}]}$$

Some participants will have reported more than one AE. For this analysis, we count participants only once if they experienced any AE(s).

As noted in Chapter 6, this calculated proportion is considered a point estimate, because it was obtained from a single sample and the estimate does not take into account any variability attributed to sampling. In most clinical study reports (and, ultimately, package inserts for marketed products), the point estimate of the proportion of individuals experiencing AEs is expressed as a percentage of individuals. This quantity can be thought of as a rate (ratio of individuals experiencing an event among those exposed to the treatment) or, in the terminology used in the discipline of epidemiology, the incidence of AEs.

Calculating the proportion (or, equivalently, the percentage) of individuals reporting any AE for all treatment groups in a study enables us to see whether AEs are more or less likely in the test treatment group than in other groups. The use of an inactive control group (for example, a placebo) in a study allows us to compare the probability attributed to the test treatment group to what can be thought of as the background risk, which is approximated for by the risk in the inactive control group.

8.7 Absolute and relative risks of participants reporting specific AEs

Similar analysis approaches are used to describe the risk, in both the absolute and relative (comparative) sense, of individuals reporting specific AEs. These analyses are much more useful clinically because not all AEs are created equal. One example is to estimate the proportion of individuals in a given group who reported a headache. To do this in a standardized manner it is necessary to "code" the AE descriptions (for example, "tension headache", "achy head"). The use of the MedDRA coding dictionary for this purpose is now widely accepted, and in some instances may be required. Coding is performed before statistical analysis and the "coded" terms are used in statistical summaries that require counting of participants reporting each event.

The proportion from the sample in the study can be estimated as:

[Number of participants who received the treatment and reported a headache during the study]

[Number of participants who received the treatment].

For example, if 25 participants received treatment A and, among them, 5 reported a headache, the estimated proportion of participants reporting a headache is 5/25 = 0.20, which can also be expressed as 20%. When such an analysis is repeated for all AEs reported, and the quantities are expressed as percentages and displayed in tabular form in a package insert, it is relatively easy for prescribing physicians and their potential patients to answer their questions.

Suppose that an investigational antihypertensive drug is evaluated at multiple doses in a parallel-group placebo-controlled study. Participants in this therapeutic exploratory study were randomly assigned to receive either placebo or one of three possible doses of the test treatment (low, medium, or high). The treatment period was for 6 weeks. The number and percentage of participants experiencing any AE, and particular AEs, are displayed in Table 8.2.

We now have data with which to begin to answer the question: How likely is a patient to experience an AE after use of the new treatment? As this study included three doses of the test treatment, we need to consider the dose in our answer. Examining the top row in Table 8.2, it seems that the overall chance of observing an AE at all doses of the active treatment is similar to that for the placebo group: The percentages for "Any event" range from 10% to 13% across the groups with no apparent relationship to dose. From these data, our best guess as to the probability of an individual treated with the test treatment experiencing any AE is between 10% and 13%. However, the probability of experiencing

Table 8.2 Number and percentage of participants reporting adverse events (AEs) by group

AE	Placebo (n = 98)	Low (n = 101)	Medium (n = 104)	High (n = 97)
Any event	12 (12%)	13 (13%)	10 (10%)	12 (12%)
Headache	6 (6%)	8 (8%)	9 (9%)	8 (8%)
Dizziness	1 (1%)	3 (3%)	4 (4%)	3 (3%)
Upper respiratory infection	4 (4%)	1 (1%)	2 (2%)	2 (2%)
Nausea	1 (1%)	2 (2%)	1 (1%)	3 (3%)

an AE is almost equal to the probability of experiencing an AE after treatment with placebo. The implication of this result is that the risk of experiencing an AE after treatment with the new drug is no different than if the participant had not been treated with the drug.

Looking at the specific AEs in Table 8.2, there is really little difference among the groups with one exception, the AE of dizziness. Only 1% of participants in the placebo group reported dizziness compared with 3–4% of participants treated with the active drug. How might a regulatory reviewer interpret these data? The first conclusion is that dizziness was not reported very often in any participant group, so, if the drug is approved and marketed, most patients treated with the new drug would probably not have a problem. However, the difference in the percentage of participants might generate some concern.

Initially, the absolute difference in dizziness rates (2–3%) may not seem extreme. However, when considering the rates in relative terms, those treated with the investigational drug are three to four times as likely to experience dizziness as someone who did not receive the active drug. This measure of risk is called a relative risk and is calculated as follows:

$$\text{Relative risk} = \frac{\text{The probability of the event in group A}}{\text{The probability of the event in group B}}.$$

In many instances, the communication of a risk (probability of experiencing the event) is most clear with an absolute measure (such as the point estimate for a group) and a relative measure (such as the relative risk). The relative risk is a ratio of two probabilities, and can therefore range from zero to infinity.

8.8 Analyzing serious AEs

ICH Guidance E2A (1994) provides the following definition of a serious event: A serious adverse event (experience) or reaction is any untoward medical occurrence that at any dose:

- results in death
- is life threatening (note that the term "life threatening" in the definition of "serious"

refers to an event in which the patient was at risk of death at the time of the event; it does not refer to an event that hypothetically might have caused death if it were more severe)
- requires inpatient hospitalization or prolongation of existing hospitalization
- results in persistent or significant disability/incapacity
- is a congenital anomaly/birth defect.

A similar analysis can be performed to address another question of interest: How likely is it that an individual will experience an adverse effect that is potentially life threatening? The data used to answer this question include all of the AEs that were rated as serious at the time of reporting. We would estimate the probability by calculating the proportion of participants treated in each group who experienced a serious AE. The proportions (or, equivalently, the percentages) of patients could be compared across groups to see if there was an increased risk of a serious AE associated with the new treatment.

8.9 Concerns with potential multiplicity issues

As noted earlier, safety analyses in clinical trials tend to be largely descriptive because so many AEs and other safety parameters are evaluated. If we were to perform hypothesis tests for the large number of parameters evaluated – for example, for all AEs reported in a trial – it is probable that at least one of the tests would be nominally statistically significant at the $\alpha = 0.05$ level. In most instances the statistical analysis is planned so that the probability of making a type I error is ≤ 0.05. In Table 8.2 rates were presented for five AEs (including any event). If we were interested in identifying statistically significant differences for each active dose group versus placebo, we would need to conduct 15 hypothesis tests (three dose groups to be tested against placebo for five AEs). As we saw in Chapter 6, if we test a number of hypotheses without taking into account multiplicity of comparisons we will likely commit a type I error. For the 15 tests that could be conducted using the data in Table 8.2, it is certainly possible that one of them might have a nominal p value ≤ 0.05 by chance alone. Committing a type I error in this setting would mean concluding that the new treatment was associated with an excess risk of an AE when that really is not the case.

If a single test were considered nominally statistically significant after looking at so many other AEs, the result should be treated with a great deal of skepticism. Before making any regulatory or business decisions on the basis of such a result, medical, clinical, and statistical experts should, at a minimum, evaluate the medical and statistical plausibility of the result. Ideally, additional data would be collected to provide supporting evidence for such a finding. As we have pointed out a number of times already, statistical results such as these aid in decision-making, in concert with insights and evidence from other disciplines. This view, as it relates to analyses of safety data, is perfectly in line with the EMEA's Committee for Proprietary Medicinal Products (CPMP) (2002, p 4) guidance, *Points to Consider on Multiplicity Issues in Clinical Trials*:

> In those cases where a large number of statistical test procedures is used to serve as a flagging device to signal a potential risk caused by the investigational drug it can be generally stated that an adjustment for multiplicity is counterproductive for considerations of safety. It is clear that in this situation there is no control over the type I error for a single hypothesis and the importance and plausibility of such results will depend on prior knowledge of the pharmacology of the drug.

8.10 Accounting for sampling variation

Hypothesis tests and interval estimates of proportions are frequently presented in clinical study reports, especially in earlier studies of development when late phase studies are being planned. Accordingly, discussion now turns to analysis methods that can be used to account for sampling variation and, therefore, determine if the results observed are likely due to chance alone.

In Chapter 6 we described the basic components of hypothesis testing and interval estimation (that is, confidence intervals). One of the basic components of interval estimation is the standard error of the estimator, which quantifies how much the sample estimate would vary from sample to sample if (totally implausibly) we were to conduct the same clinical study over and over again. The larger the sample size in the trial, the smaller the standard error. Another component of an interval estimate is the reliability factor, which acts as a multiplier for the standard error. The more confidence that we require, the larger the reliability factor (multiplier). The reliability factor is determined by the shape of the sampling distribution of the statistic of interest and is the value that defines an area under the curve of $(1 - \alpha)$. In the case of a two-sided interval the reliability factor defines lower and upper tail areas of size $\alpha/2$.

If the shape of the sampling distribution is symmetric (for example, the Z or t distributions), the reliability factor used for the lower and upper limits is exactly the same, but with a change in sign. Some sampling distributions are not symmetric (for example, the F distribution for the ratio of two variances) and, therefore, the reliability factors for the lower and upper limits are not equal.

Let us now look at how we would calculate a confidence interval for a single proportion, such as a within-treatment group proportion of participants experiencing an AE.

8.11 A confidence interval for a sample proportion

The estimator for a sample proportion can be defined as follows:

$$\hat{p} = \frac{\text{number of observations with the event of interest}}{\text{total number of observations at risk of the event}},$$

which is an unbiased estimator of the unknown population proportion, P. The standard error of the estimator,

$$SE(\hat{p}) = \sqrt{\frac{\hat{p}\hat{q}}{n}},$$

where $\hat{q} = 1 - \hat{p}$, the sample proportion of observations without the event of interest. The estimator $\hat{p}$ is approximately normally distributed for large samples (that is, when $\hat{p}n > 5$) so the reliability factor for interval estimates will come from the Z distribution. For now, we will consider only two-sided confidence intervals. Hence, the reliability factor $Z_{1-\alpha/2}$ will be the specific value of Z such that an area of $(1 - [\alpha/2])$ lies to the right of the cutoff value. A two-sided $(1 - \alpha)\%$ confidence interval for a sample proportion, $\hat{p}$ is:

$$\hat{p} \pm z_{1-\alpha/2}SE(\hat{p}).$$

This is also a confidence interval for the parameter p, probability of success, of the binomial distribution. The use of the Z distribution for this interval is made possible because of the Central Limit Theorem. Consider the random variable X taking on values of 0 or 1, such that the sampling distribution of the sample mean (the proportion) is approximately normally distributed. A table of the most commonly encountered values of the standard normal distribution is provided in Table 8.3 for quick reference. Others are provided in Appendix 1.

Table 8.3 Selected values of Z for two-sided confidence intervals

α (two sided)	$Z_{1-\alpha/2}$
0.10	1.645
0.05	1.96
0.01	2.576
0.001	3.3

This methodology can be used to answer a question about the data presented in Table 8.2, where the percentages of participants reporting headache during the 6-week study were 6%, 8%, 9%, and 8% for the placebo, low-dose, medium-dose, and high-dose groups respectively. Headaches may be reported fairly often among people with hypertension as a matter of course, but these data suggest that the proportion (expressed here as a percentage) of individuals reporting headache is a bit higher for individuals treated with the active treatment than for those in the placebo group. We can calculate the 95% confidence interval for the proportion of participants in the combined active dose groups reporting a headache. We can also calculate the corresponding confidence interval for the placebo group and compare the two.

The research question

Is the risk (or probability) of experiencing a headache after treatment with the active drug (all doses combined) higher than the risk after treatment with placebo?

Study design

In this study, an investigational antihypertensive drug was evaluated at multiple doses in a parallel-group, placebo-controlled study. An important feature of the design was randomization to treatment, which provides us with unbiased (accurate) estimates of treatment differences. Another feature of the design of the statistical analysis is that we have chosen to compare the rates of one particular AE among many only after seeing the results (that is, *a posteriori*). As we have already seen, any difference between treatments that we may find at this point may be a type I error resulting from the large number of AEs that could have been selected for this particular analysis.

Data

The data for this analysis are the counts of participants treated in each group (that is, the denominator for within-group proportions) and the counts of participants within each group who reported a headache during the study (that is, the numerator for the within-group proportions). As the research question involved all active dose groups combined (that is, any dose of the drug) it is necessary to pool the data across the active dose groups to calculate the confidence interval of interest. Having done that, we now have the following data for our example: 6 out of 98 participants in the placebo group reported a headache, and 25 out of 302 participants in the combined active groups.

Statistical analysis

The statistical analysis approach is to calculate 95% confidence intervals for the proportion of participants in each group (placebo and combined active) reporting a headache. This analysis approach is reasonable because the sample size is sufficiently large (that is, the values, $\hat{p}n$, in each group are at least five). Satisfying this assumption enables us to use the Z distribution for the reliability factor.

The first step is to calculate the point estimate of the proportion. For the placebo group the proportion is 0.06. The second step is to calculate the standard error. For this estimator the standard error is calculated as follows:

$$\sqrt{\frac{(0.06)(0.94)}{98}} = 0.02.$$

The third component of the interval estimate is the reliability factor. As we are calculating a two-sided 95% confidence interval, we select the value of Z from Table 8.3 corresponding to α of 0.05, that is, 1.96.

With all of the components now available, the last step is to calculate the confidence interval. The lower limit is $0.06 - 1.96(0.02) = 0.02$. The upper limit is $0.06 + 1.96(0.02) = 0.10$. We write the 95% confidence interval as (0.02, 0.10). Repeating these steps for the combined active dose group, we obtain a 95% confidence interval of (0.04, 0.12). (We leave it to you to verify this calculation.)

Interpretation and decision-making

Using these two confidence intervals we can now make some conclusions about the unknown population proportion of participants who experience headache after exposure in each group. In the case of the placebo group, we are 95% confident that the population proportion of participants experiencing a headache is enclosed in the interval (0.02, 0.10). For the combined active dose group, we are 95% confident that the population proportion of participants experiencing a headache is enclosed in the interval (0.04, 0.12). Although it may initially have seemed that there may be an increased risk of headache associated with the active treatment,

the overlapping within-group confidence intervals suggest that there is insufficient evidence to conclude that the observed difference is real (that is, not due to chance).

8.12 Confidence intervals for the difference between two proportions

There is also another way to answer this research question. If the proportions of individuals reporting headache are the same among participants in the active dose groups and the placebo group, the difference between the two proportions would be 0. Further, because of the influence of sampling error, with which we are now very familiar, we would not necessarily expect the difference to be exactly 0 (just like we do not expect precisely equal numbers of heads and tails in a series of coin tosses). In this approach, therefore, we calculate a confidence interval about the difference in proportions for two independent groups. This interval estimate allows us to exclude implausible values of the difference. This method and others throughout this book require independence of groups (for example, two groups of participants). Examples of groups that are not considered independent are measurements on the same study participant (for example, in ophthalmology left eyes are not considered independent of right eyes in the same individual).

For this method we have sample proportions for independent groups 1 and 2 defined as above:

$$\hat{p}_1 = \frac{\text{number of observations in group 1 with the event of interest}}{\text{total number of observations in group 1 at risk of the event}} \text{ and}$$

$$\hat{p}_2 = \frac{\text{number of observations in group 2 with the event of interest}}{\text{total number of observations in group 2 at risk of the event}}.$$

The estimator for the difference in the two sample proportions is $\hat{p}_1 - \hat{p}_2$ and the standard error of $\hat{p}_1 - \hat{p}_2$ is:

$$SE(\hat{p}_1 - \hat{p}_2) = \sqrt{\frac{\hat{p}_1 \hat{q}_1}{n_1} + \frac{\hat{p}_2 \hat{q}_2}{n_2}},$$

where $\hat{q}_1 = 1 - \hat{p}_1$ and $\hat{q}_2 = 1 - \hat{p}_2$.

For large samples (that is, when $\hat{p}_1 n_1 > 5$ and $\hat{p}_2 n_2 > 5$) the estimator $\hat{p}_1 - \hat{p}_2$ is approximately normally distributed with mean,

$$p_1 - p_2$$

and variance,

$$\frac{p_1(1 - p_1)}{n_1} + \frac{p_2(1 - p_2)}{n_2}.$$

So the reliability factor for interval estimates will come from the Z distribution. Then a two-sided $(1 - \alpha)\%$ confidence interval for the difference in sample proportions, $\hat{p}_1 - \hat{p}_2$ is:

$$(\hat{p}_1 - \hat{p}_2) \pm z_{1-\alpha/2}\text{SE}(\hat{p}_1 - \hat{p}_2).$$

While this form of the confidence interval is widely used we suggest the use of a correction factor,

$$\frac{1}{2}\left(\frac{1}{n_1} + \frac{1}{n_2}\right),$$

attributed to Yates (see Fleiss et al., 2003). This continuity correction factor accounts for the fact that the normal distribution is being used as an approximation to the binomial. With the correction factor, a two-sided $(1 - \alpha)\%$ confidence interval for the difference in sample proportions, $\hat{p}_1 - \hat{p}_2$, is:

$$(\hat{p}_1 - \hat{p}_2) \pm \left(z_{1-\alpha/2}\text{SE}(\hat{p}_1 - \hat{p}_2) + \frac{1}{2}\left(\frac{1}{n_1} + \frac{1}{n_2}\right)\right).$$

As an example, we look at the headache AE data again and calculate a two-sided confidence interval for the difference in sample proportions.

Data

As above, the data are in the form of counts: 6 out of 98 participants in the placebo group reported a headache and 25 out of 302 participants in the combined active groups reported a headache.

Statistical analysis

As with the previous method, the first step is to calculate the point estimate, but this time the point estimate of the difference in sample proportions. For the placebo group the proportion is 0.06. For the active group the proportion

is 0.08. So the point estimate for the difference is $0.06 - 0.08 = -0.02$.

The next step is to calculate the standard error, which is:

$$\sqrt{\frac{(0.06)(0.94)}{98} + \frac{(0.08)(0.92)}{302}} = 0.03.$$

The third component of the interval estimate is the reliability factor. The Z value will be the same as for the previous example (that is, 1.96). For this interval estimate, we also use the continuity correction factor. The continuity correction is calculated as $0.5(1/98 + 1/302) = 0.007$.

We now have all the components of the interval calculation. The lower limit is given as follows:

$$-0.02 - 1.96(0.03) - 0.007 = -0.09.$$

The upper limit is given as follows:

$$-0.02 + 1.96(0.03) - 0.007 = 0.04.$$

Note that the calculated limits do not appear to be equidistant from the point estimate, as we might have expected. This is the result of rounding to two significant digits in the calculations. The calculated 95% confidence interval about the difference in proportion of participants reporting headache as an AE is written as follows:

$$95\% \text{ CI} = (-0.09, 0.04).$$

Interpretation and decision-making

Given its importance, it is worth restating the interpretation of this confidence interval. We are 95% confident that the true difference in proportions of individuals reporting headache as an AE is within the interval $(-0.09, 0.04)$. As the interval includes 0, there is not enough evidence to suggest that the two groups are statistically significantly different with respect to the risk of headache as an AE. Following this conclusion, we could reasonably continue with further studies in our clinical development program of the active drug, with some assurance from these limited data that the active treatment did not increase the risk of headache.

Suppose, however, that a skeptical colleague insisted that the risk of headache had to be higher for participants treated with the active drug than with placebo. Using these data, how confident could he or she be that this was really the case? What if all of the headaches in the active treated group were reported in the first week of treatment, whereas in the placebo group the events were spread evenly over the entire 6-week treatment period? Would your view of the relationship between the active treatment and the risk of headache change? A methodology called time-to-event analysis is useful here.

8.13 Time-to-event analysis

An illustration of this scenario is given in Figure 8.1, which shows data from a hypothetical study, study 1 (we discuss another hypothetical scenario, study 2, in due course). There are two treatment groups represented: Active and placebo. Suppose for this example that there are 10 participants in each group, and the length of treatment is 20 days. On the x axis of each panel is time, that is, the number of days since the start of study treatment. Different study participants are represented on the y axis of each panel. Participants numbered 1–10 are in the placebo group and participants numbered 11–20 are in the active group. The occurrence of an AE ("A") is represented with an "X." Completion of the study on day 20 without the AE is denoted by an open circle. The time to either the first report of the AE or the completion of the study is represented by the length of the line from day 1 to the event. Note that it is possible for participants to report more than one instance of the same AE, but only the first occurrence is represented in Figure 8.1.

Here is a descriptive summary of the data displayed in Figure 8.1. For both groups (placebo and active), 5 out of 10 (50%) of the participants reported the particular AE. So, if we were to report these rates and a 95% confidence interval about the difference in proportions, there would not appear to be any difference between these two groups. However, when we look at the times relative to the start of study treatment, this is not so clear any more. In the placebo group, the AE was reported on days 4, 9, 11, 14, and 18. In

contrast, the AE was reported much earlier among participants in the active group, on days 1, 2, 4, 5, and 6. The remainder of participants in both groups completed the study on day 20 without experiencing the AE. It appears as if the probability of experiencing the AE (as estimated by the proportion of participants reporting it) is the same between the groups, but that there is a temporal relationship between the start of the study treatment and the time at which the AE is reported. How might we report such a result?

One possibility that might come to mind, although it is not recommended for reasons we discuss shortly, would be to calculate the average number of days to the reported AE. This is problematic, however, because we can calculate such a quantity only for those participants who actually reported the AE. The mean number of days is 11.2 and 3.6 among participants reporting AE "A" in the placebo and active groups, respectively. This analysis completely ignores those who did not report the AE. It hardly seems accurate to exclude these individuals from our analysis. In fact, although half of the participants in both groups did not report "A," they might have eventually reported it if we had followed them longer. Such an estimate of the expected time at which an AE is reported is biased, because not all participants were part of the estimate.

This example suffers from an oversimplification that we have to deal with in the real world, namely that study participants do not always complete the study for the full length of the follow-up period. Participants may drop out of studies for a number of reasons, some of which reflect their experience with the drug (for example, it may be poorly tolerated). Therefore, the "time at risk" differs from individual to individual within the same trial, and it can differ to a considerable degree from trial to trial throughout a clinical development program.

The most important points to remember here are as follows. Simply comparing the relative frequency (that is, the proportion of participants reporting the AE) of the AE between two groups does not tell the whole story: Such an analysis does not address the potential temporal relationship between exposure to the study treatment and the AE of interest. As we saw in this

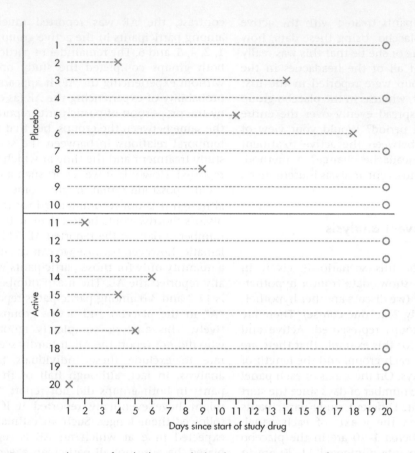

Figure 8.1   Days since the start of study drug at which adverse event "A" was first reported: Study 1 with no dropouts

example, exactly the same proportion of participants in both groups reported the AE. However, the AE occurred in the first 6 days among participants in the active group, whereas the AE reported by participants in the placebo group occurred at evenly spaced intervals over the course of the time at risk. Such a difference in times of the events would suggest that there is a cause-and-effect relationship between the active treatment and the AE.

A more informative approach would be to take into account the time of the event relative to the start of treatment. Ideally, we should use the data from all participants in this approach and should account for varying lengths of time at risk for experiencing the event. O'Neill (1987) advocated

such an approach especially for serious AEs caused by the shortcomings of simply describing the incidence (or "crude rate" as he defines it) of AEs:

> For drugs used for chronic exposure, one number or rate such as the crude rate is not likely to be informative without reference to time. To be useful as a summary measure of combined safety data from several studies and which would estimate an overall rate that describes experiences of all participants exposed for varying time periods, there is a need to stratify for time as well as other factors. (O'Neill 1987, p 20)

The next section in this chapter addresses just such a method.

8.14 Kaplan–Meier estimation of the survival function

The analysis method attributed to Kaplan and Meier (1958) enables us to analyze the time to the first reported AE while accounting for different lengths of time at risk. To illustrate this method fully, we have modified the data from the previous example slightly, as shown in Figure 8.2. We refer to this new example as study 2.

The proportion of participants with the event is still equal between the groups (this time 0.6 in both). As seen in Figure 8.2, some participants dropped out of the study before reporting the AE, which are denoted by the open circles at days before day 20. When analyzing data in this way, observations for which the event of interest was not recorded during the time at risk are called censored observations. As noted earlier it

is conceivable that, if we had followed these participants for a longer period of time, or if they had not dropped out of the study, they may have experienced the AE of interest.

When analyzing the time to the AE, we need an analytic way to deal with these censored observations. Although we do not know what would have happened for these participants, we do know that they were at risk for some period of time and "survived" their time in the study without experiencing the AE. Accordingly, the main objective of this analysis is to describe how long participants survive without experiencing the event.

The name survival analysis reflects one situation in which this type of analysis is used. When the participants in a clinical trial are very ill, the measurement of efficacy can be the length of time that they live, that is, death is the "event."

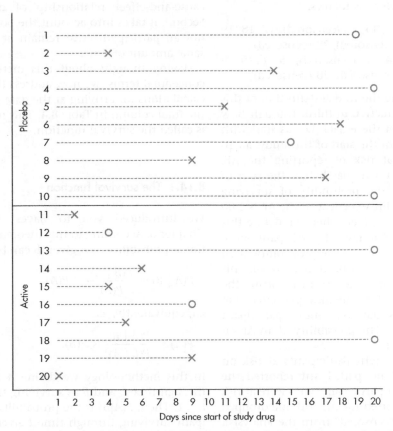

Figure 8.2   Days since the start of study drug at which adverse event "A" was first reported: Study 2 with dropouts

An example may be an oncology trial in which one group receives the investigational drug and the other receives an active control, usually the current gold standard of therapy for the specific type of cancer. Of interest is whether those receiving the investigational treatment survive longer than those receiving the active control. However, survival analysis, as will be seen in our examples, can also be used to measure the time to any defined event.

In this analytic methodology the data for each participant are expressed in a different manner. We present the event times for every participant, defined in one of two ways:

1. The day at which the participant reported the AE
2. The last day the participant was "at risk" for reporting the AE without having done so. This type of participant is labeled parenthetically as "censored."

The data are therefore as follows:

- placebo: 4, 9, 11, 14, 15 (censored), 17, 18, 19 (censored), 20 (censored), 20 (censored)
- active: 1, 2, 4, 4 (censored), 5, 6, 9, 9 (censored), 20 (censored), 20 (censored).

Before discussing the formal definition of this method, it is instructive to think through how we might interpret these data. Let us start with the active group. At the start of the study, all 10 participants are at risk of reporting the AE. Therefore, at day 0 (the day before the start of study treatment), the probability of surviving day 0 without having experienced the AE is 1.00 (we accept this as a given when we define this analysis formally). On day 1, 1 participant out of 10 at risk reported the AE. The probability of an AE on day 1 is 1/10 or 0.10 (that is, 10%). This participant is no longer at risk of reporting the AE later. On day 2 there are nine participants at risk and on this day one more participant reported the event. The probability of an AE on day 2 is 1/9 or 0.11.

This also leaves eight participants at risk on day 3. On day 3 no participant reported the event. Of the eight participants who were at risk on day 4, one reported the AE and one dropped out (that is, was "censored" from the analysis). As before, the probability of an AE occurring is

calculated relative to the number at risk, that is, 1/8 or 0.13. On day 5 there are only six participants still at risk. These data are provided in the first five columns of Table 8.4 for the active group, and the same interpretation follows through the end of the 20-day study.

The primary interest in this analysis is not what happens at a single time point, but rather what happens at time t and all points preceding time t. This leads us to the final column of Table 8.4. The numbers in this last column are the estimated probabilities of participants surviving the interval time t without having reported the AE. Given these data, it becomes possible to compare among treatments the probability of a participant not having the event of interest at any given time t.

This method has two desirable characteristics that a simple comparison of proportions does not have. First, it takes into account the variable timing of AEs, which can occur if there is a cause-and-effect relationship of drug to AE. Second, it takes into account the possibility that not all participants will remain at risk for the same amount of time.

Having thought about this methodology in conceptual terms, we now address the necessary calculations for arriving at the data presented in the final column in Table 8.4. This methodology is called the survival function.

8.14.1 The survival function

We introduced you to Bayes' theorem in Chapter 6. According to this theorem, the conditional probability of A given B can be written as:

$$P(A \mid B) = \frac{P(B \mid A)}{P(B)} \times P(A).$$

Or, equivalently, as:

$$P(A) = \frac{P(A \mid B)}{P(B \mid A)} \times P(B).$$

In this methodology we define A as surviving through time t, and B as surviving through time $t - 1$. Then, $P(A|B)$ is the probability of a participant surviving through time t given that he or she has survived through all preceding times

Table 8.4   Event times for the active group in study 2

Time (day), t	Individuals at risk for the AE before time t	Individuals reporting AE at time t	Probability of AE at time t among those at risk	Individuals dropping out at time t	Probability of surviving through time t without AE
0	10	0	0	0	1.00
1	10	1	0.10	0	0.90
2	9	1	0.11	0	0.80
3	8	0	0	0	0.80
4	8	1	0.13	1	0.70
5	6	1	0.17	0	0.58
6	5	1	0.20	0	0.46
7	4	0	0	0	0.46
8	4	0	0	0	0.46
9	4	1	0.25	1	0.35
10	2	0	0	0	0.35
11	2	0	0	0	0.35
12	2	0	0	0	0.35
13	2	0	0	0	0.35
14	2	0	0	0	0.35
15	2	0	0	0	0.35
16	2	0	0	0	0.35
17	2	0	0	0	0.35
18	2	0	0	0	0.35
19	2	0	0	0	0.35
20	2	0	0	2	0.35

$(t - 1)$, $(t - 2)$, . . . , (1). In addition, $P(B|A)$ is the probability of surviving through $t - 1$ given that the participant survived through time t. By definition, that probability is 1.00. Therefore, to calculate the conditional probability of surviving through time t, we need two pieces of information:

1. The probability of surviving through time t given that the participant survived the previous time
2. The probability of surviving the previous interval.

At day 0 (before any participants are at risk), the probability of surviving through time t is 1.00 by definition. On day 1 the probability of surviving through day 1 is the probability of surviving through day 1 given survival through day 0 (that is, 1 minus the probability of the event on day 1 among those at risk), which is equal to

$1 - 0.10 = 0.90$ times the probability of surviving through day 0 (1.00). That is, the probability is $0.90 \times 1.00 = 0.90$. Therefore, to calculate the probability in the last column we use the cumulative survival probability (last column) for the previous time and the probability of the event in the interval among those at risk.

Sometimes, these data are presented in a shorter table that displays only those time points at which an individual had an event or was censored, and thus the only values of time for which the probability of survival changes. It is more common, however, to see analyses of this type displayed graphically. The Kaplan–Meier estimate of the survival distribution is displayed for both groups in Figure 8.3. The survival curves displayed in the figure are termed "step functions" because of their appearance. We return to the interpretation of Figure 8.3 after we have fully specified the survival distribution function.

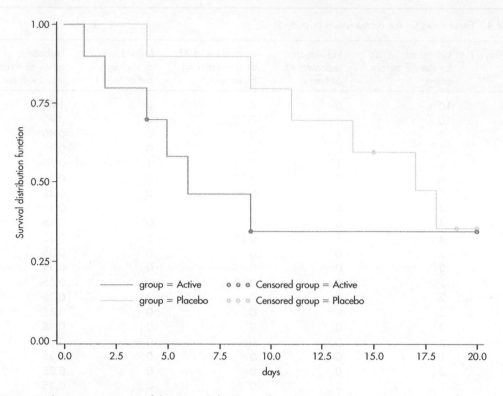

Figure 8.3   Kaplan–Meier estimate of the survival distribution for adverse event A

8.14.2 Kaplan–Meier estimation of a survival distribution

The survival function is the probability that a participant survives (that is, does not experience the event) longer than time t:

$S(t) = P$ (participant survives longer than t).

By definition, a participant cannot experience the event until he or she is at risk of the event, so will survive longer than time 0 or, equivalently, $S(0) = 1$. Also, we accept as a given that, if we waited an infinite amount of time, an individual would eventually experience the event no matter how rare. Therefore, the survival distribution at infinity is defined to be 0, or $S(\infty) = 0$. We also define the following:

- t_i is the unique event time, where $i = 1, 2, \ldots, i$.
- n_i is the number of participants who are at risk just before t_i

- m_i is the number of participants with events at time t_i
- c_i is the number of participants censored in the interval (t_i, t_{i+1}).

The Kaplan–Meier estimate of the survival function at time t is:

$$\hat{S}(t) = \prod_{t_i < t} \left(1 - \frac{m_t}{n_t}\right).$$

We can write this series of products out in full as follows:

$$\hat{S}(t) = 1 \times \left(1 - \frac{m_1}{n_1}\right) \times \left(1 - \frac{m_1}{n_1}\right)\left(1 - \frac{m_2}{n_2}\right) \times \ldots \times \left(1 - \frac{m_{t-1}}{n_{t-1}}\right)\left(1 - \frac{m_t}{n_t}\right).$$

This expression means that the probability of surviving past time t is the product of the probability of surviving time t conditional upon surviving all preceding time points and the probability of surviving all other preceding time points.

The variance of the survival distribution function at time t is:

$$\text{var}[\hat{S}(t)] = [\hat{S}(t)] \sum_{t(i)<t} \frac{m_t}{n_t(n_t - m_t)}.$$

Consequently, we can take the square root of the variance to obtain the standard error and calculate a $(1 - \alpha)\%$ confidence interval:

$$\hat{S}(t) \pm Z_{1-\alpha/2} \sqrt{\text{var}[\hat{S}(t)]}.$$

A common measure of central tendency from the Kaplan–Meier estimate is the median survival time (note that this can be estimated only if more than half the participants experience the event). The median survival time is the earliest value of t such that the probability of survival is < 0.5. Note that when observations are censored any estimate of the mean is biased because, technically, the event would eventually occur if we followed participants indefinitely.

We now return to our example to work with some of these expressions. Looking at the last column in Table 8.4 (the estimated survival distribution), we can see that the probability of surviving day 5 is 0.58. Similarly the probability of surviving day 6 is 0.46. Therefore, the estimated median time to an AE in the active group is 6 days, the earliest time at which the probability of survival is < 0.5. For a comparison, the median time to an AE is 16 days in the placebo group. The graphical representation of the survival distribution in Figure 8.3 can also be used to estimate the median time to event.

In Figure 8.3 the survival distribution is plotted against time. As can be seen from the tabular presentation of these estimates in Table 8.4, the survival estimate changes only when there is an event. In the active group on day 1 the estimate is 0.9 and then it drops down to 0.8 on day 2. An important property of the step function defined using discrete event times is that it is a discontinuous function (that is, not defined) between event times. For example, the survival distribution function is 0.46 on days 6, 7 and 8, and then at day 9 the estimate is 0.35. Looking at the Kaplan–Meier curve for the active group you could read day 9 as having an estimate of 0.35 or 0.46, but it is appropriate to remember that the outside edge of the step (right

at day 9) is discontinuous, and thus the estimated probability of survival for day 9 or later is 0.35.

Using this guideline we can read off the median survival times by drawing a reference line across Figure 8.3 at $S(t) = 0.50$ and finding the earliest value of time on the curve below the reference line. We leave it to you to verify the median times of 6 and 16 days for the active and placebo groups, respectively, using this method.

The point estimate of the probability of surviving past day 6 is 0.46 for the active group. Using the notation above, we write $\hat{S}(6) = 0.46$. We can now calculate a 95% confidence interval about this estimate. The first step is to calculate the variance about the estimate. Using the expression above and point estimate and the number of events and participants at risk at each time point before day 6, we obtain the following:

$$\text{var}[\hat{S}(6)] = (0.46)^2 \left[\frac{1}{10(9)} + \frac{1}{9(8)} + \frac{1}{8(7)} + \frac{1}{6(5)} \right]$$

$$= (0.46)^2 \left[\frac{1}{90} + \frac{1}{72} + \frac{1}{56} + \frac{1}{30} \right]$$

$$= 0.016.$$

As we have chosen a confidence level of 95%, the corresponding value of Z (the reliability factor) is 1.96. Finally, the 95% confidence interval is calculated as follows:

$$0.46 \pm 1.96 \ (0.016), \text{ i.e., } (0.43, 0.49).$$

That is, we are 95% confident that the true probability of not experiencing the event (surviving) past day 6 is in the interval (0.43, 0.49).

The Kaplan–Meier estimate is a non-parametric method that requires no distributional assumptions. The only assumption required is that the observations are independent. In the case of this example, the observations are event times (or censoring times) for each individual. Observations on unique study participants can be considered independent. The confidence interval approach described here is consistent with the stated preference for estimation and description of risks associated with new treatments. A method for testing the equality of survival distributions is discussed in Chapter 11.

8.14.3 Cox's proportional hazards model

Although we do not cover them in detail, there are parametric methods to analyze time to event data of this type, the most notable of which is Cox's proportional hazards model.

A hazard can be thought of as the risk of the event in a small interval of time, given survival up to the start of the short interval. Parametric approaches to time-to-event data such as Cox's model have a number of advantages, including the ability to adjust for other explanatory effects in a model and to extend them to recurring events for a single individual. In this case, event times would not be independent because within-participant event times would be correlated. Such an approach is appealing statistically because it makes use of more data. However, the main disadvantage of Cox's model is that the single parameter of the model, the ratio of the hazards of two groups, is assumed to be constant over time. The risk of an AE for participants treated with an active drug could vary in a nonconstant manner over time relative to the risk for placebo-treated participants, making such an assumption tenuous.

8.14.4 Considerations for the use of Kaplan–Meier estimation for AEs

We suggest the use of the Kaplan–Meier estimate for a better understanding of the risk of AEs in clinical trials for two reasons. First, the proportional hazards model has important assumptions which must be made. Secondly, the Kaplan–Meier method is easier to implement and interpret. The analysis of AEs using the Kaplan–Meier method allows us to account for the different lengths of time at risk without making any significant assumptions about the shape of the underlying distributions of the survival or hazard functions. Reviewing the rather exaggerated data from Figure 8.3 it may seem obvious that ignoring the time at risk could be problematic. Employing an appropriate method of analysis (for example, properly accounting for all individuals and calculating an interval estimate for the proportion) does not necessarily mean that the analysis is the most

appropriate one. Consideration should be given to the varying lengths of follow-up or "time at risk" when reporting AEs. It is wise to consider the denominator carefully when making any statement about probabilities.

A final word of caution here is that, although the Kaplan–Meier method (and other methods for time-to-event data) appropriately accounts for the time at risk of an event within a group, if the pattern of censoring is dependent on the treatment (for example, suppose the dropout rate is dose dependent as might be seen with chemotherapy), any treatment group comparisons of the estimate of the risk of AEs would be potentially biased. Thus, a more complete analysis would include first an assessment of censoring times (visually at a minimum) and the reason for drop out, and then the appropriate analysis to account for the time at risk. Failing to quantify the probability of an AE accurately during drug development can have significant implications for sponsors, regulatory authorities, prescribing clinicians, and patients.

8.15 Review

1. What measures are taken to ensure that AE data are of a high quality?

2. Refer to Table 8.2. Calculate a two-sided 99% confidence interval for the proportion of participants reporting any event in the:

   (a) placebo group
   (b) active dose groups combined.

3. In a therapeutic exploratory trial, 22 participants out of 140 reported an AE:

   (a) What is the 95% confidence interval for the sample proportion of participants reporting an AE?
   (b) What is the 99% confidence interval for the sample proportion of participants reporting an AE?
   (c) How confident would you be that the true population proportion of participants reporting an AE does not exceed 0.18?

4. A total of 290 participants were studied in the first therapeutic exploratory trial of an investigational antihypertensive drug. Of the 150 individuals treated with the test treatment, 32 reported fatigue. Of the 140 treated with placebo, 19 reported fatigue:

   (a) Calculate a 90% confidence interval for the difference in proportions of participants reporting fatigue.

   (b) Calculate a 95% confidence interval for the difference in proportions of participants reporting fatigue.

   (c) Calculate a 99% confidence interval for the difference in proportions of participants reporting fatigue.

   (d) What is the statistical interpretation of these results?

   (e) How might these results influence the course of future development of the drug?

5. Why is it important to account for the time that individuals are at risk of an AE?

6. Describe in your own words what a survival function is.

8.16 References

Chow S-C, Liu J-P (2004). *Design and Analysis of Clinical Trials: Concepts and methodologies*. Chichester: John Wiley & Sons.

EMEA Committee for Proprietary Medicinal Products (CPMP) (2002). *Points to Consider on Multiplicity Issues in Clinical Trials*. London: EMEA.

Fleiss JL, Paik MC, Levin B (2003). *Statistical Methods for Rates and Proportions*, 3rd edn. Chichester: John Wiley & Sons.

ICH Guidance E2A (1995). *Clinical Safety Data Management: Definitions and Standards for Expedited Reporting*. Available at: www.ich.org (accessed July 1 2007).

ICH Guidance E6 (R1) (1996). *Good Clinical Practice*. Available at: www.ich.org (accessed July 1 2007).

Kaplan EL, Meier P (1958). Nonparametric estimation from incomplete observations. *J Am Statist Assn* **53**:457–481.

Mann R, Andrews E, eds (2007). *Pharmacovigilance*, 2nd edn. Chichester: John Wiley & Sons.

O'Neill RT (1987). Statistical analyses of adverse event data from clinical trials: special emphasis on serious events. *Drug Information J* **21**:9–20.

US Food and Drug Administration (2005). *Conducting a Clinical Safety Review of a New Product Application and Preparing a Report on the Review*. Available from www.fda.gov (accessed July 1 2007).

9

Confirmatory clinical trials: Safety data II

9.1 Introduction

Chapter 8 focused on adverse event (AE) data, a large component of the overall safety data collected in clinical trials. Although AE data are often presented descriptively, we demonstrated that it is indeed possible to conduct inferential statistical analyses using AE data. This chapter discusses other safety data, including laboratory data, vital signs, and an assessment of cardiac safety that involves investigation of the cardiac QT interval (the QT interval can be identified on the ECG, as seen in Figure 9.2). In each of these cases, descriptive statistics, including measures of central tendency and dispersion, and categorical data are common forms of assessment.

9.2 Analyses of clinical laboratory data

Safety monitoring in clinical studies can be both data and labor intensive. In the context of later-stage therapeutic exploratory and therapeutic confirmatory trials, the collection of laboratory data is no exception. Typically, participants in clinical trials provide blood or urine samples at every clinic visit. There is an expansive range of clinical chemistry tests that can be conducted using these samples.

Samples may be analyzed by laboratories associated with each site (sometimes called local labs), each with its own handling procedures, assays, and reporting conventions, but this is not an optimal strategy. The use of a site's own laboratory poses no difficulties when the emphasis is on medical care, that is, the values obtained for a single individual. However, when conducting

clinical research the emphasis is on using data from a group of individuals to make optimally informed conclusions and decisions.

Differences from local lab to local lab may preclude a sponsor from meaningfully combining data from all participants across a number of investigative sites. A statistical approach to standardizing laboratory values from a number of different labs (each potentially with their own reference ranges) has been described by Chuang-Stein (1992). However, standardization is time-consuming and the use of a number of local labs can introduce unwanted sources of variability that are neither easily quantified nor accounted for.

To overcome the difficulties with using local labs the use of central laboratories (central labs) is desirable. The advantages of using a central lab are that the samples are handled in a similar fashion, the assays used are consistent over time and across individuals, and the reporting conventions (for example, units of measurement) are uniform. Techniques for proper sample collection, storage, and handling, including shipment to a central lab, should be included in study protocols. Once the samples have been obtained by the central lab they are analyzed and the data recorded in a database that includes participant identifiers, study visit, date and time of sample collection, test name, result, reporting units, and the value of the reference ("normal") range.

The determination of values for reference ranges is based on the distribution of test values in large samples. Reference ranges are determined using large databases from a general population and typically represent "2σ" limits, assuming that the values are normally distributed in the general population. The lower limit of the reference range is the value that cuts off the lowest 2.5% of values from individuals in the general population ($\mu - 2\sigma$). Likewise, the upper limit of the reference range is the value that cuts off the highest 2.5% of values from individuals in a general population ($\mu + 2\sigma$). Reference ranges for certain parameters (for example, hematocrit) may be defined specific to age and gender. Whichever approach is employed, local or central labs, the reference ranges are provided with lab values themselves to gauge the extent to which an individual's value is considered within an expected range or extreme.

In ICH Guidance E3 (1995), several analyses of clinical laboratory data are recommended. The approaches to describing clinical laboratory data include:

- measures of central tendency (for example, means or medians) for all groups at all time points examined
- shift analyses that classify laboratory values at baseline and later time points as normal, low or high relative to a reference range
- description of the number and proportion of participants for whom a change of a specified magnitude or more was reported at a particular time point. This is typically called a responders' analysis
- graphical displays of each subject's baseline value plotted against an on-treatment and/or end-of-study value
- identification of individual values that are so extreme that they would be considered clinically significant.

9.2.1 Measures of central tendency at each time point

Laboratory values are summarized descriptively for continuous measures by displaying the sample size, measures of central tendency (including the mean and median), the standard deviation, and the minimum and maximum values. A sample of such a descriptive display is provided in Table 9.1.

As the primary comparison is among or between treatment groups, the groups are displayed in the columns. Values of each test over time are of secondary interest and, therefore, are placed on the rows of the table. Reading between columns, we can see if the typical value (for example, the mean) for a parameter differs between groups. It is also possible to read down the column (that is, across time within a group) to see how the typical values vary over time. Provision of the minimum and maximum values allows the reviewer to identify any extreme values that might be considered out of the normal range. On occasion, similar analyses may also be presented for change from baseline values (typically calculated as endpoint value minus baseline value). If there are consistent and systematic changes from the start of the study, they may be apparent by examining the mean values and looking for values that deviate considerably from zero.

It may be of interest to provide a confidence interval for the change from baseline value within a group where an interval estimate that

Table 9.1   Summary of hemoglobin values (g/dL)

Visit	Statistic	Treatment group	
		Placebo	Active
Baseline	n	20	20
	Mean (SD)	13.78 (1.97)	14.61 (2.05)
	Median	13.5	14.6
	Min., Max.	11.0, 17.3	11.2, 17.7
Endpoint (last visit)	n	20	20
	Mean (SD)	13.41 (2.07)	13.75 (2.00)
	Median	13.3	13.5
	Min., Max.	10.6, 16.9	10.4, 17.2

excludes zero represents evidence of a change in mean value that exceeds what might be observed by chance alone. Similarly, confidence intervals may be calculated to provide an estimate of the between-group difference in a laboratory parameter. Comparison with a control group can be especially important when there is a laboratory test that changes as a result of study procedures (for example, decreases in hematocrit or hemoglobin as a consequence of frequent blood sampling). A summary of the change from baseline at the last visit is provided in Table 9.2.

9.2.2 A confidence interval for a mean with unknown variance

For a sample size of n observations of a random variable, the sample mean, an estimator of the population mean, is calculated as:

$$\bar{x} = \frac{\sum\limits_{i=1}^{n} x_i}{n}$$

and the sample standard deviation, s, an estimator of the population standard deviation is calculated as:

$$s = \sqrt{\frac{\sum\limits_{i=1}^{n} (x_i - \bar{x})^2}{n - 1}}.$$

The standard error of the sample mean is then calculated as:

$$SE(\bar{x}) = \frac{s}{\sqrt{n}}.$$

Finally, assuming that the random variable is normally distributed (or at least symmetrically distributed with a sample size ≥ 30), a $(1 - \alpha/2)\%$ confidence interval is:

$$\bar{x} \pm t_{1-\alpha/2, n-1} SE(\bar{x}),$$

where $t_{1-\alpha/2, n-1}$ represents the reliability factor and is the value of the t distribution with $n - 1$ degrees of freedom (df) to the left of which is $(1 - \alpha/2)\%$ of the area under the curve. These values are provided in Appendix 2.

As an example, let us calculate a 95% two-sided confidence interval for the mean hemoglobin value at the end of the study for the active group using data in Table 9.1.

Data

The data are 20 hemoglobin values from individuals treated with the active drug, obtained from blood samples collected at the last visit of the study. The mean and standard deviation were calculated as 13.75 and 2.00, respectively, and these values serve as the basis of the confidence interval.

Statistical analysis

As the population variance is unknown and is therefore being estimated by the sample variance, we use the t distribution for a reliability factor. The use of the t distribution requires us to assume that the underlying distribution of hemoglobin values is approximately normally distributed, or at least symmetrically distributed. The standard error of the sample mean is calculated as:

Table 9.2   Summary of change from baseline hemoglobin values (g/dL)

| Visit | Statistic | Treatment group | |
		Placebo	Active
Endpoint (last visit)	n	20	20
	Mean (SD)	−0.37 (1.47)	−0.86 (1.67)
	Median	−0.4	−0.8
	Min., Max.	−3.8, 2.1	−4.5, 1.4

$$SE(\bar{x}) = \frac{s}{\sqrt{n}} = \frac{2.00}{\sqrt{20}} = 0.44.$$

As we are interested in a 95% two-sided confidence interval, the value of the variate that cuts off the upper 2.5% of area from the t distribution with 19 df is 2.093. Therefore, the 95% confidence interval for the mean hemoglobin is calculated as follows:

$$13.75 \pm 2.093 (0.44) = (12.83, 14.67).$$

Interpretation and decision-making

From the confidence interval we can conclude with 95% confidence that the true population mean hemoglobin is in the interval (12.83, 14.67). Assuming that the reference range is 12–15 g/dL for females and 14–17 g/dL for males, we can proceed with development of the new drug with some degree of assurance although gender-specific intervals would be more informative.

9.2.3 A confidence interval for the difference in two means with equal unknown variance

Within-group confidence intervals can be informative, but usually the primary interest in a clinical trial is to compare the effect of one treatment with that of another. Therefore, a confidence interval for the difference in two means can better address the goals of the research.

For two independent groups 1 and 2, a sample size of n_1 observations of a random variable from group 1 and n_2 observations of a random variable from group 2, the sample means from each group are:

$$\bar{x}_1 = \frac{\sum\limits_{i=1}^{n_1} x_{1i}}{n_1} \text{ and}$$

$$\bar{x}_2 = \frac{\sum\limits_{j=1}^{n_2} x_{2j}}{n_2}, \text{ respectively.}$$

The within-group sample variances are estimated as:

$$s_1^2 = \frac{\sum\limits_{i=1}^{n_1} (x_{1i} - \bar{x}_1)^2}{n_1 - 1} \text{ and}$$

$$s_2^2 = \frac{\sum\limits_{j=1}^{n_2} (x_{2j} - \bar{x}_2)^2}{n_2 - 1}, \text{ respectively.}$$

As before, these sample statistics are estimates of the unknown population parameters, the population means, and the population variances. If the population variances are assumed to be equal, each sample statistic is a different estimate of the same population variance. It is then reasonable to average or "pool" these estimates to obtain the following:

$$s_p^2 = \frac{(n_1 - 1)s_1^2 + (n_1 - 1)s_2^2}{(n_1 + n_1 - 2)}.$$

The standard error of the difference in sample means is:

$$SE(\bar{x}_1 - \bar{x}_2) = s_p \sqrt{\frac{1}{n_1} + \frac{1}{n_2}}.$$

Calculation of a confidence interval for the difference in means requires an assumption of normal data (or, alternately, symmetrical distributions with sample sizes of 30 or more). If the population variances are assumed to be equal, a two-sided $(1 - \alpha)$% confidence interval is:

$$(\bar{x}_1 - \bar{x}_2) \pm t_{1-\alpha/2,n_1+n_2-2} SE(\bar{x}_1 - \bar{x}_2),$$

where $t_{1-\alpha/2,n_1+n_2-2}$ represents the reliability factor and is the value of the t distribution with n_1+n_2-2 df to the left of which is $(1 - \alpha/2)$% of the area under the curve.

To illustrate this methodology we use the data from Table 9.2 to calculate a between-group difference in the mean change from baseline hemoglobin at the end of the study.

Data

The description of the data for this analysis is provided in Section 9.2.1.

Statistical analysis

For this analysis we are required to use the t distribution, and therefore to make the assumption that the distribution of change from baseline values is normally or approximately normally distributed. When calculating a between-group confidence interval, it is very important to understand how the difference is being calculated and what the interpretation of the interval is, given the direction of the difference.

In this case, each change from baseline value is calculated as "endpoint minus baseline." Therefore, a mean value of change from baseline that was > 0 would imply an increase from baseline, whereas a mean change from baseline value that was < 0 would imply a decrease from baseline. In this instance we are interested in the between-group difference in mean change from baseline. We interpret the calculated confidence interval accordingly.

To start, the point estimate for the between-group (active minus placebo) difference in mean change from baseline is $(-0.86) - (-0.37) = -0.49$. To calculate the standard error we first need to obtain an estimate of the pooled variance, which is calculated as follows:

$$s_p^2 = \frac{(20-1)1.67^2 + (20-1)1.47^2}{(20+20-2)} = \frac{(19)2.79 + (19)2.16}{38} = 2.47.$$

The pooled standard deviation is calculated as:

$$\sqrt{2.47} = 1.57.$$

The standard error of the difference in means is calculated as:

$$SE(\bar{x}_1 - \bar{x}_2) = 1.57\sqrt{\frac{1}{20} + \frac{1}{20}} = 0.50.$$

The final component is to obtain the reliability factor from the t distribution with 38 df, which

is 2.02. The 95% confidence interval for the difference in means is therefore calculated as:

$$-0.49 \pm 2.02(0.50) = (-1.5, 0.52).$$

Interpretation and decision-making

On the basis of this confidence interval, there does not appear to be much of a difference between the groups with respect to a change in hemoglobin from baseline to the end of the study, particularly because the confidence interval includes the value 0.

9.2.4 Shift analysis

Another method used to analyze clinical laboratory data is called a shift analysis. For this analysis the data themselves are not the actual numeric values of the laboratory test, but a categorical ordinal variable that indicates whether the value was within the reference range (normal), low relative to the reference range (low), or high relative to the reference range (high). With these classifications on observations from baseline and some other post-randomization time point (for example, end of study), the primary interest is in the proportion of individuals who shifted from normal to high or normal to low. Depending on the parameter being investigated, a shift from high to low or low to high may also be of interest.

A typical summary table representing this kind of analysis is provided in Table 9.3. As seen there 25% of participants in the placebo group who had normal values at baseline had low values at the last visit. In the active group 20% of participants experienced this shift from baseline to last visit.

9.2.5 Responders' analysis

We noted earlier in this book that there is no such thing as an effective drug without some associated risks. Some drugs may be known to be

Table 9.3   Shift analysis of hemoglobin values

| | Baseline value | | | | | |
| | Placebo ($n = 20$) | | | Active ($n = 20$) | | |
Last visit	Low	Normal	High	Low	Normal	High
Low	3 (15%)	5 (25%)	0	1 (5%)	4 (20%)	1 (5%)
Normal	2 (10%)	7 (35%)	2 (10%)	1 (5%)	11 (55%)	0
High	0	1 (5%)	0	0	0	2 (10%)

associated with a small but consistent change in a clinical laboratory parameter (for example, treatment with hydrochlorothiazide is often associated with increases in blood glucose). Imagine a scenario in which a small change is not troubling in itself. A concern may then be: What is the chance that an individual who receives the test treatment will have a change in the lab test above a certain threshold, one that would no longer be trivial?

An analysis approach that may be informatively used here is to calculate a change from baseline for each observation and then categorize the change from baseline value as either a responder (that is, someone whose change from baseline was less or greater than a specified value) or a non-responder (that is, someone whose change from baseline was within the tolerable values of change). Whether or not a decrease or increase in the lab value is indicative of harm depends on the laboratory test itself. The descriptive analysis for this type of data includes the presentation of counts and percentages (recall that these can be represented as proportions) of responders in each group. As there usually are a number of visits at which the lab test is performed, the analysis may be presented for all post-baseline visits, the last visit, or both.

An extension of the responder analysis described above would be to categorize the change from baseline values into several (> 2) categories (for example, no change, increase $\leq X$, increase $> X$).

9.2.6 Graphical displays of end-of-study values plotted against baseline

One common element shared by a number of the analyses of laboratory data that we have described is that the magnitude of change from the start to the end of the study is important, but so is the final value itself. In addition, the relative frequency of such outcomes is of vital interest when gauging the overall risk of treatment with a new drug. One descriptive approach to address several of these issues is a graphical one.

A scatter plot of each individual's baseline value plotted against his or her end-of-study value enables us to see how many individuals (in the absolute or relative sense) had end-of-study values beyond a normal level or changes from baseline to end-of-study that represent a significant health risk. As an example, hemoglobin values at the end of the study have been plotted against the baseline value for two treatment groups (placebo and active) in Figure 9.1.

Note the diagonal line in each plot that connects all points for which the baseline value is equal to the end-of-study value. With the end-of-study value on the y axis, points above the diagonal line represent an increase from baseline and points below represent a decrease from baseline. Larger vertical deviations from the diagonal line represent larger changes from baseline values. Thus, the need to interpret a number of quantities at once is satisfied by one graphical display.

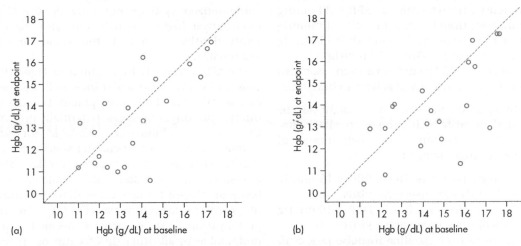

Figure 9.1   Scatterplot of hemoglobin values at baseline and end of study: (a) Placebo; (b) active

9.2.7 Clinically significant laboratory values

A graphical display such as the one in Figure 9.1, or a table of summary descriptive statistics including the minimum and maximum, may reveal values that are so extreme that they merit additional scrutiny. This is typically accomplished with the use of a listing that provides all values of the laboratory test, the dates and times of the sample collection, and the characteristics of the participant. Such an analysis is not based on aggregate information but rather on an individual observation. If a clinically significant observation were noted a medical reviewer would look to see if the participant's values returned to normal levels or remained abnormal, and if there were any accompanying AEs.

9.3 Vital signs

Vital signs typically measured in clinical trials are blood pressure (both systolic or SBP and diastolic or DBP) and heart rate, often measured as pulse rate, in beats per minute. Weight might also be of interest. In our ongoing scenario of

the development of a new antihypertensive drug, blood pressure measurements are efficacy measurements, not safety measures as such. However, we discuss the use of blood pressures in safety assessment here because this is so common in the development of non-antihypertensive drugs.

As for laboratory data, both continuous and categorical data analytical methods can be employed here. Measures of central tendency and dispersion are appropriate for continuous data. Categories of interest, and the associated categorical data, can take various forms. Imagine a trial in which the treatment phase is 12 weeks and participants visit their investigational site every 2 weeks – that is, a baseline value taken before treatment commences is followed by six values measured during the treatment phase. It may be of interest to know how many individuals show clinically significant vital sign changes during the treatment period. In this case a precise definition of clinically significant must be provided in the study protocol. The following hypothetical changes in vital signs might be considered of clinical significance by clinicians on the study team if they occurred at any of the six measurement points in the treatment phase:

- an increase from baseline in SBP ≥ 20 mmHg
- an increase from baseline in DBP ≥ 12 mmHg
- an increase from baseline in SBP ≥ 15 mmHg and an increase in DBP ≥ 10 mmHg
- a pulse rate ≥ 120 beats/min and an associated increase from baseline of at least 15 beats/min.

The clinicians on the study team might also be interested in sustained changes in vital signs. Hypothetical examples of definitions of sustained changes might be:

- an increase from baseline in SBP ≥ 15 mmHg at each of three consecutive visits
- an increase from baseline in DBP ≥ 10 mmHg at each of three consecutive visits
- an increase from baseline in pulse rate ≥ 10 beats/min at each of three consecutive visits.

Appropriate categorical analyses could then be used with these data.

9.4 QT interval prolongation and torsades de pointes liability

The ECG is a very recognizable pattern of biological activity. The ECG consists of the P wave, the QRS complex, and the T wave. These components, represented in Figure 9.2, are associated with different aspects of the cardiac cycle: Atrial activity, excitation of the ventricles, and repolarization of the ventricles, respectively. Modern

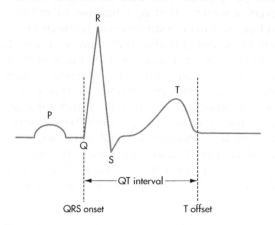

Figure 9.2 Stylized representation of the ECG, showing the QT interval

computerized systems not only display these electrophysiological signals but also concurrently digitize them and store them for later examination.

The QT interval is highlighted in Figure 9.2. This interval is of particular interest in assessing cardiac safety in drug development, because QT interval prolongation is one potentially informative surrogate biomarker available for very serious cardiac events including sudden cardiac death. (This section focuses on cardiac safety assessment in all systemically available drugs being developed for uses other than the control of cardiac arrhythmias: QT/QT_c interval prolongation – an occurrence deemed highly undesirable in all other drugs – can occur with antiarrhythmic drugs as a consequence of their mechanism of clinical efficacy [ICH Guidance E14, 2005].) The ICH Guidance E14 addresses the evaluation of QT intervals in clinical development programs.

The time interval between the onset of the QRS complex and the offset of the T wave is defined as the QT interval. Consider an individual with a steady heart rate of 60 beats/min, a number chosen to make the math easy in this example. This represents one heart beat/second, and so the total length (in the time domain) of all ECG segments during one beat would add up to 1 second, represented in this research field as 1000 milliseconds (ms). Each component of the ECG can therefore be assigned a length, or duration, in milliseconds. The length of the QT interval can be obtained by measurement from inspecting the ECG and identifying the QRS onset and the T-wave offset.

As the heart beats faster (heart rate increases), the duration of an individual cardiac cycle decreases, because more cardiac cycles now occur in the same time. Therefore, as the cardiac cycle shortens, so do each of the components of the cardiac cycle. This means that the QT interval will tend to be shorter at a higher heart rate. As it is of interest to examine the QT interval at various heart rates, the interval can be "corrected" for heart rate. This leads to the term QT_c, which is calculated (by one of several methods including two corrections attributed to Bazett and Fridericia), taking into account the actual QT and the heart rate (the duration of the entire cardiac cycle, sometimes referred to as the RR interval) at that point. The title of ICH Guidance E14 uses the term "QT/QT_c interval" to indicate that both QT and QT_c are of interest: In this book, the term "QT interval" represents both QT and QT_c.

It is of considerable interest in drug development to determine whether the investigational drug under development leads to prolongation of the QT interval: Although QT interval prolongation can be congenital, it can also be acquired, for example, induced by drug therapy. QT prolongation, which represents delayed cardiac repolarization of the myocardial cells, is regarded as a potentially very informative surrogate marker for certain dangerous cardiac arrhythmias, namely polymorphic ventricular tachycardia and torsades de pointes, and sudden cardiac death. Extensive ECG monitoring during preapproval clinical trials is therefore a critical part of clinical development programs, and results from this testing must be presented to a regulatory agency to obtain marketing approval. One of the biggest causes of delay in getting a new drug approved by a regulatory agency, or failure to be given marketing approval, is cardiac safety issues, and therefore the choice of the correct study design, appropriate methodology for collecting optimum quality data, and appropriate statistical analyses are of tremendous importance.

Although ICH Guidance E14 (2005) provides guidance on each of these considerations, we focus here on the statistical approaches that should be taken in the investigation of QT prolongation. As this guidance noted (p 9), "The QT/QT_c interval data should be presented both as analyses of central tendency (for example, means, medians) and categorical analyses. Both can provide relevant information on clinical risk assessment." The effect of the investigational drug on the QT intervals is most commonly analyzed using the largest time-matched mean difference between the drug and placebo (adjusted for baseline) over the data collection period.

Categorical analyses are based on the number and the percentage of individuals who meet or exceed a predefined upper limit. Such limits can be stated in the study protocol in terms of either absolute QT interval prolongation values or changes from baseline. At this time, there is no consensus concerning what is the "best" choice of these upper limit values. ICH Guidance 14 therefore suggested that multiple analyses using several predefined limits is a reasonable approach in light of this lack of consensus. For absolute QT interval data, the guidance suggests providing absolute numbers and percentages of individuals whose QT intervals exceed 450, 480, and 500 ms. For change-from-baseline QT interval data, the same information might be provided for increases exceeding 30 ms and those exceeding 60 ms. The design and analysis of studies intended to evaluate changes in QT can be rather difficult to implement. Some of the difficulties and areas for further research brought to light by ICH Guidance E14 are discussed in a recent paper (Pharmaceutical Research and Manufacturers of America QT Statistics Expert Working Team, 2005).

For further discussion of QT/QT_c interval prolongation and other cardiac safety assessments for noncardiac drugs, see Morganroth and Gussak (2005) and Turner and Durham (2008).

9.5 Concluding comments on safety assessments in clinical trials

In this chapter we have seen that the goal of safety analyses is to cast a wide net in the hopes of identifying any events that may be attributable to treatment with the new drug. Such a broad search, however, also has a significant disadvantage: If we look at so many outcomes, we might find one that looks problematic just by chance alone. Rather than rely solely on statistical approaches to limit the chance of this occurring, a sensible approach is to substantiate such a finding with additional data, either a similar result in a different study or some data on the medical explanation for the event (the mechanism of action).

The analysis tools that we have described in this chapter provide ways to evaluate the risk of the new drug, given the constraints of sample sizes obtainable in clinical development. The limitations of relatively little human experience before marketing approval have to be considered, especially when reviewing clinical safety data. Thus far, regulatory agencies have not required pharmaceutical companies to increase the sizes of their studies to find the best way to uncover safety risks that would otherwise be hard to find. Rather, the emphasis has been to use more modern tools (for example, genetics and candidate screening) to identify potentially dangerous drugs before there are a large number of participant exposures (US Department of Health and Human Services, FDA, 2004). The role of postmarketing surveillance will continue to be important (see also ICH Guidance E2E, 2004; Strom, 2005; Mann and Andrews, 2007). This is especially true when we think of the relative homogeneity of participants in clinical trials compared with patients in the real world and the implications of the law of large numbers (recall discussions in Chapter 6).

As a final note to this chapter, any potential risks to individuals treated with a new drug have to be considered and cannot automatically be considered trivial. The acceptability of the magnitude of the risk depends largely on a statistical demonstration of the expected benefit of the new treatment, which is the topic of Chapters 10 and 11.

9.6 Review

1. What are some advantages and disadvantages of the various analytical approaches cited from ICH Guidance E3 listed in Section 9.2?

2. Refer to the data in Table 9.1:

   (a) Calculate a two-sided 90% confidence interval for the difference in mean hemoglobin value at endpoint (last visit).

   (b) Calculate a two-sided 95% confidence interval for the difference in mean hemoglobin value at endpoint (last visit).

   (c) Calculate a two-sided 99% confidence interval for the difference in mean hemoglobin value at endpoint (last visit).

   (d) What is the statistical interpretation of these results?

3. What is the statistical and clinical interpretation (or relevance) of the following 95% confidence intervals for the between-group difference (for example, test group minus placebo) in mean change from baseline hemoglobin (g/dL) at endpoint (last visit)?

   (a) $(-1.2, 2.6)$
   (b) $(1.7, 3.4)$
   (c) $(-6.2, -2.3)$.

9.7 References

Chuang-Stein C (1992). Summarizing laboratory data with different reference ranges in multi-center trials. *Drug Information J* **26**:74–84.

ICH Guidance E2E (2004). *Pharmacovigilance Planning*. Available at: www.ich.org (accessed July 1 2007).

ICH Guidance E3 (1995). *Structure and Content of Clinical Study Reports*. Available at: www.ich.org (accessed July 1 2007).

ICH Guidance E14 (2005). *The Clinical Evaluation of QT/QTc Interval Prolongation and Proarrhythmic Potential for Non-Antiarrhythmic Drugs*. Available at: www.ich.org (accessed July 1 2007).

Mann R, Andrews E, eds (2007). *Pharmacovigilance*, 2nd edn. Chichester: John Wiley & Sons.

Morganroth J, Gussak I, eds (2005). *Cardiac Safety of Noncardiac Drugs: Practical guidelines for clinical research and drug development*. Totowa, NJ: Humana Press.

Pharmaceutical Research and Manufacturers of America QT Statistics Expert Working Team (2005). Investigating drug-induced QT and QTc prolongation in the clinic: a review of statistical design and analysis considerations: report from the Pharmaceutical Research and Manufacturers of America QT Statistics Expert Team. *Drug Information J* 39:243–266.

Strom BL, ed. (2005). *Pharmacoepidemiology*, 4th edn. Chichester: John Wiley & Sons.

Turner JR, Durham TA (2008). *Integrated Cardiac Safety: Assessment methodologies for noncardiac drugs in discovery, development, and postmarketing surveillance*. Hoboken, NJ: John Wiley & Sons, in press.

US Department of Health and Human Services, Food and Drug Administration (2004). *Challenge and Opportunity on the Critical Path to New Medical Products*. Available from www.fda.gov (accessed July 1 2007).

10

Confirmatory clinical trials: Analysis of categorical efficacy data

10.1 Introduction: Regulatory views of substantial evidence

When thinking about the use of statistics in clinical trials, the first thing that comes to mind for many people is the process of hypothesis testing and the associated use of p values. This is very reasonable, because the role of a chance outcome is of utmost importance in study design and the interpretation of results from a study. A sponsor's objective is to develop an effective therapy that can be marketed to patients with a certain disease or condition. From a public health perspective, the benefits of a new treatment cannot be separated from the risks that are tied to it. Regulatory agencies must protect public health by ensuring that a new treatment has "definitively" been demonstrated to have a beneficial effect. The meaning of the word "definitively" as used here is rather broad, but we discuss what it means in this context – that is, we operationally define the term "definitively" as it applies to study design, data analysis, and interpretation in new drug development.

Most of this chapter is devoted to describing various types of data and the corresponding analytical strategies that can be used to demonstrate that an investigational drug, or test treatment, is efficacious. First, however, it is informative to discuss the international standards for demonstrating efficacy of a new product, and examine how regulatory agencies have interpreted these guidelines. ICH Guidance E9 (1998, p 4) addresses therapeutic confirmatory studies and provides the following definition:

A confirmatory trial is an adequately controlled trial in which the hypotheses are stated in advance and evaluated. As a rule, confirmatory trials are necessary to provide firm evidence of efficacy or safety. In such trials the key hypothesis of interest follows directly from the trial's primary objective, is always pre-defined, and is the hypothesis that is subsequently tested when the trial is complete. In a confirmatory trial it is equally important to estimate with due precision the size of the effects attributable to the treatment of interest and to relate these effects to their clinical significance.

It is common practice to use earlier phase studies such as therapeutic exploratory studies to characterize the size of the treatment effect, while acknowledging that the effect size found in these studies is associated with a certain amount of error. As noted earlier, confidence intervals can be helpful for planning confirmatory studies. The knowledge and experience gained in these earlier studies can lead to hypotheses that we wish to test (and hopefully confirm) in a therapeutic confirmatory trial, for example, the mean reduction in systolic blood pressure (SBP) for the test treatment is 20 mmHg greater than the mean reduction in SBP for placebo. As we have seen, a positive result from a single earlier trial could be a type I error, so a second study is useful in substantiating that result.

The description of a confirmatory study in ICH Guidance E9 (1998) also illustrates the importance of the study design employed. The study should be designed with several important characteristics:

- It should test a specific hypothesis.
- It should be appropriately sized.
- It should be able to differentiate treatment effects from other sources of variation (for

example, time trends, regression to the mean, bias).

• The size of the treatment effect that is being confirmed should be clinically relevant.

The clinical relevance, or clinical significance, of a treatment effect is an extremely important consideration. The size of a treatment effect that is deemed clinically relevant is best defined by medical, clinical, and regulatory specialists.

Precise description of the study design and adherence to the study procedures detailed in the study protocol are particularly important for confirmatory studies. Quoting again from ICH Guidance E9 (1998, p 4):

> Confirmatory trials are intended to provide firm evidence in support of claims and hence adherence to protocols and standard operating procedures is particularly important; unavoidable changes should be explained and documented, and their effect examined. A justification of the design of each such trial, and of other important statistical aspects such as the principal features of the planned analysis, should be set out in the protocol. Each trial should address only a limited number of questions.

Confirmatory studies should also provide quantitative evidence that substantiates claims in the product label (for example, the package insert) as they relate to an appropriate population of patients. In the following quote from ICH Guidance E9 (1998, p 4), the elements of statistical and clinical inference can be seen:

> Firm evidence in support of claims requires that the results of the confirmatory trials demonstrate that the investigational product under test has clinical benefits. The confirmatory trials should therefore be sufficient to answer each key clinical question relevant to the efficacy or safety claim clearly and definitively. In addition, it is important that the basis for generalisation . . . to the intended patient population is understood and explained; this may also influence the number and type (e.g. specialist or general practitioner) of centres and/or trials needed. The results of the confirmatory trial(s) should be robust. In some circumstances the weight of evidence from a single confirmatory trial may be sufficient.

The terms "firm evidence" and "robust" do not have explicit definitions. However, as clinical trials have been conducted and reported in recent years, some practical (operational) definitions have emerged, and these are discussed shortly.

In its guidance document *Providing Clinical Evidence of Effectiveness for Human Drug and Biological Products*, the US Food and Drug Administration (US Department of Health and Human Services, FDA, 1998) describes the introduction of an effectiveness requirement according to a standard of "substantial evidence" in the Federal Food, Drug, and Cosmetic Act (the FDC Act) of 1962:

> *Substantial evidence* was defined in section 505(d) of the Act as "evidence consisting of adequate and well-controlled investigations, including clinical investigations, by experts qualified by scientific training and experience to evaluate the effectiveness of the drug involved, on the basis of which it could fairly and responsibly be concluded by such experts that the drug will have the effect it purports or is represented to have under the conditions of use prescribed, recommended, or suggested in the labeling or proposed labeling thereof."
>
> US Department of Health and Human Services, FDA (1998, p 3)

The phrase "adequate and well-controlled investigations" has typically been interpreted as at least two studies that clearly demonstrated that the drug has the effect claimed by the sponsor submitting a marketing approval. Furthermore, a type I error of 0.05 has typically been adopted as a reasonable standard upon which data from clinical studies are judged. That is, it was widely believed that the intent of the FDC Act of 1962 was to state that a drug could be concluded to be effective if the treatment effect was clinically relevant and statistically significant at the $\alpha = 0.05$ level in two independent studies.

The ICH Guidance E8 (1998, p 4) clarified this issue:

> The usual requirement for more than one adequate and well-controlled investigation reflects the need for *independent substantiation*

of experimental results. A single clinical experimental finding of efficacy, unsupported by other independent evidence, has not usually been considered adequate scientific support for a conclusion of effectiveness. The reasons for this include the following:

- Any clinical trial may be subject to unanticipated, undetected, systematic biases. These biases may operate despite the best intentions of sponsors and investigators, and may lead to flawed conclusions. In addition, some investigators may bring conscious biases to evaluations.
- The inherent variability in biological systems may produce a positive trial result by chance alone. This possibility is acknowledged, and quantified to some extent, in the statistical evaluation of the result of a single efficacy trial. It should be noted, however, that hundreds of randomized clinical efficacy trials are conducted each year with the intent of submitting favorable results to the FDA. Even if all drugs tested in such trials were ineffective, one would expect one in forty of those trials to "demonstrate" efficacy by chance alone at conventional levels of statistical significance. It is probable, therefore, that false positive findings (that is, the chance appearance of efficacy with an ineffective drug) will occur and be submitted to FDA as evidence of effectiveness. Independent substantiation of a favorable result protects against the possibility that a chance occurrence in a single study will lead to an erroneous conclusion that a treatment is effective.
- Results obtained in a single center may be dependent on site or investigator-specific factors (for example, disease definition, concomitant treatment, diet). In such cases, the results, although correct, may not be generalizable to the intended population. This possibility is the primary basis for emphasizing the need for independence in substantiating studies.
- Rarely, favorable efficacy results are the product of scientific fraud.

Although there are statistical, methodologic, and other safeguards to address the identified problems, they are often inadequate to address these problems in a single trial. Independent substantiation of experimental results addresses such problems by providing consistency across more than one study, thus greatly reducing the possibility that a biased, chance, site-specific, or fraudulent result will lead to an erroneous conclusion that a drug is effective.

This guidance further clarified that the need for substantiation does not necessarily require two or more identically designed trials:

> Precise replication of a trial is only one of a number of possible means of obtaining independent substantiation of a clinical finding and, at times, can be less than optimal as it could leave the conclusions vulnerable to any systematic biases inherent to the particular study design. Results that are obtained from studies that are of different design and independent in execution, perhaps evaluating different populations, endpoints, or dosage forms, may provide support for a conclusion of effectiveness that is as convincing as, or more convincing than, a repetition of the same study.

ICH Guidance E8 (1998, p 5)

Regulatory agencies have traditionally accepted only two-sided hypotheses because, theoretically, one could not rule out harm (as opposed to simply no effect) associated with the test treatment. If the value of a test statistic (for example, the Z-test statistic) is in the critical region at the extreme left or extreme right of the distribution (that is, < -1.96 or > 1.96), the probability of such an outcome by chance alone under the null hypothesis of no difference is 0.05. However, the probability of such an outcome in the direction indicative of a treatment benefit is half of 0.05, that is, 0.025. This led to a common statistical definition of "firm" or "substantial" evidence as the effect was unlikely to have occurred by chance alone, and it could therefore be attributed to the test treatment. Assuming that two studies of the test treatment had two-sided p values < 0.05 with the direction of the treatment effect in favor of a benefit, the probability of the two results occurring by chance alone would be 0.025×0.025, that is, 0.000625 (which can also be expressed as 1/1600).

It is important to note here that this standard is not written into any regulation. Therefore, there may be occasions where this statistical standard is not met. In fact, it is possible to redefine the statistical standard using one large well-designed trial, an approach that has been described by Fisher (1999).

Whether the substantial evidence comes from one or more than one trial, the basis for concluding that the evidence is indeed substantial is statistical in nature. That is, the regulatory agency must agree with the sponsor on several key points in order to approve a drug for marketing:

- The effect claimed cannot be explained by other phenomena such as regression to the mean, time trends, or bias. This highlights the need for appropriate study design and data acquisition.
- The effect claimed is not likely a chance outcome. That is, the results associated with a primary objective have a small *p* value, indicating a low probability of a type I error.
- The effect claimed is large enough to be important to patients, that is, clinically relevant. The magnitude of the effect must account for sampling during the trial(s).

A clinical development program contains various studies that are designed to provide the quantity and quality of evidence required to satisfy regulatory agencies, which have the considerable responsibility of protecting public health. The requirements for the demonstration of substantial evidence highlight the importance of study design and analytic strategies. Appropriate study design features such as concurrent controls, randomization, standardization of data collection, and treatment blinding help to provide compelling evidence that an observed treatment effect cannot be explained by other phenomena. Selection of the appropriate analytical strategy maximizes the precision and efficiency of the statistical test employed. The employment of appropriate study design and analytical strategies provides the opportunity for an investigational drug to be deemed effective if a certain treatment effect is observed in clinical trials.

10.2 Objectives of therapeutic confirmatory trials

Table 10.1 provides a general taxonomy of the objectives of confirmatory trials and specific research questions corresponding to each. Confirmatory trials typically have one primary objective that varies by the type of trial. In the case of a new antihypertensive it may be sufficient to demonstrate simply that the reduction in blood pressure is greater for the test treatment than for the placebo. A superiority trial is appropriate in this instance. However, in other therapeutic areas – for example, oncology – other designs are appropriate. In these therapeutic areas it is not ethical to withhold life-extending therapies to certain individuals by randomizing them to a placebo treatment if there is already an existing treatment for the disease or condition.

In such cases, it is appropriate to employ trials with the objective of demonstrating that the clinical response to the test treatment is equivalent (that is, no better or worse) to that of an existing effective therapy. These trials are called

Table 10.1 Taxonomy of therapeutic confirmatory trial objectives

Objective of trial	Example indication	Example research question
Demonstrate superiority	Hypercholesterolemia	Is the magnitude of LDL reduction for the test treatment greater than for placebo?
Demonstrate equivalence	Oncology	Is the test treatment at worst trivially inferior to and at best slightly better than the active control with respect to the rate of partial tumor response?
Demonstrate noninferiority	Anti-infective	Is the microbial eradication rate for the test treatment at least not unacceptably worse than for the active control?

equivalence trials. A question that arises here is: Why would we want to develop another drug if there is already an existing effective treatment? The answer is that we believe the test treatment offers other advantages (for example, convenience, tolerability, or cost) to justify its development. Another type of trial is the noninferiority trial. These trials are intended only to demonstrate that a test treatment is not unacceptably worse (noninferior) than an active control. Again, the test treatment may provide advantages other than greater therapeutic response such as fewer adverse effects or greater convenience.

Equivalence and noninferiority trials are quite different from superiority trials in their design, analysis, and interpretation (although exactly the same methodological considerations apply to collect optimum quality data in these trials). Superiority trials continue to be our focus in this book, but it is important that you are aware of other designs too. Therefore, in Chapter 12 we discuss some of the unique features of these other design types.

10.3 Moving from research questions to research objectives: Identification of endpoints

There is an important relationship between research questions and study objectives, and it is relatively straightforward to restate research questions such as those in Table 10.1 in terms of study objectives. As stated in ICH Guidance E9, a confirmatory study should be designed to address at most a few objectives. If a treatment effect can be quantified by an appropriate statistical measure, study objectives can be translated into statistical hypotheses. For example, the extent of low-density lipoprotein (LDL)-cholesterol reduction can be measured by the mean change from baseline to end-of-treatment, or by the proportion of study participants who attain a goal level of LDL according to a treatment guideline. The efficacy of a cardiovascular intervention may be measured according to the median survival time after treatment. For many drugs, identification of an appropriate measure

of the participant-level response (for example, reported pain severity using a visual analog scale) is not difficult. However, there may be instances when the use of a surrogate endpoint can be justified on the basis of statistical, biological and practical considerations. Measuring HIV viral load as a surrogate endpoint for occurrence of AIDS is an example.

Identification of the endpoint of interest is one of the many cases in clinical research that initially seem obvious and simple. We know exactly what disease or condition we are interested in treating, and it should be easy to identify an endpoint that will tell us if we have been successful. In reality, the establishment of an appropriate endpoint, whether it is the most clinically relevant endpoint or a surrogate endpoint, can be difficult. Some of the statistical criteria used to judge the acceptability of surrogate endpoints are described by Fleming and DeMets (1996), who caution against their use in confirmatory trials. One might argue that the most clinically relevant endpoint for a antihypertensive is the survival time from myocardial infarction, stroke, or death. Fortunately, the incidence of these events is relatively low during the typical observation period of clinical trials. The use of SBP as a surrogate endpoint enables the use of shorter and smaller studies than would be required if the true clinical endpoint had to be evaluated. For present purposes, we assume the simplest scenario: The characteristic that we are going to measure (blood pressure) is uncontroversial and universally accepted, and a clinically relevant benefit is acknowledged to be associated with a relative change in blood pressure for the test treatment compared with the control.

Common measures of the efficacy of a test treatment compared with a placebo include the differences in means, in proportions, and in survival distributions. How the treatment effect is measured and analyzed in a clinical trial should be a prominent feature of the study protocol and should be agreed upon with regulatory authorities before the trial begins. In this chapter we describe between-group differences in general terms. It is acceptable to calculate the difference in two quantities, *A* and *B* as "*A* minus *B*" or "*B* minus *A*" as long as the procedure chosen is identified unambiguously.

10.4 A brief review of hypothesis testing

We discussed hypothesis testing in some detail in Chapter 6. For present purposes, the role of hypothesis testing in confirmatory clinical trials can be restated simply as follows:

Hypothesis testing provides an objective way to make a decision to proceed as if the drug is either effective or not effective based on the sample data, while also limiting the probability of making either decision in error.

For a superiority trial the null hypothesis is that the treatment effect is zero. Sponsors of drug trials would like to generate sufficient evidence, in the form of the test statistic, to reject the null hypothesis in favor of the alternate hypothesis, thereby providing compelling evidence that the treatment effect is not zero. The null hypothesis may be rejected if the treatment effect favors the test drug, and also if it favors the placebo (as discussed, we have to acknowledge this possibility).

The decision to reject the null hypothesis depends on the value of the test statistic relative to the distribution of its values under the null hypothesis. Rejection of the null hypothesis means one of two things:

1. There really is a difference between the two treatments, that is, the alternate hypothesis is true.
2. An unusually rare event has occurred, that is, a type I error has been committed, meaning that we reject the null hypothesis given that it is true.

Regulatory authorities have many reasons to be concerned about type I errors. As a review at the end of this chapter, the reader is encouraged to think about the implications for a pharmaceutical company of committing a type I or II error at the conclusion of a confirmatory efficacy study.

The test statistic is dependent on the analysis method, which is dependent on the study design; this, in turn, is dependent on a precisely stated research question. By now, you have seen

us state this fundamental point several times, but it really cannot be emphasized enough. In our experience, especially with unplanned data analyses, researchers can be so anxious to know "What's the p value?" that they forget to consider the possibility that **the study that generated the data was not adequately designed to answer the specific question of interest**. The steps that lead toward optimally informed decision-making in confirmatory trials on the basis of hypothesis testing are as follows:

1. State the research question.
2. Formulate the research question in the form of null and alternate statistical hypotheses.
3. Design the study to minimize bias, maximize precision, and limit the chance of committing a type I or II error. As part of the study design, prespecify the primary analysis method that will be used to test the hypothesis. Depending on the nature of the data and the size of the study, consider whether a parametric or nonparametric approach is appropriate.
4. Collect optimum-quality data using optimum-quality experimental methodology.
5. Carry out the primary statistical analysis using the prespecified method.
6. Report the results of the primary statistical analysis.
7. Make a decision to proceed as if the drug is either effective or ineffective:

   (a) If you decide that it is effective based on the results of this study, you may choose to move on to conduct the next study in your clinical development plan, or, if this is the final study in your development plan, to submit a dossier (for example, NDA [new drug application], MAA [marketing authorisation application]) to a regulatory agency.
   (b) If you decide that it is ineffective based on the results of this study, you may choose to refine the original research question and conduct a new study, or to abandon the development of this investigational new drug.

10.5 Hypothesis tests for two or more proportions

The research question of interest in some studies can be phrased: Does the test treatment result in a higher probability of attaining a desired state than the control? Examples of such applications include:

- survival after 1 year following a cardiovascular intervention
- avoiding hospitalization associated with asthmatic exacerbations over the course of 6 months
- attaining a specific targeted level of LDL according to one's background risk.

In a confirmatory trial of an antihypertensive, for example, a sponsor might like to know if the test treatment results in a higher proportion of hypertensive individuals (which can be interpreted as a probability) reaching an SBP < 140 mmHg.

10.5.1 Hypothesis test for two proportions: The Z approximation

In the case of a hypothesis test for two proportions the null and alternate statistical hypotheses can be stated as follows:

$$H_0: p_1 - p_2 = 0$$
$$H_A: p_1 - p_2 \neq 0$$

where the population proportions for each of two independent groups are represented by p_1 and p_2.

The sample proportions will be used to estimate the population proportions and, as in Chapter 8, are defined as:

$$\hat{p}_1 = \frac{\text{number of observations in group 1 with the event of interest}}{\text{total number of observations in group 1 at risk of the event}}$$

and

$$\hat{p}_2 = \frac{\text{number of observations in group 2 with the event of interest}}{\text{total number of observations in group 2 at risk of the event}}$$

The estimator for the difference in the two sample proportions is $\hat{p}_1 - \hat{p}_2$ and the standard error of the difference $\hat{p}_1 - \hat{p}_2$ is:

$$SE(\hat{p}_1 - \hat{p}_2) = \sqrt{\frac{\hat{p}_1 \hat{q}_1}{n_1} + \frac{\hat{p}_2 \hat{q}_2}{n_2}},$$

where $\hat{q}_1 = 1 - \hat{p}_1$ and $\hat{q}_2 = 1 - \hat{p}_2$. The test statistic for the test of two proportions is equal to:

$$Z = \frac{(\hat{p}_1 - \hat{p}_2)}{SE(\hat{p}_1 - \hat{p}_2)}.$$

Use of a correction factor may be useful as well, especially with smaller sample sizes. A test statistic that makes use of the correction factor is:

$$Z = \frac{|\hat{p}_1 - \hat{p}_2| - \frac{1}{2}\left(\frac{1}{n_1} + \frac{1}{n_2}\right)}{SE(\hat{p}_1 - \hat{p}_2)}.$$

For large samples (that is, when $\hat{p}_1 n_1 \geqslant 5$ and $\hat{p}_2 n_2 \geqslant 5$), these test statistics follow a standard normal distribution under the null hypothesis. Values of the test statistic that are far away from zero would contradict the null hypothesis and lead to rejection. In particular, for a two-sided test of size α, the critical region (that is, those values of the test statistic that would lead to rejection of the null hypothesis) is defined by $Z < Z_{\alpha/2}$ or $Z > Z_{1-\alpha/2}$. If the calculated value of the test statistic is in the critical region, the null hypothesis is rejected in favor of the alternate hypothesis. If the calculated value of the test statistic is outside the critical region, the null hypothesis is not rejected.

As an illustration of this hypothesis test, consider the following hypothetical data from a confirmatory study of a new antihypertensive. In a randomized, double-blind, 12-week study, the test treatment was compared with placebo. The primary endpoint of the study was the proportion of participants who attained an SBP goal < 140 mmHg. Of 146 participants assigned to placebo, 34 attained an SBP < 140 mmHg at week 12. Of 154 assigned to test treatment, 82 attained the goal. Let us look at how these results can help us to make a decision based on the information provided. We go through the steps needed to do this.

The research question

Is the test treatment associated with a higher rate of achieving target SBP?

Study design

As noted, the study is a randomized, double-blind, placebo-controlled, 12-week study of an investigational antihypertensive drug.

Data

The data from this study are in the form of counts. We have a count of the number of participants in each treatment group, and, for both of these groups, we have a count of the number of participants who experienced the event of interest. As the research question pertains to a probability, or risk, we use the count data to estimate the probability of a proportion of participants attaining the goal SBP.

Hypotheses and statistical analysis

The null and alternate statistical hypotheses in this case can be stated as:

$$H_0: p_{TEST} - p_{PLACEBO} = 0$$
$$H_A: p_{TEST} - p_{PLACEBO} \neq 0$$

where the population proportions for each group are represented by p_{TEST} and $p_{PLACEBO}$. As the response is attaining a lower SBP, the group with the greater proportion of responses will be regarded as the treatment with a more favorable response. The difference in proportions is calculated as "test minus placebo." Positive values of the test statistic will favor the test treatment.

As the samples are large according to the definition given earlier, the test of the two proportions using the Z approximation is appropriate. For a two-sided test of size 0.05 the critical region is defined by $Z < -1.96$ or $Z > 1.96$. The value of the test statistic is calculated as:

$$Z = \frac{\hat{p}_{TEST} - \hat{p}_{PLACEBO}}{SE(\hat{p}_{TEST} - \hat{p}_{PLACEBO})}.$$

The difference in sample proportions is calculated as:

$$\hat{p}_{TEST} - \hat{p}_{PLACEBO} = \frac{82}{154} - \frac{34}{146} = 0.5325 - 0.2329 = 0.2996.$$

The standard error of the difference in sample proportions is calculated as:

$$SE(\hat{p}_{TEST} - \hat{p}_{PLACEBO}) = \sqrt{\frac{(0.5325)(0.4675)}{154} + \frac{(0.2329)(0.7671)}{146}} = 0.0533.$$

Using these calculated values, the value of the test statistic is:

$$Z = \frac{0.2996}{0.0533} = 5.62.$$

The test statistic using a correction factor is obtained as:

$$Z = \frac{0.2996 - \frac{1}{2}\left(\frac{1}{154} + \frac{1}{146}\right)}{0.0533} = 5.50.$$

Interpretation and decision-making

As the value of test statistic – that is, 5.62 – is in the critical region (5.62 > 1.96), the null hypothesis is rejected in favor of the alternate hypothesis. Note that the value of the test statistic using the correction factor was also in the critical region. The probability of attaining the SBP goal is greater for those receiving the test treatment than for those receiving placebo.

It is fairly common to report a p value from such an analysis. As we have seen, the p value is the probability (under the null hypothesis) of observing the result obtained or one that is more extreme. In this analytical strategy we refer to a table of Z scores and the tail areas associated with each to find the sum of the two areas (that is, probabilities) to the left of -5.62 (a result as extreme as the observed or more so) and to the right of 5.62 (the result observed and those more extreme). A Z score of this magnitude is way out in the right-hand tail of the distribution, leading to a p value < 0.0001.

The results of this study may lead the sponsor to decide to conduct a second confirmatory trial, being confident that the drug is efficacious. Alternately, if the entire set of clinical data are satisfactory, the sponsor may decide to apply for marketing approval.

10.5.2 Hypothesis test for two (or more) proportions: χ^2 test of homogeneity

An alternative method to the Z approximation for the comparison of two proportions from independent groups is called the χ^2 test, which is considered a goodness-of-fit test; this quantifies the extent to which count data (for example, the number of individuals with and without the response of interest) deviate from counts that would be expected under a particular mathematical model. The mathematical model used in clinical studies for goodness-of-fit tests is that of homogeneity. That is, if a particular response is homogeneous with respect to treatment, we would expect all the responses of interest to be proportionally distributed among all treatment groups. The assumption of homogeneity will allow us to calculate the cell counts that would be expected. These will then be compared with what was actually observed. The more the expected counts under the particular model of interest (for example, homogeneity) deviate from what is observed, the greater the value of the test statistic, and therefore the more the data do not represent goodness of fit. The χ^2 test is useful because it can be used to test homogeneity across two or more treatment groups. We first describe the case of two groups and the more general case is described in Section 10.5.3.

If there are two independent groups of interest (for example, treatment groups in a clinical trial) each representing an appropriate population, the proportions of participants with the characteristic or event of interest are represented by $\hat{p}_1 = m_1/n_1$ and $\hat{p}_2 = m_2/n_2$. The counts of participants with events and nonevents can be displayed in a contingency table with two columns and two rows, representing the numbers of observations with (m_1 and m_2) and without ($n_1 - m_1$ and $n_2 - m_2$) the characteristic of interest. The marginal total of individuals with events (the sum across the two groups) is denoted by $R = m_1 + m_2$. The marginal total of individuals without the events (sum across the two groups) is denoted by $S = (n_1 + n_2) - (m_1 + m_2)$.

Finally, the total sample size (sum across the two groups) is denoted by $N = n_1 + n_2$. The overall proportion of responses of interest across both groups is $\hat{p} = R/N$. The complementary proportion of responses is $\hat{q} = S/N$. A sample contingency table displaying the observed counts is represented in Table 10.2.

Table 10.2 Sample contingency table for two groups and two responses (2 × 2)

Event or characteristic?	Group		
	1	2	Total
Yes	m_1	m_2	R
No	$n_1 - m_1$	$n_2 - m_2$	S
	n_1	n_2	N

The null hypothesis for the χ^2 test of homogeneity for two groups is stated as:

H_0: The distribution of the response of interest is homogeneous with respect to the two treatment groups. Equivalently, the proportion of "yes" responses is equal across the two groups.

The alternate hypothesis is:

H_A: The distribution of the response of interest is not homogeneous with respect to the two treatment groups.

If the null hypothesis is true – that is, the proportion of participants with the event of interest is similar across the two groups – the expected count of responses in groups 1 and 2 would be in the same proportion as observed across all groups. That is, the expected cell count in row 1 (participants with events of interest) for group 1 is:

$$E_{1,1} = \hat{p}n_1.$$

Likewise, the expected cell count in row 1 (participants with events of interest) for group 2 is:

$$E_{1,2} = \hat{p}n_2.$$

Similarly, the expected cell count in row 2 (participants without the event of interest) for group 1 is:

$$E_{2,1} = \hat{q}n_1.$$

Lastly, the expected cell count in row 2 (participants without the event of interest) for group 2 is:

$$E_{2,2} = \hat{q} n_2.$$

The corresponding observed counts in Table 10.2 are:

$$O_{1,1} = m_1,$$
$$O_{1,2} = m_2,$$
$$O_{2,1} = n_1 - m_1,$$

and

$$O_{2,2} = n_2 - m_2.$$

The test statistic χ^2 is calculated as the sum of squared differences between the observed and expected counts divided by the expected count for all four cells (two groups and two responses) of the contingency table:

$$X^2 = \sum_{i=1}^{2} \sum_{r=1}^{2} \frac{(O_{r,i} - E_{r,i})^2}{E_{r,i}}.$$

Under the null hypothesis of homogeneity, the test statistic, X^2, for two groups and two responses (for example, interest is in the proportion) is approximately distributed as a χ^2 with 1 degree of freedom (df). Only large values of the test statistic are indicative of a departure from the null hypothesis. Therefore, the χ^2 test is implicitly a one-sided test. Values of the test statistic that lie in the critical region are those with $X^2 > \chi_1^2$.

The notation in this section tends to be more complex than we have encountered in previous chapters. A worked example using the data from Section 10.5.1 may clarify the description. In a randomized, double-blind, 12-week study, the test treatment was compared with placebo. The primary endpoint of the study was the proportion of participants who attained an SBP goal < 140 mmHg. Of 146 participants assigned to placebo, 34 attained an SBP < 140 mmHg at week 12. Of 154 assigned to test treatment, 82 attained the goal.

The research question

Are participants who take the test treatment more likely than placebo participants to attain their SBP goal?

Study design

The study is a randomized, double-blind, placebo-controlled, 12-week study of an investigational antihypertensive drug.

Data

The data from the study are represented as the contingency table displayed in Table 10.3.

Table 10.3   Contingency table for individuals attaining goal SBP

Attained SBP < 140?	Placebo	Test	Total
Yes	34	82	116
No	112	72	184
	146	154	300

Statistical analysis

The null and alternate statistical hypotheses can be stated as follows:

H_0: The proportion of individuals who attained SBP < 140 mmHg is homogeneous (equal) across the two treatment groups.

H_A: The proportion of individuals who attained SBP < 140 mmHg is not homogeneous across the two treatment groups.

In cases where there are only two categories, such as in this one, we need to know only how many individuals are in the "yes" row, because the number in the "no" row can be obtained by subtraction from the sample size within each group.

To calculate the test statistic, we first need to know the expected cell counts. These can be calculated as the product of the marginal row total and the marginal column total divided by the total sample size. The expected cell counts under the null hypothesis of homogeneity are provided in Table 10.4. The expected cell count for the placebo group in the first row ("Yes") was calculated as: $(146)(116)/300 = 56.453$. The expected cell count for the test treatment group in the second row ("No") was calculated as: $(154)(184)/300 = 94.453$. You are encouraged to verify the remaining two cell counts using the same methodology.

Table 10.4 Expected cell counts for χ^2 test of homogeneity

Attained SBP < 140?	Placebo	Test	Total
Yes	56.453	59.547	116
No	89.547	94.453	184
	146	154	300

Now that we have calculated the expected cell counts, we can calculate the test statistic using these expected cell counts in conjunction with the observed cell counts:

$$X^2 = \frac{(34-56.453)^2}{56.453} + \frac{(82-59.547)^2}{59.547} + \frac{(112-89.547)^2}{89.547} + \frac{(72-94.453)^2}{94.453}$$

$$= 28.3646$$

Tabled values to determine critical regions are not as concise as those for the standard normal distribution, because there is not just one χ^2 distribution but many of them. However, the χ^2 distribution with 1 df is quite frequently encountered as 2 × 2 contingency tables. Hence, for reference, values of the χ^2 distribution for 1 df that cut off various areas in the right-hand tail are provided in Table 10.5. Additional values of $\chi^2_{1-\alpha}$ are provided in Appendix 3.

Table 10.5 Critical values for the χ^2 distribution with 1 degree of freedom

α (one sided)	$\chi^2_{(1-\alpha),1}$
0.10	2.706
0.05	3.841
0.01	6.635
0.001	10.38

For a test of size 0.05 the value of the test statistic, 28.3646, is much greater than the critical value of 3.841.

Interpretation and decision-making

Just as the hypothesis test using the Z approximation resulted in a rejection of the null hypothesis, so does this χ^2 test. We can also tell from the critical values in Table 10.5 that the p value must be < 0.001 because less than 0.001 of the area under the 1 df χ^2 distribution lies to the right of the value 10.38 and the calculated test statistic, 28.3646 lies to the right of that value.

10.5.2.1 Odds ratio as a measure of association from 2 × 2 contingency tables

Many articles published in medical journals cite a measure of association called an odds ratio, which is an estimate of the relative risk of the event or outcome of interest, a concept that was introduced in Chapter 8. If the probability of an outcome of interest for group 1 is estimated as $\hat{p}_1$ the odds of the event are:

$$\text{Odds of the event for group 1} = \frac{\hat{p}_1}{1-\hat{p}_1}.$$

Similarly:

$$\text{Odds of the event for group 2} = \frac{\hat{p}_2}{1-\hat{p}_2}.$$

Then the estimated odds ratio is calculated as:

$$\text{Odds ratio} = \frac{\hat{p}_1(1-\hat{p}_2)}{\hat{p}_2(1-\hat{p}_1)}.$$

Note that an equivalent definition of the odds ratio using the observed counts from the 2 × 2 contingency table in Section 10.5.2 is:

$$\text{Odds ratio} = \frac{O_{1,1}O_{2,2}}{O_{1,2}O_{2,1}}.$$

A standard error may be calculated for purposes of constructing a confidence interval for the odds ratio, but it requires an iterative solution. Statistical software is useful for this purpose. Interested readers will find a wealth of information on the odds ratio in Fleiss et al. (2003).

If the estimated probabilities of the event are the same (or similar) between the two groups, the odds ratio will have a value around 1 (unity). Thus an assumption of no association in a 2 × 2 table implies that the odds ratio is equal to 1.

This also means that the χ^2 test for binary outcomes from Section 10.5.2 can be considered a test of the null hypothesis that the population odds ratio = 1. Values of the odds ratio appropriately < 1 or appropriately > 1 are suggestive of an association between the group and the outcome.

Using the data from Table 10.3 as presented and using the formula for observed cell counts, the estimated odds ratio is calculated as:

$$\text{Odds ratio} = \frac{(34)(72)}{(112)(82)} = 0.27.$$

Interpreting this value as an estimate of the relative risk of attaining the target SBP level, we would say that patients treated with placebo are 0.27 times as likely as patients treated with the active drug to attain the SBP goal. This statement may seem awkward (we would not disagree), which points out a potentially difficult aspect of the odds ratio. As the name implies it is a ratio scaled quantity so the odds ratio can be expressed as *a/b* or *b/a*. Keeping in mind that the odds ratio is an estimate of the relative risk, selecting the more appropriate method will aid the clinical interpretation of the result. In this case the response of interest is a favorable outcome, so a relative risk > 1 would imply that a favorable outcome was more likely after treatment with the active drug than the placebo. Similarly, if the response of interest is a bad outcome (for example, serious adverse event) a relative risk < 1 would suggest that the probability of a bad outcome was less for the active drug than the placebo.

Hence we can make more sense of this calculated value by taking its inverse as $1/0.27 = 3.75$. This expression is more appealing and an accurate interpretation in that patients treated with the test drug are 3.75 times more likely to attain the SBP goal than those treated with placebo. One can also obtain this result by switching the order of the columns in Table 10.3 and performing the calculation as:

$$\text{Odds ratio} = \frac{(82)(112)}{(72)(34)} = 3.75.$$

Odds ratios are one of the most common statistics cited from logistic regression analyses.

Logistic regression is an advanced topic and therefore not included in this book. An overly simple description is that it is an analysis method by which binary outcomes are modeled (or explained) using various predictor variables. The proper interpretation of odds ratios from logistic regression models will depend on the way in which the predictors were used in the statistical model. However, the general concept is the same as in this example. The odds ratio represents the relative increase in risk of a particular event for one group versus another. We recommend two excellent texts on logistic regression by Hosmer and Lemeshow (2000) and Kleinbaum and Klein (2002).

10.5.2.2 Use of the χ^2 test for two proportions

The χ^2 test of homogeneity is useful for comparing two proportions under the following circumstances:

- The groups need to be independent.
- The responses need to be mutually exclusive.
- The expected cell counts are reasonably sized.

With regard to the last of these requirements, we need to operationally define "reasonably sized." A commonly accepted guideline is that the χ^2 test is appropriate when at least 80% of the cells have expected counts of at least five. In the case of the worked example, the use of the χ^2 test is appropriate on the basis of independence (no participant was treated with both placebo and test treatment) and sample size. If a participant can be counted in only one response category the responses are considered mutually exclusive or non-overlapping, as was the case here.

The χ^2 test of homogeneity is a special case because it can be used for any number of groups. The more general case is discussed in the following section.

10.5.3 Hypothesis test for *g* proportions: χ^2 test of homogeneity

If there are *g* independent groups of interest (for example, treatment groups in a clinical trial) each representing relevant populations, the proportion of individuals with the characteristic or event of interest is represented by:

$$\hat{p}_i = \frac{m_i}{n_i}$$

for $i = 1, 2, \ldots g$, where g represents the number of groups. The counts of individuals with events and nonevents can be displayed in a contingency table with g columns and two rows representing the numbers of observations with (m_i) and without ($n_i - m_i$) the characteristic of interest. The marginal total of individuals with events (the sum across the g groups) is denoted by:

$$R = \sum_{i=1}^{g} m_i .$$

The marginal total of individuals without the events (sum across the g groups) is denoted by:

$$S = \sum_{i=1}^{g} n_i - m_i .$$

Finally, the total sample size (sum across the g groups) is denoted by:

$$N - \sum_{i=1}^{g} n_i .$$

The overall proportion of responses across all groups is:

$$\hat{p} = \frac{R}{N}.$$

A sample contingency table displaying the observed counts in this more general case is represented in Table 10.6.

As before with the case of two groups, the null hypothesis is stated as:

> H_0: The distribution of the response of interest is homogeneous with respect to the g treatment groups. Equivalently, the proportion of "yes" responses is equal across all g groups.

The alternate hypothesis is:

> H_A: The distribution of the response of interest is not homogeneous with respect to the g treatment groups.

If the null hypothesis is true, that is, the proportion of individuals with the event of interest is similar across the groups, the expected count of responses in group i will be in the same proportion as observed across all groups. That is, the expected cell count in row 1 (individuals with events of interest) for group i is:

$$E_{1,i} = \hat{p} n_i .$$

Similarly, the expected cell count in row 2 (individuals without the event of interest) for group i is:

$$E_{2,i} = \hat{q} n_i.$$

The expected cell counts are calculated in this manner for all $2g$ cells of the contingency table. The corresponding observed counts for groups $i = 1, 2, \ldots, g$, in Table 10.6 are:

$$O_{1,i} = m_i$$

and

$$O_{2,i} = n_i - m_i.$$

The test statistic X^2 is calculated as the sum of squared differences between the observed and expected counts divided by the expected count

Table 10.6 Sample contingency table for g groups and two responses ($g \times 2$)

Event or characteristic?	Group				Total
	1	2	. . .	g	
Yes	m_1	m_2	. . .	m_g	R
No	$n_1 - m_1$	$n_2 - m_2$	. . .	$n_g - m_g$	S
	n_1	n_2	. . .	n_g	N

for all $2g$ cells (g groups and 2 responses) of the contingency table:

$$X^2 = \sum_{i=1}^{g} \sum_{r=1}^{2} \frac{(O_{i,g} - E_{i,g})^2}{E_{i,g}}.$$

Under the null hypothesis of homogeneity, the test statistic, X^2, for g groups and two responses is approximately distributed as a χ^2 with $(g-1)$ df. Values of the test statistic that lie in the critical region are those with $X^2 > \chi^2_{g-1}$.

10.5.4 Hypothesis test for r responses from g groups

The χ^2 test can be applied to more general situations, including data with r response levels and g independent groups. When there are more than two response categories, however, the null and alternate hypotheses cannot be stated simply in terms of one proportion, but need to be stated in terms of the distribution of response categories.

One example containing more than two groups would be an evaluation of the following three categories of response: Worsening, no change, and improvement. It would not be sufficient to state the null hypothesis in terms of the proportion of individuals with a response of worsening because there are two other responses of interest. We highlight this point because the χ^2 test is used extensively in clinical research, and it can be correctly applied to multilevel responses and multiple groups. If we use the more general terminology, "distribution of responses is homogeneous with respect to treatment group," we are always correct no matter how many responses there were or how many groups.

The specific methodology associated with these more general cases is beyond the scope of our text. The most appropriate and efficient analyses of data of this type can depend on the hypothesis of interest and whether or not the response categories are ordered. Additional details can be found in two excellent texts by Stokes et al. (2001) and Agresti (2007).

10.5.5 Hypothesis test for two proportions: Fisher's exact test

The two methods described earlier, the Z approximation and the χ^2 test of homogeneity, are appropriate when the sample sizes are large enough. There are times, however, when the sample sizes in each group are not large enough or the proportion of events is low such that $n\hat{p} < 5$. In such cases another analysis method, one that does not require any approximation, is appropriate.

An alternate hypothesis test for two proportions is attributed to Fisher. Fisher's exact test is applicable to contingency tables with two or more responses in two or more independent groups. We consider one case, 2×2 tables, represented by counts of individuals with and without the characteristic of interest (two rows) in each of two treatment groups (two columns), for which the cell counts are small. For this test the row and column marginal totals are considered fixed. That is, one assumes that the total number of individuals with events is fixed as well as the number in each group. The extent to which the two groups are similar or dissimilar accounts for the distribution of events between the two groups. For any 2×2 table, the probability of the particular distribution of response counts, assuming the fixed marginal totals, can be calculated exactly via something called the hypergeometric distribution (we do not go into details here). Using slightly different notation from the examples above, the cell counts and marginal totals of a general 2×2 table are displayed in Table 10.7. The total number of

Table 10.7 Cell counts and marginal totals from a general 2×2 table

Event or characteristic of interest?	Group 1	Group 2	Total
Yes	Y_1	Y_2	$Y.$
No	N_1	N_2	$N.$
	n_1	n_2	n

"yes" responses is denoted by the symbol, $Y_.$, where the dot in the index means that the count is obtained by summing the responses over the two columns, that is, $Y_1 + Y_2$. Likewise, the total number of "no" responses is denoted by the symbol, $N_.$, the sum over groups 1 and 2.

Given the fixed margins as indicated in Table 10.7, the probability of the distribution of responses in the 2×2 table is calculated from the hypergeometric distribution as:

$$P(Y_1, Y_2, N_1, N_2 \mid Y_., N_., n_1, n_2, n) = \frac{Y_.! N_.! n_1! n_2!}{n! Y_1! Y_2! N_1! N_2!}.$$

The null and alternate hypotheses in this case are as follows:

H_0: The proportion of responses is independent of the group.

H_A: The proportion of responses is not independent of the group.

If the null hypothesis is rejected, the alternate hypothesis is better supported by the data.

For this test there is no test statistic as such, because this test is considered an exact test. Therefore, we need not compare the value of a test statistic to a distribution. Instead, the p value is calculated directly and compared with the predefined α level. Recall that a p value is the probability, under the null hypothesis, of observing the obtained results or those more extreme, that is, results contradicting the null hypothesis. The calculation of the p value for this exact test entails the following three steps:

1. Calculate the probability of the observed cell counts using the expression above.
2. For all other permutations of 2×2 tables with the same marginal totals, calculate the probability of observed cell counts in a similar manner.
3. Calculate the p value as the sum of the observed probability (from the first step) and all probabilities for other permutations that are less than the probability for the observed table.

As a consequence, the p value represents the likelihood of observing, by chance alone, the actual result or those more extreme. The calculated p value is compared with the value of α and we either reject or fail to reject the null hypothesis.

As an example of Fisher's exact test, we consider other data from the antihypertensive trial introduced in Section 10.5.1. These data are presented in Table 10.8.

Table 10.8 Contingency table for individuals attaining SBP < 120 mmHg

Attained SBP < 120?	Placebo	Test	Total
Yes	1	3	4
No	145	151	296
	146	154	300

The research question

Is there sufficient evidence at the $\alpha = 0.05$ level to conclude that the probability of attaining a SBP < 120 mmHg (a remarkable response for a hypertensive person!) is greater for people receiving the test treatment than for those receiving the placebo?

Study design

The study is a randomized, double-blind, placebo-controlled, 12-week study of an investigational antihypertensive drug.

Data

The data from the study are represented as a contingency table as displayed in Table 10.8. As seen in Table 10.8, only four individuals had the event of interest. Neither the Z approximation nor the χ^2 test would be appropriate given the small cell sizes of one and three.

Statistical analysis

The null and alternate statistical hypotheses can be stated as:

H_0: The proportion of individuals who attained SBP < 120 mmHg is independent of treatment group.

H_A: The proportion of participants who attained SBP < 120 mmHg is not independent of treatment group.

In this instance, independence means that the probability of the response is no more or less likely for one group versus the other. In his original paper, Fisher stated the null hypothesis slightly differently (although equivalent mathematically). The null hypothesis, after Fisher, can be stated in this form: The population odds ratio of response to nonresponse for one group versus the other is equal to one.

In Figure 10.1 all of the possible permutations of cell counts, given the marginal totals, are displayed. To be concise, the row and column labels are not included. The calculated probability from the hypergeometric distribution is provided to the right of each arrangement of cell counts. The probabilities in Figure 10.1 are included to illustrate the calculation. Note that by definition, 0! = 1. For this particular dataset it is manageable to calculate each probability with a calculator, but in many instances this particular test should be done using statistical software. When calculating these probabilities by hand it is helpful to re-write the factorial expressions in a way so that numerator and denominator terms "cancel out." For example, writing 154! as 154*153*152*151! allows us to cancel 151! from the numerator and denominator of the probability associated with the observed result.

The calculated p value is the probability from the observed result plus all probabilities less than the probability associated with the observed result. For this example the exact p value is:

$$p \text{ value} = 0.263453 + 0.236537 + 0.068119 + 0.054910 = 0.623019.$$

Rounding to three significant digits, this can be expressed as p value = 0.623.

Interpretation and decision-making

Comparing the p value of 0.623 to $\alpha = 0.05$, the statistical conclusion is not to reject the null hypothesis. There is insufficient evidence to conclude that the alternate hypothesis is true. If the goal of a new antihypertensive therapy were to

0	4
146	150

$$P = \frac{4! \, 296! \, 146! \, 154!}{0! \, 4! \, 146! \, 150! \, 300!} = 0.068119$$

1	3
145	151

$$P = \frac{4! \, 296! \, 146! \, 154!}{1! \, 3! \, 145! \, 151! \, 300!} = 0.263453 \text{ (observed result)}$$

2	2
144	152

$$P = \frac{4! \, 296! \, 146! \, 154!}{2! \, 2! \, 144! \, 152! \, 300!} = 0.376981$$

3	1
143	153

$$P = \frac{4! \, 296! \, 146! \, 154!}{3! \, 1! \, 145! \, 151! \, 300!} = 0.236537$$

4	0
142	154

$$P = \frac{4! \, 296! \, 146! \, 154!}{4! \, 0! \, 142! \, 154! \, 300!} = 0.054910$$

Figure 10.1   All permutations of response counts given fixed marginal totals and probabilities of each

reduce SBP to levels < 120 mmHg, such a result would be disappointing and may lead to a decision to halt the clinical development program. However, the study was not designed to answer such a question. In fact, the research question, having been formulated as an exploratory analysis, may not be well suited for the study that was actually conducted. Perhaps a greater dose or more frequent administration of the investigational antihypertensive drug would increase the rate of the desired response. In any case, as the analysis earlier in the chapter illustrated, the new drug does seem to lower SBP to levels that would be considered clinically important (< 140 mmHg).

10.5.6 Test of two proportions from stratified samples: The Mantel–Haenszel method

Confirmatory efficacy studies typically involve a number of investigative centers and, accordingly, are known as multicenter trials. Multicenter trials have a number of benefits, which are discussed later. A common analysis method used in multicenter trials is to account for differences from center to center by including them in the analysis. Stratifying the randomization to treatment assignment by investigative center ensures that there are approximately equal numbers of participants assigned to test or placebo within each center. Analyses from studies with this design typically account for center as it is conceivably another source of variation. This is accomplished by calculating a summary test statistic within each center and then pooling or calculating weighted averages of the within-center statistics across all centers, thereby removing the effect of the centers from the overall test statistic.

The weights used in the analysis are chosen at the trial statistician's discretion, which provides a good example of the "art" of Statistics, because the statistician must make a well-informed judgment call. Some commonly employed choices of weights are as follows:

- equal weights for all centers
- weights proportional to the size of the center
- weights that are related to the standard error of the within-center statistic (for example,

more precise estimates have more weight than less precise estimates).

One method applicable to the difference of two proportions, originally described by Mantel and Haenszel (1959) and well described by Fleiss et al. (2003), utilizes weights that are proportional to the size of each stratum (in this case, centers) to calculate a test statistic that follows approximately a χ^2 distribution.

Assume that there are h strata of interest, and within each of the strata ($h = 1, 2, \ldots, H$) there are n_{h1} observations for group 1 (for example, treatment group 1) and n_{h2} observations for group 2 (for example, treatment group 2). The proportion of observations with the characteristic of interest within each stratum for the two groups is denoted by $\hat{p}_{h1}$ and $\hat{p}_{h2}$, respectively. The overall proportion of participants with the characteristic of interest within each stratum is denoted by $\bar{p}_h$; the overall proportion without the characteristic of interest with each stratum is denoted by $\bar{q}_h = 1 - \bar{p}_h$.

The null hypothesis tested by the Mantel–Haenszel method is as follows:

H$_0$: There is no overall association between response and group after accounting for the stratification factor.

If the null hypothesis is rejected, the data favor the following alternate hypothesis:

H$_A$: There is an overall association between response and group after accounting for the stratification factor.

The test statistic for the Mantel–Haenszel method is:

$$X^2_{MH} = \frac{\left(\left| \sum_{h=1}^{H} \frac{n_{h1} \, n_{h2}}{n_h} (\hat{p}_{h1} - \hat{p}_{h2}) \right| - 0.5 \right)^2}{\sum_{h=1}^{H} \frac{n_{h1} \, n_{h2}}{n_h - 1} \bar{p}_h \bar{q}_h}.$$

Note that the differences in proportions, $\hat{p}_{h1} - \hat{p}_{h2}$, are weighted by the quantities $\frac{n_{h1} n_{h2}}{n_h}$.

This test statistic utilizes a continuity correction factor of 0.5 as well. As described by Fleiss et al. (2003), the test performs well when expected cell counts within each of H 2 × 2 tables differ by at least 5 (maximum – minimum). The test statistic that is computed in this manner is approximately distributed as a χ^2 with 1 df.

A similar test statistic, Cochran's statistic, originally attributed to Cochran (1954), is described by Fleiss et al. (2003):

$$X^2_{CMH} = \frac{\left(\sum_{h=1}^{H} \frac{n_{h1} \, n_{h2}}{n_h} (\hat{p}_{h1} - \hat{p}_{h2}) \right)^2}{\sum_{h=1}^{H} \frac{n_{h1} \, n_{h2}}{n_h} \bar{p}_h \bar{q}_h}.$$

Note that Cochran's statistic does not use a correction factor and the denominator of the stratum weights is n_h instead of $(n_h - 1)$. We mention Cochran's statistic because it is used by some statistical software packages instead of the Mantel–Haenszel statistic. Fleiss points out that the difference between the Mantel–Haenszel statistic and Cochran's statistic is small when the sample sizes are large, but considerable when the sample sizes within each of the strata are small.

As an illustration of the Mantel–Haenszel method, we take the data from our example as detailed in Section 10.5.1 and separate them into data collected at each of three centers, which in this case represent the three strata.

The research question

Is there sufficient evidence at the $\alpha = 0.05$ level to conclude that the probability of attaining a goal SBP level is greater for individuals receiving test treatment than for those receiving the placebo after accounting for differences in response among centers?

Study design

The study is a randomized, double-blind, placebo-controlled, 12-week study of an investigational antihypertensive drug.

Data

The data from the study are represented as three contingency tables, one for each of the centers in Table 10.9.

Table 10.9   Contingency table for individuals attaining goal SBP by center

Center 1 Attained SBP < 140?	Placebo	Test	Total
Yes	12	24	36
No	34	21	55
	46	45	91
Center 2 Attained SBP < 140?	Placebo	Test	Total
Yes	15	31	46
No	29	19	48
	44	50	94
Center 3 Attained SBP < 140?	Placebo	Test	Total
Yes	7	27	34
No	49	32	81
	56	59	115
Overall Attained SBP < 140?	Placebo	Test	Total
Yes	34	82	116
No	112	72	184
	146	154	300

Statistical analysis

The null and alternate statistical hypotheses can be stated as:

H_0: There is no overall association between the response (attaining SBP < 140 mmHg) and treatment group after accounting for center.
H_A: There is an overall association between the response and treatment group after accounting for center.

For a test of size $\alpha = 0.05$, a χ^2 test with 1 df has a critical value of 3.841.

The differences in the proportions of interest (test minus placebo) are as follows:

- Center 1: $(0.533 - 0.261) = 0.272$
- Center 2: $(0.620 - 0.341) = 0.279$
- Center 3: $(0.458 - 0.125) = 0.333$.

The overall response rates for the event of interest and their complements are:

Center 1: $\bar{p}_1 = \dfrac{36}{91} = 0.396$ and $\bar{q}_1 = \dfrac{55}{91} = 0.604$

Center 2: $\bar{p}_2 = \dfrac{46}{94} = 0.489$ and $\bar{q}_2 = \dfrac{48}{94} = 0.511$

Center 3: $\bar{p}_3 = \dfrac{34}{115} = 0.296$ and $\bar{q}_3 = \dfrac{81}{115} = 0.704$.

The test statistic is then computed as:

$$X_{MH}^2 = \frac{\left| \left| \left[\left(\frac{46 * 45}{91} \right)(0.272) + \left(\frac{44 * 50}{94} \right)(0.279) + \left(\frac{56 * 59}{115} \right)(0.333) \right] \right| - 0.5 \right|^2}{\left(\frac{46 * 45}{90} \right)(0.396)(0.604) + \left(\frac{44 * 50}{93} \right)(0.489)(0.511) + \left(\frac{56 * 59}{114} \right)(0.296)(0.704)}$$

$$= 27.21$$

Although the calculation details are not shown here, the value of Cochran's statistic for this example is 28.47, which is consistent with the result obtained for the Mantel–Haenszel statistic.

Interpretation and decision-making

The value of the test statistic is much greater than the critical value of 3.841. Hence the statistical decision is to reject the null hypothesis of no association after accounting for center differences. The proportion of responders is significantly higher among those receiving the test treatment. The p value associated with the test can be obtained from statistical software. However, we know from the sample of critical values in Table 10.5 that the p value must be < 0.001. As before, a pharmaceutical company would be encouraged by such results.

10.6 Concluding comments on hypothesis tests for categorical data

All of the methods described in this chapter are applicable to data that are in the form of "binary"

events, that is, either the event or characteristic occurred for a given individual or it did not. For binary data, the summary statistic representing each treatment group is a sample proportion. To account for variation from sample to sample, hypothesis-testing methods allow a researcher to draw an inference about the underlying population difference in proportions. Although not covered in great detail, some of the methods can also be expanded to more than two categories.

In contrast, the methods described in Chapter 11 are applicable to data with outcomes that are continuous in nature. In those cases, other summary statistics are required to describe the typical effect in each group and the typical effect expected for the population under study.

10.7 Review

1. What constitutes "compelling evidence" of a beneficial treatment effect?

2. Consider a pharmaceutical company that has just completed a confirmatory efficacy study. What are the implications for the company of committing a type I error? What are the implications for the company of committing a type II error?

3. The equality of two proportions is being tested with the null hypothesis, H_0: $P_{TEST} - P_{PLACEBO} = 0$. Given that this is a two-sided test and using the following information, would the null hypothesis be rejected or not rejected?

   (a) $\alpha = 0.05$, Z approximation test statistic $= 1.74$
   (b) $\alpha = 0.10$, Z approximation test statistic $= 1.74$
   (c) $\alpha = 0.05$, Z approximation test statistic $= 4.23$
   (d) $\alpha = 0.01$, Z approximation test statistic $= 4.23$
   (e) $\alpha = 0.05$, χ^2 test statistic $= 1.74$
   (f) $\alpha = 0.10$, χ^2 test statistic $= 1.74$
   (g) $\alpha = 0.05$, χ^2 test statistic $= 4.23$
   (h) $\alpha = 0.01$, χ^2 test statistic $= 4.23$.

4. The equality of two proportions is being tested with the null hypothesis, H_0: $P_{TEST} - P_{PLACEBO} = 0$. Given that this is a two-sided test, what is the p value that corresponds to the following values of the Z approximation test statistic?

   (a) -1.56
   (b) -2.67

(c) 3.29

(d) 1.00.

5. The term "responders' analysis" was first introduced in Chapter 9 with regard to clinical laboratory data. A responders' analysis approach can be used in the context of efficacy data, as well. Consider a double-blind, placebo-controlled, therapeutic confirmatory trial of an investigational antihypertensive ("test drug"). Based on earlier experience, a period of 12 weeks is considered sufficient to observe a clinically meaningful treatment effect that can be sustained for many months. In this study, a participant whose SBP is reduced by at least 10 mmHg after 12 weeks of treatment is considered a responder. Similarly, a participant whose SBP is not reduced by at least 10 mmHg after 12 weeks is considered a non-responder. A total of 1000 participants were studied: 502 on placebo and 498 on test drug. Among the placebo participants, 117 were responders. Among those on the test drug, 152 were responders.

(a) Summarize these results in a 2 × 2 contingency table.

(b) The sponsor's research question of interest is: Are individuals treated with the test drug more likely to respond than those treated with placebo? What are the null and alternate statistical hypotheses corresponding to this research question?

(c) What statistical tests may be used to test the null hypothesis? Are any more appropriate than others?

(d) Is there sufficient evidence to reject the null hypothesis using a test of size $\alpha = 0.05$? Describe any assumptions necessary and show the calculation of the test statistic.

(e) Calculate the odds ratio from the contingency table. What is the interpretation of the calculated odds ratio?

6. When would the Mantel–Haenszel χ^2 test be more useful than the χ^2 test?

10.8 References

Agresti A (2007). *An Introduction to Categorical Data Analysis*, 2nd edn. Chichester: John Wiley & Sons.

Cochran WG (1954). Some methods of strengthening the common χ^2 tests. *Biometrics* **10**:417–451.

Fisher LD (1999). One large, well-designed, multicenter study as an alternative to the usual FDA paradigm. *Drug Information J* **33**:265–271.

Fleiss JL, Paik MC, Levin B (2003). *Statistical Methods for Rates and Proportions*, 3rd edn. Chichester: John Wiley & Sons.

Fleming TR, DeMets DL (1996). Surrogate end points in clinical trials: are we being misled? *Ann Intern Med* **125**:605–613.

Hosmer DW, Lemeshow S (2000). *Applied Logistic Regression*, 2nd edn. Chichester: John Wiley & Sons.

ICH Guidance E8 (1997). *General Consideration of Clinical Trials*. Available at: www.ich.org (accessed July 1 2007).

ICH Guidance E9 (1998). *Statistical Principles for Clinical Trials*. Available at: www.ich.org (accessed July 1 2007).

Kleinbaum DG, Klein M (2002). *Logistic Regression: A self-learning text*, 2nd edn. New York: Springer.

Mantel N, Haenszel W (1959). Statistical aspects of the analysis of data from retrospective studies of disease. *J Natl Cancer Instit* **22**:719–748.

Stokes ME, Davis CS, Koch GG (2001). *Categorical Data Analysis using the SAS System*, 2nd edn. Chichester: Wiley & Sons.

US Department of Health and Human Services, Food and Drug Administration (1998). *Providing Clinical Evidence of Effectiveness for Human Drug and Biological Products*. Available from www.fda.gov (accessed July 1 2007).

11

Confirmatory clinical trials: Analysis of continuous efficacy data

11.1 Introduction

As we have seen, several summary measures of central tendency can be used for continuous outcomes. The most common of these measures is the mean. In clinical trials we calculate sample statistics, and these serve to estimate the unknown population means. When developing a new drug, the estimated treatment effect is measured by the difference in sample means for the test treatment and the placebo. If we can infer (conclude) that the corresponding population means differ by an amount that is considered clinically important (that is, in the positive direction and of a certain magnitude) the test treatment will be considered efficacious.

In Chapter 10 we saw that there are various methods for the analysis of categorical (and mostly binary) efficacy data. The same is true here. There are different methods that are appropriate for continuous data in certain circumstances, and not every method that we discuss is appropriate for every situation. A careful assessment of the data type, the shape of the distribution (which can be examined through a relative frequency histogram or a stem-and-leaf plot), and the sample size can help justify the most appropriate analysis approach. For example, if the shape of the distribution of the random variable is symmetric or the sample size is large (> 30) the sample mean would be considered a "reasonable" estimate of the population mean. Parametric analysis approaches such as the two-sample t test or an analysis of variance (ANOVA) would then be appropriate. However, when the distribution is severely asymmetric, or skewed, the sample mean is a poor estimate of the population mean. In such cases a nonparametric approach would be more appropriate.

It should be emphasized at this point that the term "nonparametric" is not a quality judgment compared with the term "parametric." The nomenclature simply serves to delineate two types of analyses. Nonparametric tests are not "less good" than parametric tests. Indeed, if it were appropriate to use a nonparametric approach in a certain circumstance, that test would have higher statistical power than a parametric approach. We respectfully feel that the differentiation between parametric and nonparametric approaches in many introductory Statistics textbooks is misleading, and does tend to imply that nonparametric tests are naturally inferior to the other: Nonparametric tests are commonly discussed separately, often toward the end of the book, leaving the reader feeling that the books' authors regarded these discussions as unwanted but obligatory. We encourage you as your first step to consider what valid and appropriate analyses there are for a given situation, and then to select the most efficient analysis method from among them. We have reinforced this notion by including nonparametric analysis approaches side by side with parametric approaches.

11.2 Hypothesis test of two means: Two-sample t test or independent groups t test

A common measure of central tendency of continuous outcomes is the mean. In clinical studies employing measurement of continuous variables such as blood pressure, the typical response among participants in a treatment group is represented by this summary descriptive statistic. As we have seen, sample statistics, by definition, vary from sample to sample. When developing new drugs we would like to make an inference about the magnitude of the difference between two population means, typically represented by the symbol μ, one for a test treatment and the other for a control. If the difference in means exceeds the typical variability that would be expected from sample to sample, we can conclude that the difference is unlikely to be due to chance. More specifically, when comparing two population means, we are interested in testing the null hypothesis,

$$H_0: \mu_1 - \mu_2 = 0.$$

If the null hypothesis is rejected the following alternate hypothesis is better supported by the data:

$$H_A: \mu_1 - \mu_2 \neq 0.$$

Treatment group 1 is represented by n_1 observations, $x_{11}, x_{12}, x_{13}, \ldots, x_{1n_1}$. Similarly, treatment group 2 has n_2 observations, $x_{21}, x_{22}, x_{23}, \ldots, x_{2n_2}$. For this statistical test these two groups must be independent. The population means, μ_1 and μ_2, are estimated by the sample means from each group, $\bar{x}_1$ and $\bar{x}_2$:

$$\bar{x}_1 = \frac{\sum_{i=1}^{n_1} x_{1i}}{n_1},$$

$$\bar{x}_2 = \frac{\sum_{i=1}^{n_2} x_{2i}}{n_2}.$$

The population variances, σ_1^2 and σ_2^2, are estimated by the sample variances:

$$s_1^2 = \frac{\sum_{i=1}^{n_1} (x_{1i} - \bar{x}_1)^2}{n_1 - 1},$$

$$s_2^2 = \frac{\sum_{i=1}^{n_2} (x_{2i} - \bar{x}_2)^2}{n_2 - 1}.$$

Assuming that the two populations have the same, albeit unknown, population variance, an average or pooled estimate of the sample variances is an estimator of the unknown population variance. The pooled variance, s_p^2, is obtained as:

$$s_p^2 = \frac{s_1^2(n_1 - 1) + s_2^2(n_2 - 1)}{n_1 + n_2 - 2}.$$

Finally, the pooled standard deviation, s_p, is the square root of the variance:

$$s_p = \sqrt{s_p^2}.$$

The estimator for the difference in population means is the difference in sample means, that is, $\bar{x}_1 - \bar{x}_2$. The standard error of the estimator, $\text{SE}(\bar{x}_1 - \bar{x}_2)$, is calculated as:

$$\text{SE}(\bar{x}_1 - \bar{x}_2) = s_p \sqrt{\frac{1}{n_1} + \frac{1}{n_2}}.$$

The test statistic for the two-sample t test is:

$$t = \frac{\bar{x}_1 - \bar{x}_2}{\text{SE}(\bar{x}_1 - \bar{x}_2)}.$$

Under the null hypothesis of equal population means, the test statistic follows a t distribution with $n_1 + n_2 - 2$ degrees of freedom (df), assuming that the sample size in each group is large (that is, > 30) or the underlying distribution is at least mound shaped and somewhat symmetric. As the sample size in each group approaches 200, the shape of the t distribution becomes more like a standard normal distribution. Values of the test statistic that are far away from zero would contradict the null hypothesis and lead to its rejection. In particular, for a two-sided test of size α, the critical region (that is, those values of the test statistic that would lead to rejection of the null hypothesis) is defined by $t < t_{\alpha/2, n1+n2-2}$ or $t > t_{1-\alpha/2, n1+n2-2}$. Note that as t distributions are symmetric, $|t_{\alpha/2}| = t_{1-\alpha/2}$. If the calculated value of the test statistic is in the critical region, the null hypothesis is rejected in favor of the alternate hypothesis. If the calculated value of the test statistic is outside the critical region, the null hypothesis is not rejected.

As there are an infinite number of t distributions there is no concise way to display all possible values that may be encountered. However, as can be seen in Table 11.1, the value of the t distribution that cuts off the upper 2.5%

area of the distribution becomes smaller with increasing sample sizes (and therefore increasing df). Tabled values in Appendix 2 are provided for other values of α.

Table 11.1 Sample values from t distributions for a two-sided test of $\alpha = 0.05$

Degrees of freedom $(n_1 + n_2 - 2)$	$t_{0.975}$
10	2.2281
30	2.0423
50	2.0086
100	1.9840
200	1.9719

The use of the two-sample t test is illustrated here with sample data from a clinical trial of an investigational antihypertensive drug.

The research question

Does the test treatment lower SBP more than placebo?

Study design

In a randomized, double-blind, 12-week study, the test treatment, one tablet taken once a day, was compared with placebo (taken in the same manner). The primary endpoint of the study was the mean change from baseline SBP. The primary analysis will be based on a two-sample t test with $\alpha = 0.05$ (two-sided).

Data

In the placebo group (146 individuals) the mean change from baseline was -3.4 mmHg with a standard deviation of 17.4 mmHg. In the test treatment group (154 individuals) the mean change from baseline was -19.2 mmHg with a standard deviation of 16.9 mmHg.

Statistical analysis

The null and alternate statistical hypotheses can be stated as:

$$H_0: \mu_{TEST} - \mu_{PLACEBO} = 0.$$
$$H_A: \mu_{TEST} - \mu_{PLACEBO} \neq 0.$$

The pooled sample variance is calculated as:

$$s_p^2 = \frac{17.4^2(145) + 16.9^2(153)}{146 + 154 - 2} = 293.95.$$

It follows from this that the pooled standard deviation is:

$$s_p = \sqrt{293.95} = 17.1.$$

The estimate of the difference in mean change from baseline is:

$$\bar{x}_{TEST} - \bar{x}_{PLACEBO} = -19.2 - (-3.4) = -15.8.$$

The standard error of the difference is calculated as:

$$SE(\bar{x}_{TEST} - \bar{x}_{PLACEBO}) = 17.1\sqrt{\frac{1}{146} + \frac{1}{154}} = 1.98.$$

The test statistic is then calculated using these values:

$$t = \frac{-15.8}{1.98} = -7.98$$

Under the null hypothesis of no difference in population means, and assuming somewhat symmetric distributions, the test statistic follows a t distribution with 298 (that is, $146 + 154 - 2$) df. Therefore the critical region (values of the test statistic that lead to rejection) is defined as $t < -1.968$ and $t > 1.968$. Note that this particular entry is not in Appendix 2, but the closest is for 300 df.

Interpretation and decision-making

As $-7.98 < -1.968$, the null hypothesis is rejected in favor of the alternate one. The mean change from baseline for the test treatment group is significantly different from the placebo group's at the $\alpha = 0.05$ level. To determine the p value associated with this test, we need statistical software or an extensive look-up table. Given the large sample size in this example, we can use the percentiles of the standard normal distribution to approximate the p value. These study results allow us to conclude that the test treatment is efficacious. The difference between treatments in the magnitude of the change in SBP was unlikely to be the result of chance. Therefore the sponsor can submit these data as substantial statistical evidence of the test treatment's efficacy.

11.3 Hypothesis test of the location of two distributions: Wilcoxon rank sum test

The two-sample t test is useful on many occasions, but there are occasions when its use is not justified. One reason is that the sample size is small (< 30 per group). Although small studies are certainly encountered frequently in clinical research, most confirmatory efficacy studies are sizable, and so this reason is not applicable here. A second reason is, however, applicable. The most common reason why a two-sample t test would not be appropriate is a heavily skewed distribution, whether or not the sample size is large.

The sample mean is a poor measure of central tendency when the distribution is heavily skewed. Despite our best efforts at designing well-controlled clinical trials, the data that are generated do not always compare with the (deliberately chosen) tidy examples featured in this book. When we wish to make an inference about the difference in typical values among two or more independent populations, but the distributions of the random variables or outcomes are not reasonably symmetric, nonparametric methods are more appropriate. Unlike parametric methods such as the two-sample t test, nonparametric methods do not require any assumption about the shape of a distribution for them to be used in a valid manner. As the next analysis method illustrates, nonparametric methods do not rely directly on the value of the random variable. Rather, they make use of the rank order of the value of the random variable.

It is appropriate to note here that performing an analysis on an assigned rank instead of on the raw data results in a loss of information. Think of the related example of receiving a grade A on an assignment. If a grade A is given for any mark between 90% and 100%, the grade alone does not tell you how well you have actually done on the assignment: A score of 91% is assigned the same grade as a score of 100%. If the mark for this assignment is the first one of several in a course that will ultimately be combined to yield your final grade in some manner, you may very legitimately be interested in your actual (raw) score. Nevertheless, in clinical trials there can be a sound rationale for not using raw data in certain circumstances.

When rather extreme departures from required assumptions are noted, our choice of an appropriate statistical method should be one of first **validity** and second **efficiency**. The difference between an extreme departure from required assumptions and any departure from required assumptions is again a matter of judgment. It should be noted that many of the parametric methods in this book are robust to departures from distributional assumptions, meaning that the results are valid under a number of conditions. This is especially true with the larger sample sizes encountered in therapeutic exploratory and confirmatory trials. We should also note that all the methods described in this book require that observations in the analysis are independent. There are statistical methods to be used for dependent data, but they are not described in this book.

In our opinion, therefore, nonparametric methods should be chosen when assumptions (such as normality for the t test) are clearly not met and the sample sizes are so small that there is very little confidence about the properties of the underlying distribution. The nonparametric method discussed in this section is a test of a shift in the distribution between two populations with a common variance represented by two samples, and it will always be valid when comparing two independent groups.

The two-sample t test was based on the assumption that the two samples were drawn from an underlying normal population with the same (assumed) population variance. A rejection of the null hypothesis in the setting of the two-sample t test would imply that the two populations from which the samples were drawn were represented by two normal distributions with the same variance (shape), but with different means. The Wilcoxon rank sum test does not require the assumption of the normal distribution, but does require that the samples be drawn from the same population. The Wilcoxon rank sum test tests a similar hypothesis such that, if it is rejected, the two populations from which the samples were drawn had the same shape (not necessarily normal or otherwise symmetric), but differed by some distance. That is, a rejection of the null hypothesis in the setting of Wilcoxon's rank sum test would imply that the two population distributions were shifted, that is, not overlapping.

Although this approach has its advantages, one disadvantage is that no single numerical estimate, either a point estimate or an interval estimate, can convey the extent to which the populations differ because the test of the location shift is based on relative rank and not the original scale.

Using the Wilcoxon rank sum test, interest is in a location shift between two population distributions so the following null hypothesis is tested:

H_0: The location of the distribution of the random variable in population 1 does not differ from the location of the random variable for population 2.

If the null hypothesis is rejected the following alternate hypothesis is better supported by the data:

H_A: The location of the distribution of the random variable in population 1 is different from the location for population 2.

Treatment group 1 (representing population 1) is represented by n_1 observations measured on a continuous scale, $x_{11}, x_{12}, x_{13}, \ldots, x_{1n_1}$. Similarly, treatment group 2 (representing population 2) has n_2 observations measured in a continuous scale, $x_{21}, x_{22}, x_{23}, \ldots, x_{2n_2}$. The total sample size of the two groups is $n_1 + n_2$. The first step in calculating the test statistic is to order the values of all observations from smallest to largest, without regard to the treatment group. Then, a rank is assigned to each observation, starting with 1 for the smallest value after sorting, then 2, and so on for all $n_1 + n_2$ observations. If two or more observations are tied, the assigned rank will be the average of the ranks that would have been assigned if there were no ties. For example,

if the third, fourth, and fifth sorted observations were all tied, the assigned rank for each of the three observations would be $[3 + 4 + 5]/3 = 4$. The next largest value would then be assigned a rank of 6.

At this stage, we now have n_1 ranks for treatment group 1, $r_{11}, r_{12}, r_{13}, \ldots, r_{1n_1}$. Similarly, treatment group 2 has n_2 ranks, $r_{21}, r_{22}, r_{23}, \ldots, r_{2n_2}$. The test statistic for the Wilcoxon rank sum test is the sum of the ranks in group 1:

$$S_1 = \sum_{i=1}^{n_1} r_{1i}.$$

Only the ranks from group 1 are required because, if the values from group 1 tend to be smaller than those from group 2, the sum of ranks will be small, leading to rejection of the null hypothesis. Similarly, if the values from group 1 tend to be larger than those from group 2 the sum or ranks will be a large number and will also lead to rejection.

The null hypothesis will be rejected if the test statistic is less than or equal to or greater than or equal to cut points obtained from a table (which need not be provided here) – that is, the null hypothesis will be rejected if $S_1 \le W_L$ or $S_1 \ge W_U$. Other authors (Schork and Remington, 2000) have suggested a large sample approximation, which is possible because the test statistic, S_1, is approximately normally distributed with mean $[n_1(n_1 + n_2 + 1)]/2$ and variance $[n_1 n_2(n_1 + n_2 + 1)]/12$. The derivation of these two parameters is beyond the scope of this text. Applying a familiar mathematical operation (standardization of a normally distributed random variable), we obtain an alternate test statistic, which has an approximate standard normal distribution:

$$Z = \frac{S_1 - \dfrac{n_1(n_1 + n_2 + 1)}{2}}{\sqrt{\dfrac{n_1 n_2(n_1 + n_2 + 1)}{12}}}.$$

Values of this test statistic can then be compared with the more familiar critical values of the standard normal distribution.

To illustrate this method, consider the following example that (deliberately) has a small dataset.

The research question

Does the test treatment lower SBP more than placebo?

Study design

In a randomized, double-blind, 6-week study, the test treatment (one tablet taken once a day) was compared with placebo. The primary endpoint of the study was the mean change from baseline SBP. Given the small sample size of the study, the primary analysis is based on the Wilcoxon rank sum test with $\alpha = 0.05$ (two-sided).

Data

Each value listed below represents change from baseline SBP for a participant in a clinical trial comparing a new antihypertensive treatment with placebo. Lower values indicate a greater reduction in blood pressure from baseline, the favored outcome.

Test treatment ($n = 10$):
$-8, -1, 0, 2, -20, -18, -12, -17, -14, -11.$
Placebo ($n = 10$):
$-9, 0, -4, -4, -3, 1, -7, 1, 2, -3.$

Statistical analysis

After ordering all observations from highest to lowest within the two groups, we have the following:

Test	-20	-18	-17	-14	-12	-11	-8	-1	0	2
Placebo	-9	-7	-4	-4	-3	-3	0	1	1	2

Then ranking each observation across groups, accounting for ties as described above, we obtain the following ranks:

Test	1	2	3	4	5	6	8	14	15.5	19.5
Placebo	7	9	10.5	10.5	12.5	12.5	15.5	17.5	17.5	19.5

The test statistic is computed as the sum of the ranks for the test treatment group:

$$S_1 = 1+2+3+4+5+6+8+14+15.5+19.5 = 78.$$

When testing the null hypothesis at the two-sided $\alpha = 0.05$ level and a sample size of 10 in each group, the critical region is any value of $S_1 \le 78$ or ≥ 132.

Interpretation and decision-making

As the value of the test statistic is in the rejection region (only just, but still in it), the null hypothesis is rejected. The conclusion is that the distributions of the two populations from which the samples were selected differ in their location. The test treatment is associated with a greater reduction in SBP than placebo.

Alternately, if we were to use the test statistic based on a normal approximation, it would be:

$$Z = \frac{78 - \dfrac{10(10 + 10 + 1)}{2}}{\sqrt{\dfrac{10 * 10(10 + 10 + 1)}{12}}} = -2.007.$$

Under the null hypothesis, this test statistic follows a standard normal distribution. The null hypothesis is rejected because the test statistic falls in the rejection region for a two-sided test of $\alpha = 0.05$ based on the standard normal distribution ($Z < -1.96$ or $Z > 1.96$).

11.4 Hypothesis tests of more than two means: Analysis of variance

The t tests are extremely helpful, commonly used tests, but they do have one noteworthy limitation: They can address only the equality of two means. In the present context, they can compare only the results from two treatment groups. Situations that require us to test the equality of more than two means occur quite frequently, and so a test that can be used with two or more groups is needed.

In many instances in drug development, two or more doses may seem to be promising based on results from earlier phases of clinical development. The question of interest therefore becomes: Of all the doses studied, which has the greatest beneficial effect? Confirmatory efficacy studies aim to answer this question. As in other study designs that we have discussed, the sponsor would like to minimize the chance of committing a type I or II error. We therefore need an appropriate statistical method that can identify the best dose (among a number of them), while accounting for the inherent variability in the data and limiting the chances of committing an error in the final decision-making process. Analysis of variance (ANOVA) is well suited to this task.

Assume that there are k independent groups ($k > 2$), each of which represents populations of interest, for example, individuals given a particular treatment. An important objective of many clinical trials is to determine if there is any difference among the treatments administered with regard to the underlying population means. The null hypothesis for such an objective is:

$$H_0: \mu_1 = \mu_2 = \ldots = \mu_k.$$

If there is sufficient evidence to conclude that the null hypothesis should be rejected, the alternate hypothesis that would be favored is that there was at least one difference among all $[k(k - 1)]/2$ pairs of population means:

$$H_A: \mu_1 \neq \mu_2 \text{ or } \ldots \mu_1 \neq \mu_k \text{ or } \ldots \mu_{k-1} \neq \mu_k.$$

Each treatment group j ($j = 1, 2, \ldots, k$) is represented by n_j observations, $x_{1j}, x_{2j}, x_{3j}, \ldots, x_{nj}$. The sample sizes for each of the groups need not be equal. For each group the population mean, μ_j, is estimated by the sample mean, $\bar{x}_j$:

$$\bar{x}_j = \frac{\sum_{i=1}^{n_j} x_{ij}}{n_j}.$$

We can calculate the mean of all values across the k groups, the grand mean, as:

$$\bar{x}. = \frac{\sum_{j=1}^{k} \sum_{i=1}^{n_j} x_{ij}}{n},$$

where

$$n = \sum_{j=1}^{k} n_j,$$

the overall sample size. The total variability across all $n = n_1 + n_2 + \ldots n_k$ observations is the sum of the squared difference between each

observation and the grand mean divided by the number of df:

$$V_T = \frac{\sum_{j=1}^{k} \sum_{i=1}^{n_j} (x_{ij} - \bar{x}.)^2}{n - 1}.$$

The sum of the squared deviations of each observation from the overall mean (the numerator) is also called the "total sums of squares."

The population variance for each group, σ_j^2, is estimated by the sample variance:

$$s_j^2 = \frac{\sum_{i=1}^{n_j} (x_{ij} - \bar{x}_j)^2}{n_j - 1}.$$

While the notation here is a little more complicated than we have seen before (because of the addition of the subscript j) the basic principle is exactly the same. All we have done to this point in this example is to calculate the sample means and variances for each group in the study.

An estimate of the average variance over all k groups represents the "typical" spread of data over the entire study or experiment. This variability is often referred to as random variation or noise. In the ANOVA strategy this number is called the within-group variance (or mean square error), and is calculated as a weighted average of the sample variances:

$$\text{Within-group variance } (V_w) = \frac{\sum_{j=1}^{k} (n_j - 1)s_j^2}{n - k}.$$

The denominator – that is, the df – in this calculation may be puzzling at first, but, again, the principle is the same as we have seen before. Recall that, when estimating the sample variance, the df value is $n - 1$. This is because the sum of deviations has to equal 0. Given knowledge of $n - 1$ observations in the sample, we can determine the last observation: It is the value that will ensure that the sum of all deviations adds to 0. In this case, the "minus 1" is applied for all k groups. This leads to:

$$(n_1 - 1) + (n_2 - 1) + \ldots (n_k - 1) = (n_1 + n_2 + \ldots n_k) - k = n - k.$$

As there are also k sample means, each representing an estimate of the typical value of the population (that is, the population mean), those estimates may also vary from sample to sample. The variance of the means across all groups is called the among-group variance (or the mean square among groups), and is calculated as a weighted average (weighted by the sample size) of the squared differences of each sample mean from the grand mean:

$$\text{Among-group variance } (V_A) = \frac{\sum_{j=1}^{k} n_j (\bar{x}_j - \bar{x}.)^2}{k - 1}.$$

where

$$\bar{x}. = \frac{\sum_{j=1}^{k} \sum_{i=1}^{n_j} x_{ij}}{n},$$

the grand mean, as before. The total variability in the data can be split or partitioned as the within-group variability (the background variability) and the among-group variability of means (how much the sample means vary from the overall mean):

$$V_T = V_A + V_W.$$

As we have seen with a number of methods so far (most notably, the two-sample t test) the extent to which point estimates differ is measured against the typical variability of means from sample to sample. In the case of an ANOVA, we have an analogous method by which we can evaluate the extent to which the means differ. If the variance among the samples greatly exceeds the typical variance of the data in general there is an indication that the typical difference in means is not the result of random variation, but of systematic variation. If the variance among the samples is similar to the variance of the data in general such a result suggests that, whatever the difference in means, it is just like what happens by chance alone.

The test statistic (F) for this comparison in the ANOVA takes the form of a ratio of the among-sample variance to the within-sample variance:

$$F = \frac{V_A}{V_W}.$$

This test statistic is not well defined in all cases, which means that a rejection region is not automatically defined from a known distribution. However, if some assumptions are made about the distribution of the random variable X, the distribution of the test statistic can be defined. The following assumptions are required for an appropriate use of ANOVA:

- Each group represents a simple random sample from each of k populations and the observations are statistically independent.
- The random variable, X, is normally distributed within each population.
- The variance of the random variable, X, is equal among all k populations.

Given these assumptions the test statistic, F, follows an F distribution with $(k - 1)$ numerator df and $(n - k)$ denominator df. This is written in shorthand as $F_{k-1, n-k}$. Although we do not describe this distribution in detail, its essential characteristics are that it is a two-parameter distribution (that is, the numerator and denominator df) and it is asymmetric. As you might imagine, this distribution is not nearly as convenient to work with as the standard normal distribution. Defining the critical region for a given situation is best accomplished using statistical software because there are countless F distributions, each requiring a table. Similarly, calculating the sums of squares is best left to software (it can certainly be done by hand, but the required calculations are tedious).

ANOVA can be extended to situations where the experimental units (in our context, study participants) are classified on a number of factors. When they are classified on the basis of one factor, it is referred to as a one-way ANOVA. The result of partitioning the total variance into its components, in this case among and within samples defined by one factor, is displayed in Table 11.2.

The F distribution with $(k - 1)$ numerator df and $(n - k)$ denominator df is used to define the rejection region for a test of size α. The critical region may be obtained from a table of values or provided by statistical software. Tabled F values

Table 11.2 General one-way ANOVA table

Source	Sum of squares	Degrees of freedom	Mean square	F
Among samples	$\displaystyle\sum_{j=1}^{k} n_j(\bar{x}_j - \bar{x}.)^2$ $= SSA$	$k - 1$	$\dfrac{\displaystyle\sum_{j=1}^{k} n_j(\bar{x}_j - \bar{x}.)^2}{k - 1}$ $= V_A$	$\dfrac{V_A}{V_W}$
Within samples	$\displaystyle\sum_{j=1}^{k} (n_j - 1)s_j^2$ $= SSW$	$n - k$	$\dfrac{\displaystyle\sum_{j=1}^{k} (n_j - 1)s_j^2}{n - k}$ $= V_W$	
Total	$\displaystyle\sum_{j=1}^{k}\sum_{i=1}^{n_j} (x_{ij} - \bar{x}.)^2$ $= SST$	$n - 1$	$\dfrac{\displaystyle\sum_{j=1}^{k}\sum_{i=1}^{n_j} (x_{ij} - \bar{x}.)^2}{n - 1}$ $= V_T$	

for a number of combinations of α, numerator and denominator df are provided in Appendix 4. The null hypothesis of no difference among means will be rejected only if the value of the test statistic, F, is larger than the cut point specified from the parameters of the distribution. Therefore, the test is inherently one sided – that is, the rejection region is any value $F \geq F_{(k-1),(n-k)}$.

Rejection of the null hypothesis means only that there is at least one difference among all pairwise comparisons of means. This conclusion is hardly satisfactory in the world of drug development because the decisions to be made typically require the selection of a dose or treatment regimen for purposes of designing another study or proposing a dose for marketing approval.

11.5 A worked example with a small dataset

Since, as noted, the calculations involved in ANOVA are fairly tedious, we illustrate the method using an overly simplistic example with a small dataset. This example is for illustrative

purposes: In reality, datasets for which ANOVA is most appropriate have large sample sizes and are analyzed using statistical software. However, once you have a conceptual understanding of ANOVA you can interpret ANOVA tables for a wide variety of study designs.

The research question

Does the reduction in SBP differ among three doses of an investigational antihypertensive drug?

Study design

A clinical study was conducted to investigate three doses of an investigational antihypertensive drug. Fifteen participants were recruited (five per group), and randomized to three treatment groups: 10 mg, 20 mg, and 30 mg. Each treatment was taken once a day. SBP was measured 5 min before the administration of the drug (baseline) and again 30 min after. A "change from baseline score" was calculated for each participant by subtracting the baseline value from the post-treatment value.

Data

The change from baseline scores for the 15 participants are displayed below:

- 10 mg treatment group: $-6, -5, -6, -7, -6$
- 20 mg treatment group: $-8, -9, -8, -9, -6$
- 30 mg treatment group: $-10, -8, -10, -8, -9$.

Statistical analysis

A one-factor ANOVA is the appropriate analysis here assuming that the data are normal: The only factor of interest is the dose of drug given. There are three levels of this factor: 10, 20, and 30 mg. Following convention, the results of an ANOVA are displayed in an ANOVA summary table such as the model in Table 11.3. In the following calculations the values are presented without their units of measurement (mmHg) simply for convenience. At the end of the calculations, however, it is very important to remember that the numerical terms represent values measured in mmHg. The calculations needed are as follows.

1. Calculate the group means and the grand mean:

- 10 mg group mean $= \bar{x}_{10} = \dfrac{-30}{5} = -6$

- 20 mg group mean $= \bar{x}_{20} = \dfrac{-40}{5} = -8$

- 30 mg group mean $= \bar{x}_{30} = \dfrac{-45}{5} = -9$

- grand mean $= \bar{x} = \dfrac{(-6) + (-8) + (-9)}{3} = -7.67$.

2. Calculate the group sample variances:

- 10 mg group sample variance =

$$s_{10}^2 = \frac{((-6) - (-6))^2 + ((-5) - (-6))^2 + ((-6) - (-6))^2 + ((-7) - (-6))^2 + ((-6) - (-6))^2}{4} = 0.50$$

- 20 mg group sample variance =

$$s_{20}^2 = \frac{((-8) - (-8))^2 + ((-9) - (-8))^2 + ((-8) - (-8))^2 + ((-9) - (-8))^2 + ((-6) - (-8))^2}{4} = 1.50$$

- 30 mg group sample variance =

$$s_{30}^2 = \frac{((-10) - (-9))^2 + ((-8) - (-9))^2 + ((-10) - (-9))^2 + ((-8) - (-9))^2 + ((-9) - (-9))^2}{4} = 1.00$$

3. Calculate the total sums of squares (SST): The total sums of squares is the variability of observations across all three groups. It is calculated by summing the squared difference of each observation (in this case 15 of them) from the grand mean, -7.67. For brevity, the calculation is not written out here. We suggest that you verify the calculations with software:

- $SST = 35.33$.

4. Calculate the among-sample sums of squares (SSA):

$$SSA = 5((-6) - (-7.67))^2 + 5((-8) - (-7.67))^2 + 5((-9) - (-7.67))^2 = 23.33.$$

5. Calculate the within-sample sums of squares (SSW):

- $SSW = (4)(0.50) + (4)(1.50) + (4)(1.00) = 12$.

As expected, the total sums of squares is the sum of the among-sample sums of squares and the within-sample sums of squares.

6. Calculate the df:

- Total: We started with 15 scores. To get the same grand mean, 14 of these can vary, but number 15 cannot. Therefore, there are $(n - 1)$ df:

  df (total) $= 15 - 1 = 14$.

- Among samples: There are three groups, and thus three sample means. These must also average to the grand mean. Once two have been determined, the third can be only one value (that is, it cannot vary). Again, therefore, there are $(k - 1)$ df:

df (among) $= 3 - 1 = 2$.

- Within samples: By exactly the same logic that we saw for the within-groups sums of squares, we can calculate these df as:

df (within) = df (total) − df (among) = $14 - 2 = 12$.

(Note: There is also another way to think of this. Within each sample there are five values. Therefore, there are four df per sample. There are three samples. The total within-samples df is the total of the df within each sample, or $4 + 4 + 4 = 12$.)

7. Construct the ANOVA table: Having calculated the total sums of squares from all sources of variation, along with their degrees of freedom, we can now start to construct the ANOVA table. The only other calculations required are the mean squares for among-samples and within-samples (divide each sums of squares by its associated df) and the test statistic, F (divide among-samples mean square by within-samples mean square). All of this information is shown in the partial ANOVA table presented as Table 11.3.

8. Determine if the test statistic is in the rejection region: As always, we need to determine if the test statistic F falls in the rejection region. So far, we have not determined the

rejection region for this test. As noted earlier, the F distribution has two parameters that determine its shape and, therefore, the F values that cut off tail areas of the distribution. The two parameters are the numerator df (associated with the numerator of the F ratio or the among-sample source of variation) and the denominator df (associated with the denominator of the F ratio or the within-samples source of variation). In this case, the numerator df is 2 and the denominator df is 12. This is written as:

$F(2,12) = 11.67$.

Tables with values of F for several distributions are used to determine the significance of this result, or the critical values can be obtained from statistical software. We have provided a table in Appendix 4. For a test of size $\alpha = 0.05$, the critical value associated with 2 numerator df and 12 denominator df that cuts off the upper 5% of the distribution is 3.89. Although tabled values are helpful at identifying nominal p values (for example, ≤ 0.01) statistical software is required to report the specific p value. Using statistical software, you will find that the actual p value is 0.002. Table 11.4 shows the completed ANOVA table for this example. You will see that the p value is commonly included in a complete ANOVA table.

Table 11.3 One-way ANOVA table for the SBP study (partially complete)

Source	Sum of squares	Degrees of freedom	Mean square	F
Among samples	23.33	2	11.67	11.67
Within samples	12.00	12	1.00	
Total	35.33	14		

Table 11.4 Completed one-way ANOVA table for the SBP study

Source	Sum of squares	Degrees of freedom	Mean square	F	p value
Among samples	23.33	2	11.67	11.67	0.002
Within samples	12.00	12	1.00		
Total	35.33	14			

It is important to recognize that the actual p value, not simply $p < 0.05$, is stated in the table. Regulatory reviewers and journal editors prefer this practice, because the actual value provides more information than simply a statement that the value is less than 0.05.

Interpretation and decision-making

As the value of the test statistic, 11.67, is in the rejection region for this test of size $\alpha = 0.05$ (that is, $11.67 > 3.89$), the null hypothesis is rejected in favor of the alternate, which means that at least one pair of the population means is not equal.

Recall the original research question: Does the reduction in SBP differ among three doses of a new antihypertensive? The results of the one-way ANOVA that we have conducted so far are interpreted in the following manner:

- There is evidence at the $\alpha = 0.05$ level that the levels of the factor "dose of drug" differ. Therefore, there is a statistically significant difference in SBP change scores between the groups. (The p value of 0.002 indicates that the null hypothesis would also have been rejected at smaller α levels, for example, at the $\alpha = 0.01$ level.)

The above statement by itself does not, however, tell us anything about which group showed the greatest change score, or indeed how any specific group compared with any of the other groups. Consideration of the group means is necessary to do this. These means, with the associated units of measurement reinserted, are:

- 10 mg group = -6 mmHg
- 20 mg group = -8 mmHg
- 30 mg group = -9 mmHg.

Therefore, we can now state that the 30 mg group showed the greatest mean decrease in SBP, the 20 mg group the second greatest mean decrease, and the 10 mg group the least mean decrease. However, a full answer to the research question has still not been supplied, at least not in terms of determining possible statistical differences between specific pairs of dose levels.

The ANOVA test statistic revealed that, overall, the groups differed statistically significantly, but, as there are more than two groups, it cannot reveal the precise pattern of statistical significance. For any three groups (call them D, E, and F) there are $C_2^3 = 3$ possible comparisons between pairs of groups: D can be compared with E; D can be compared with F; and E can be compared with F. These three comparisons can lead to the following patterns of outcomes:

- All groups differ statistically significantly from each other.
- None of the groups differs statistically significantly from any other group.
- D and E both differ statistically significantly from F, but do not differ statistically significantly from each other.
- D and F both differ statistically significantly from E, but do not differ statistically significantly from each other.
- E and F both differ statistically significantly from D, but do not differ statistically significantly from each other.

To determine which pattern of outcomes occurred in any given situation, an additional statistical test is needed. In situations such as this, where we have a partial answer to our original research question, multiple comparisons are performed. These are tests that allow us to compare the means of each pair of groups to see which pairs (if any) differ statistically significantly from each other. Multiple comparisons therefore provide a more detailed understanding of our data than the overall test (referred to as the omnibus test) provided by the ANOVA. If the omnibus test yields a nonsignificant result, multiple comparisons are not necessary, because, in fact, none of them would be significant. In the case of a significant omnibus test, the second option above is not actually a possible outcome, whereas all of the others are. This means that we need a method of determining which of the other possibilities is the case – that is, we need a statistical methodology that will allow us to conduct multiple comparisons, and to use this methodology before we can provide the full answer to our original research question. The full answer is provided in Section 11.10, but first we need to look at another issue.

11.6 A statistical methodology for conducting multiple comparisons

In clinical studies, the probability of declaring a treatment efficacious when in reality it is not efficacious is termed α. This is the probability of detecting a false positive, or committing a type I error. As we have seen, the probability of committing a type I error should be limited to a specific value so that erroneous conclusions are not made very often. For a sponsor, committing a type I error could result in investing significant amounts of money on a drug that really does not work. For a regulatory agency, committing a type I error (approving a drug that is not efficacious) could result in many people taking a drug that does not offer a meaningful treatment benefit and may carry some risk (every drug has a side-effect profile). It is therefore important to constrain the probability of committing a type I error to an acceptable level. Traditionally, this acceptable level has been and is still regarded as the $\alpha = 0.05$ level, but, as noted before, we can choose other values when we consider them appropriate.

The important point to note here is that the $\alpha = 0.05$ level is deemed appropriate when a single test is being conducted. Multiple comparisons, by definition, mean that more that one test is being conducted. When testing a number of pairwise comparisons – for example, after an ANOVA where the null hypothesis has been rejected – it is not acceptable to test each pairwise comparison at the $\alpha = 0.05$ level because of the potential inflation of the overall type I error rate.

When three treatment groups are evaluated in a clinical study, there are three possible pairwise comparisons of means (D vs E, D vs F, and E vs F). If each mean is tested at the $\alpha = 0.05$ level, and assuming that they are mutually exclusive, the probability of declaring at least one of the pairs significantly different is equal to 1 minus the probability of accepting all three (by the complement rule). Assuming that the comparisons are independent, the probability of accepting all three null hypotheses is the probability of accepting the first null hypothesis multiplied by the probability of accepting the second multiplied by the probability of accepting the third. When testing each at the $\alpha = 0.05$ level, this probability becomes:

P (incorrectly rejecting at least one hypothesis)
$= 1 - (0.95)(0.95)(0.95) = 1 - 0.95^3 = 0.14.$

That is, instead of a type I error rate of $\alpha = 0.05$, this analysis has resulted in a higher probability of committing a type I error, just by chance alone.

In fact, the comparisons made here cannot be thought of as independent because each group is compared with two others in this case. It is more correct to use an inequality sign to say that the probability is no more than 0.14, that is, ≤ 0.14. However, this technicality is of little comfort because, to make sound decisions, we would really like to limit that probability to a reasonable level. In general, if C comparisons are each made at the α level, the probability of rejecting at least one by chance alone is:

P (rejecting at least one of c hypotheses)
$\leq (1 - (1 - \alpha)^c)$

Table 11.5 lists the probability of rejecting at least one hypothesis for a number of values of C, the number of hypothesis tests performed at the conventional $\alpha = 0.05$ level.

Table 11.5 Maximum probability of committing a type I error when each hypothesis is tested at $\alpha = 0.05$

C: No. of hypotheses tested at $\alpha = 0.05$	Maximum probability of type I error
1	0.050
2	0.098
3	0.143
4	0.185
5	0.226
6	0.265
7	0.302
8	0.337
9	0.370
10	0.401
15	0.537
20	0.642

Suppose that a clinical trial has to evaluate four doses of a test treatment and a placebo (a total of five groups) on relieving headache pain. The study was carefully designed and conducted, and the data are now ready for the statistical analysis. A one-way ANOVA is conducted, and the conclusion from the omnibus F test (comparison of the among-sample variance with the within-sample variance) is that the population means are not all equal. Five treatment groups give rise to $C_2^5 = 10$ pairwise group comparisons. Suppose that one of the researchers failed to get input from the trial statistician, and hurriedly (and mathematically correctly) analyzed all 10 pairwise comparisons of means performed using 10 two-sample t tests. The researcher takes his or her results to the study director and the rest of the study team and points out with tremendous excitement that the pairwise comparison of the lowest dose with the placebo yielded a p value of 0.023, a statistically significant result at the $\alpha = 0.05$ level. A surge of positive energy fills the room as everyone but the statistician declares, "We have found our lowest effective dose! On to the confirmatory trial!"

As you have probably realized by now, there would actually be little reason for enthusiasm, as the study statistician would very soon point out. The problem is this: While each of the 10 two-sample t tests had been conducted mathematically correctly, it is not appropriate statistical methodology to use 10 two-sample t tests in this setting. The analytic strategy employed did not limit the type I error rate to 0.05. Rather, as seen in Table 11.5, when 10 such pairwise comparisons are made – that is, 10 hypotheses are tested – the probability of rejecting at least one of the hypotheses is limited to 0.401, a value considerably greater in magnitude than 0.05. In other words, use of this naïve analytic strategy has resulted in an inflated type I error. There is up to a 40% chance of being misled by one test with a nominal p value ≤ 0.05.

The issue of type I error inflation caused by multiple testing appears in many guises in the realm of new drug development. This issue is of great importance to decision-makers, and we discuss this topic again later in the chapter. For now, we have not yet provided a full answer to our research question; our description of analysis of variance is incomplete without a discussion of at least one analysis method that controls the overall type I error rate when evaluating pairwise comparisons from an ANOVA.

11.7 Bonferroni's test

Bonferroni's test is the most straightforward of several statistical methodologies that can appropriately be used in the context of multiple comparisons. That is, Bonferroni's test can appropriately be used to compare pairs of means after rejection of the null hypothesis following a significant omnibus F test. Imagine that we have c groups in total. Bonferroni's method makes use of the following inequality:

$$P(R_1 \text{ or } R_2 \text{ or } R_3 \text{ or } \ldots \text{ or } R_c)$$
$$\leq P(R_1) + P(R_2) + P(R_3) + \ldots + P(R_c).$$

This means that the probability of rejecting at least one of c hypotheses is less than or equal to (thus the term "inequality") the sum of the probabilities of rejecting each hypothesis. This inequality is true even if the events, in this case rejecting one of c null hypotheses, are not independent. Recall from Section 6.2 that, when events are not independent, the probability of intersecting events should be subtracted. Using Bonferroni's method, testing each pair of means with an α level of $\alpha_B = \frac{\alpha}{c}$ will ensure that the overall type I error rate does not exceed the desired value of α. It follows that the probability of rejecting at least one of c null hypotheses can be expressed as follows:

$$p(\text{rejecting at least one of } c \text{ hypotheses at } \alpha_B \text{ level}) \leq c\left(\frac{\alpha}{c}\right) = \alpha.$$

It is important to note that the researcher in our scenario in Section 11.6 who hurriedly conducted 10 pairwise comparisons using 10 two-sample t tests and rejoiced in one particular finding was not completely out of line in the analytic strategy chosen. It is indeed possible to approach this situation (the need for 10 pairwise comparisons) with the intent to conduct 10 two-sample t tests. However, a correction must be made to the α level used to determine statistical significance. In the scenario as told in Section 11.6 the researcher did not perform this critical step.

In practice, then, we can carry out each of a series of pairwise comparisons of means using a two-sample t test for each comparison, but the α level must be modified accordingly. When deciding whether or not to reject the null hypothesis associated with each comparison, we need to use an α level of $\alpha_B = \frac{\alpha}{c}$ instead of the naïve choice of α. Note that this is equivalent to defining a rejection region for each test as:

$$t < t_{\alpha/2c, n-k} \text{ or } t > t_{1-(\alpha/2c), n-k}$$

which makes sense as the tail areas in the left and right of the t distribution are smaller than those obtained using the two-sided test of size α.

Consider the two-sample t-test statistic again:

$$t = \frac{(\bar{x}_1 - \bar{x}_2)}{s_p \sqrt{\frac{1}{n_1} + \frac{1}{n_2}}}.$$

In an ANOVA involving more than two groups, we estimate the underlying variability from more than two samples, and yet we are interested in the extent to which (only) two of the means differ from each other. Therefore, when comparing the means of two samples, the pooled standard deviation from the two-sample case, s_p, is replaced by an estimate that captures the variability across all groups in the analysis – the mean square error or the within-samples mean square. Recall from Section 11.4 that this quantity has the same interpretation as the pooled standard deviation, the typical spread of data across all observations.

When using Bonferroni's method, the null hypothesis associated with a pairwise comparison is rejected if the calculated test statistic, that is,

$$t = \frac{\bar{x}_1 - \bar{x}_2}{\sqrt{V_w \left(\frac{1}{n_1} + \frac{1}{n_2} \right)}}$$

is in the rejection region defined as $t < t_{(\alpha/2c), n-k}$ or $t > t_{1-(\alpha/2c), n-k}$.

Remember that V_w comes from the ANOVA table and it is the mean square error, which has also been referred to as the within-samples variability or, more informally, the background noise. This is analogous to s_p^2 in the two-sample case. As we assume equal variances, we use the estimator that uses the most data and therefore gives the most precise estimate.

The critical value can be determined from a table or software (using a two-sided test of size

α/c). The estimate of the underlying variability, V_w, comes from the ANOVA table, and the sample sizes for each group are known *and equal*. Then we can define a quantity, the minimally significant difference (MSD), which is the smallest difference (in absolute value) between any two sample means that could be considered statistically significant at the α level. (Note that when sample sizes are not equal the MSD is not defined, but there are other methods available.)

$$\text{MSD} = t_{1-(\alpha/2c), n-k} \sqrt{V_w \left(\frac{1}{n_1} + \frac{1}{n_2} \right)}.$$

Once the value of MSD has been determined, the absolute value of the difference in means will be compared with the MSD. If the absolute value of the difference in means, $|(\bar{x}_1 - \bar{x}_2)|$, is greater than or equal to the MSD the null hypothesis will be rejected.

11.8 Employing Bonferroni's test in our example

Having introduced Bonferroni's test, we can now return to our earlier example to see how to apply Bonferroni's method to our pairwise comparisons of treatment group means.

Statistical analysis

The significant result of the omnibus F test led to the rejection of the null hypothesis of no significant differences, thereby revealing the presence of a significant difference between at least one pair of means. It is now of interest to determine precisely which pair or pairs of means are significantly different.

Given that the decisions made from this trial could result in sizeable further investment in the development of the investigational antihypertensive drug, the company would like to minimize its chances of committing a type I error. That is, it would like to maintain an overall type I error of 0.05. As we have just seen in Section 11.7, one analysis that will maintain this desired type I error of 0.05 is Bonferroni's method.

In our example of three treatment groups there are three pairwise comparisons of interest. Therefore, each pairwise comparison will be tested at an α level of 0.05/3 = 0.01667. This α level will require defining a critical value from the t distribution with 12 (that is, 15 − 3) df that cuts off an area of 0.00833 (half of 0.01667) in the right-hand tail. Use of statistical software reveals that the critical value is 2.77947. From inspection of the ANOVA table presented as Table 11.4 the within-samples mean square (mean square error) can be seen to be 1. The final component needed for the MSD is:

$$\sqrt{\frac{1}{n_1} + \frac{1}{n_2}} = \sqrt{0.4} = 0.632.$$

Then the MSD is equal to:

$$MSD = (2.77947)(1)(0.632) = 1.757.$$

The mean values for each group are −6 mmHg (10 mg), −8 mmHg (20 mg), and −9 mmHg (30 mg). The absolute values of the three differences in means are displayed in Table 11.6.

Table 11.6   Absolute values of differences in means

	20 mg treatment group	30 mg treatment group
10 mg treatment group	2	3
20 mg treatment group		1

Each cell represents the differences in means for the groups represented by each row and column. The differences between the 10 mg and 20 mg groups and the 10 mg and 30 mg groups were both greater than the MSD (1.757). Therefore, these differences are considered statistically significant at the α = 0.05 level. The difference between the 20 mg and 30 mg groups was not significant, however, because it was less than the MSD.

Interpretation and decision-making

We are now in a position to provide a full answer to our research question of interest as expressed at the start of Section 11.5: Will the reduction in SBP differ among three doses of an investigational antihypertensive drug?

The first step in our analytical strategy was to conduct an ANOVA. This ANOVA tested the null hypothesis that there were no differences among the three means. The null hypothesis was tested at an α level of 0.05, and was rejected on the basis of the significant omnibus F test.

The second step in our analytical strategy was to determine which of the pairs of means were significantly different from each other. Testing each of the three hypotheses at an α level of 0.05 would have resulted in a probability of committing a type I error possibly > 0.05 (the desired level). Bonferroni's inequality was therefore used to test each of the three hypotheses at an α level of 0.05/3 = 0.01667. Using the critical value for this α level resulted in two pairs of means being declared significantly different at the 0.05 level.

The full interpretation of the study, therefore, is that the magnitude of the reduction in SBP does indeed differ according to different dose levels. The 20 mg and 30 mg doses both resulted in a statistically significantly greater SBP reduction than the 10 mg dose. There was insufficient evidence to claim that there is a statistically significant difference between the 20 mg and 30 mg doses.

What are the implications of this interpretation? First, if we decided that it would be useful to continue the clinical development program with another trial, it would be salient to note that, in terms of efficacy, the 10 mg dose was inferior to the other two. Therefore, if continuing, it is likely that we would not include the 10 mg dose in further trials. What else would help us to decide to continue with the clinical development program? The safety and tolerability of the 20 and 30 mg doses would need to be examined and deemed acceptable. Examining the safety and tolerability data from the participants in these two treatment groups would provide the evidence on which to base this decision (the safety and tolerability data from participants in the 10 mg treatment group would not be informative at this point). If there were no safety or tolerability concerns with the 20 or 30 mg doses, the next stage in development could be to continue to investigate both of these doses. Another possible interpretation is discussed in Section 11.10.

11.9 Tukey's honestly significant difference test

Bonferroni's method that we have just discussed is perhaps one of the most easily understood methods to maintain an overall type I error, which is one of its advantages. In addition, Bonferroni's method does indeed control the overall type I error rate well, such that it is guaranteed to be $\leq \alpha$. However, like many items that we discuss in this book, it has its disadvantages as well as its advantages.

Bonferroni's test is overly conservative, in that the critical values required for rejection need not be as large as they are. In other words, using a less conservative method may result in more null hypotheses being rejected. The reason that Bonferroni's method is so conservative is that it does not in any way account for the extent of correlation among the various hypotheses being tested. If a method could take into account the overlap, or lack thereof, of the various hypotheses, the critical values would not need to be defined as narrowly as with Bonferroni's. In this section, we therefore discuss another analytical strategy for multiple comparisons, Tukey's honestly significant difference (HSD) test.

Bonferroni's method for testing pairs of means (maintaining an overall type I error rate of α) involved comparing the absolute differences in means to the MSD, which was defined as a function of:

- the critical value from a t distribution with a combined area of α/c in the tails of the distribution
- the within-samples variability
- the sample sizes in each group.

Once a value of the MSD was determined each difference in means was calculated and compared with the MSD. Any difference that was equal to or greater than the MSD was considered statistically significant. Tukey's HSD test is carried out in a similar manner. A value called

the honestly significant difference is determined as a function of three things:

1. The critical value from the studentized range statistic
2. The within-samples variability
3. The sample sizes in each group.

The studentized range statistic, called q in the following description of the test, has a limited use for us now and we shall not spend any additional time characterizing it, except to say that the value of q does account for the relative size of differences among the normalized means, resulting in a test with an overall type I error of exactly 0.05. The value, q, is often provided in tables and to look it up we need to know the number of groups (k from the ANOVA description), and the number of df associated with the within-samples mean square ($n - k$). Statistical software packages also supply this number. The HSD (or, equivalently, the MSD_T for minimum significant difference – Tukey) is defined as:

$$\text{HSD} \equiv \text{MSD}_T = q \sqrt{\frac{V_W}{n}}.$$

In this expression n represents the per-group sample size which, for the moment, we require to be equal.

Once the value of HSD has been determined, the absolute value of the difference in means is compared with it. If the absolute value of the difference in means, $|(\bar{x}_1 - \bar{x}_2)|$, is greater than or equal to the HSD the null hypothesis is rejected.

The quantity represented by the letter "q" is determined from a table of values used just for this test. Two characteristics are needed to determine the appropriate value of q each time that it is used. These characteristics are represented by the letters "a" and "v." The letter a represents the number of groups, which in this example is 3. The letter v represents the df, which in this test is the df associated with the within-samples mean square. In this case, the value of v is 12, as calculated for and shown in the ANOVA summary table in Table 11.4. From the table of q values for Tukey's test (provided in Appendix 5) the value of q associated with an

(a, v) value of $(3, 12)$ is 3.77. HSD is then calculated as follows:

$$HSD = 3.77 \sqrt{\frac{1}{5}} = 1.686.$$

The absolute values of the three differences in means were displayed in Table 11.6. The differences between the 10 mg and 20 mg groups and the 10 mg and 30 mg groups were both greater than the HSD (1.686). Therefore, these differences are considered statistically significant at the 0.05 level. The difference between the 20 mg and 30 mg groups was not significant, however, because it was less than the HSD.

Although Tukey's method does not require equal sizes among the groups, imbalanced group sizes do require a different calculation of HSD. When the sample sizes are unequal among all groups being compared, there is not one common value of HSD because this value relies on the sample size per group. For the comparison of any two means with group sample sizes of n_1 and n_2, the value of HSD corresponding to that particular comparison is:

$$HSD = \frac{q}{\sqrt{2}} \sqrt{V_w \left(\frac{1}{n_1} + \frac{1}{n_2} \right)}.$$

In the case that n_1 and n_2 are equal this expression simplifies to the one we originally presented.

Interpretation and decision-making

Having gone through the calculations necessary for Tukey's test, we can look at how these results would lead to decision-making, and also compare the interpretation and decision-making with those that followed from using Bonferroni's methodology on the same dataset.

The statistical interpretations of these results are the same as with Bonferroni's method. The 20 and 30 mg doses both resulted in a statistically significantly greater SBP reduction than the 10 mg dose. There was insufficient evidence to claim that there is a statistically significant difference between the 20 mg and the 30 mg doses.

11.10 Implications of the methodology chosen for multiple comparisons

The most important lesson to be learned from our discussions of various analytic methodologies for multiple comparisons is that the method chosen can have a major impact on the risk of making incorrect decisions.

Consider the absolute difference in any two means that was required to reject a null hypothesis of H_0: $\mu_1 - \mu_2 = 0$ after rejection of the omnibus F test. In the case of the naïve approach, which was to test each pair of means separately and use an α level of 0.05 in each case, the minimum significant difference would be 1.126, but the overall type I error could be guaranteed to be bounded only by 0.143 (see Table 10.5). The use of Bonferroni's method resulted in a minimum significant difference of 1.757, but it is overly conservative and the overall type I error rate would be guaranteed to be < 0.050. Tukey's method, which accounts for the actual distribution of differences through q, resulted in a minimum significant difference of 1.686 and guaranteed that the overall type I error rate $= 0.050$, resulting in a more powerful test than Bonferroni's method. Given their importance, these characteristics are summarized in Table 11.7.

Lastly, it is important to note that differences such as these underscore the importance of declaring the primary analysis approach in a study protocol or statistical analysis plan. Committing to the most appropriate analysis from first principles is not only good scientific discipline, it is also necessary to withstand regulatory scrutiny.

It should be noted that these are not the only acceptable methods applicable to multiple comparisons from an ANOVA. In each individual case, the choice among possible approaches is largely dependent on the study design. For example, Dunnett's test can be used when the only comparisons of interest are each test treatment versus a control (for example, in a placebo-controlled, dose-ranging study). Like Tukey's test, Dunnett's method is more powerful than Bonferroni's. In general, other methods gain power compared with Bonferroni's method by

Table 11.7   Characteristics of the methods to test the three pairwise comparisons of means in the ANOVA example

Method	Minimally significant difference	Overall type I error rate: P(rejecting at least one null hypothesis)
Naïve approach (incorrect)	1.126	≤ 0.143
Bonferroni's test (correct but conservative)	1.757	< 0.050
Tukey's HSD test (correct, and more powerful than Bonferroni's)	1.686	$= 0.050$

using methods that account for the correlation of tests (for example, Tukey's HSD test) or by reducing the number of tests about which we would like to make an inference (for example, Dunnett's test). When conducting these types of analyses, it is theoretically possible (although not common) to report a significant overall F test, but not declare any pairwise comparison as statistically significant as a result of the multiple comparison procedure.

Consideration of the possible clinical interpretation of these results is also worthwhile. The interpretations given in the above sections are the full statistical interpretations from the statistical analyses that were performed on the data collected in this study. In real clinical trials, these results are also interpreted clinically, that is, their clinical significance is discussed. Making these clinical efficacy interpretations is the province of the clinicians on the study team. As we emphasized earlier in this book, we are not clinicians, and these "hypothetical comments" concerning the potential clinical significance of hypothetical data must be regarded in this light.

First, the clinical significance of a decrease in SBP of 6 mmHg versus a decrease of 8 or 9 mmHg would need to be considered. As these numerical values are all relatively close, let us create some hypothetical values that conform to the same overall pattern of significance but are more different from each other. Suppose that these mean decreases in SBP were observed using the same doses of a different antihypertensive drug:

- 10 mg group mean = -6 mmHg
- 20 mg group mean = -18 mmHg
- 30 mg group mean = -19 mmHg.

Suppose also that Tukey's test provided evidence of the same pattern of statistical significance:

- 10 versus 20 mg = $-6-(-18) = 12$; $p < 0.05$
- 10 versus 30 mg = $-6-(-19) = 13$; $p < 0.05$
- 20 versus 30 mg = $-18-(-19) = 1$; not significant (ns).

In this scenario, the clinical significance of a decrease in SBP of 6 mmHg versus a decrease of 18 or 19 mmHg would need to be considered. Suppose that decreases of 18 and 19 mmHg are both considered to be much more clinically significant than a decrease of 6 mmHg. Suppose also that the 20 mg dose had a good (and therefore acceptable) safety profile, whereas the safety profile of the 30 mg dose was not so good. Of relevance in this scenario is that there was not a statistically significant difference in efficacy between these two dose groups. It is true that the mean decrease in the 20 mg group was numerically less than the mean decrease in the 30 mg group, but it was not statistically significantly less. Therefore, it might be the case that, when input had been received from all members of the study team, including statisticians and clinicians, a decision would be made to progress only the 20 mg dose to further trials: The 10 mg dose is statistically significantly less effective, and the 30 mg dose has a less desirable safety profile while also not being statistically significantly more effective (see Turner, 2007).

This scenario illustrates several key points:

- Decision-making is not necessarily straightforward.
- The empirical evidence from our clinical trials provides the basis for rational decision-making.

- In most cases many members of the study team, including statisticians and clinicians, are needed to make the optimum decision.

In real life, clinical interpretations are vital to balance the relative weight of safety and efficacy considerations. If a higher dose of a given drug is considerably more efficacious than a lower dose and leads to only a minimal increase in very mild side-effects, a clinician may decide that, on balance, it is worth recommending the higher dose. Conversely, if a higher dose of a given drug is only minimally more efficacious than a lower dose and leads to a considerable increase in moderate or severe side-effects, a clinician may recommend the lower dose.

11.11 Additional considerations about ANOVA

Before completing our discussions of ANOVA, there are several additional points that we would like to address, because these questions may have occurred to you as you have read the preceding descriptions of the use of ANOVA and multiple comparisons in this chapter.

11.11.1 ANOVAs with only two groups

A one-way ANOVA containing three levels was used as the worked example in this section because a t test cannot address a design with more than two levels. However, the one-way ANOVA can certainly be used in situations involving only two levels. A reasonable question, therefore, is: In situations involving only two levels, where the only possible comparison is between one level and the other, is there any advantage in using the one-way ANOVA instead of the t test?

The answer is no. In cases where there are only two levels, either test is applicable. The values obtained in the calculations of the respective tests will be different, but the tests will give precisely the same answer in terms of the degree of statistical significance obtained by the respective test statistic. That is, the t value and F value will not be the same (the F-test statistic will be square of the t-test statistic), but the associated p values will be identical. The advantage of the ANOVA lies with its ability to address situations involving more than two levels, which are very common in clinical research.

11.11.2 Only collect data that you intend to analyze

Consider a scenario where a series of possible comparisons exists, but the investigator is genuinely interested only in one of these comparisons. Such a hypothetical scenario might involve a study employing four groups, with participants in each group receiving one of four dose levels (1, 2, 3, and 4) of a particular drug, and primary interest lay with comparing dose levels 1 and 4 – that is, out of the possible six comparisons, interest lay only with the comparison of dose levels 1 and 4. A question that arises here is: Is it possible to argue that this one comparison could be made without having to adopt a more conservative approach? The correct answer from a purely statistical computational viewpoint is yes, this argument can successfully be made. The individual test may be undertaken using a t test at the $\alpha = 0.05$ level, that is, without adopting a more conservative approach, because this one particular comparison of interest was specified from first principles. However, this is not the final answer here.

Although this argument is perfectly satisfactory from a purely computational view, another question begs to be asked: If the investigator was interested only in comparing dose levels 1 and 4, why were dose levels 2 and 3 included in the study? This question is pertinent in several ways. It costs a lot of time and money to collect such clinical data, and the costs associated with participants in two of the four experimental groups would be wasted. Much more important than the unnecessary costs, however, would be that the participants in the dose level 2 and 3 treatment groups would have taken part in the study for no useful reason, a gross violation of experimental ethics.

A much more realistic scenario is one in which four doses are included in such a study because the investigator does not have clear logical ideas (hypotheses) about the relative merits (perhaps relative efficacy) of the doses. In this case, an original omnibus analysis such as the one-factor ANOVA provides a very efficient initial test for differences among the groups. If a statistically significant result is given by the ANOVA, the investigator can then proceed to comparing pairs of groups in formal (and appropriate) multiple comparison testing.

11.12 Nonparametric analyses of continuous data

There are times when the required assumptions for ANOVA, a parametric test, are not met. One example would be if the underlying distributions are non-normal. In these cases, nonparametric tests are very useful and informative. For example, we saw in Section 11.3 that a nonparametric analog to the two-sample t test, Wilcoxon's rank sum test, makes use of the ranks of observations rather than the scores themselves. When a one-factor ANOVA is not appropriate in a particular case a corresponding nonparametric approach called the Kruskal–Wallis test can be used. This test is a hypothesis test of the location of (more than) two distributions.

11.13 The Kruskal–Wallis test

All that is required for this test to be employed is that the observations classified into k groups are independently sampled from populations and the random variable is continuous with the same variability across the populations represented by the samples. Importantly, no assumption about the shape of the underlying distribution is required, making this test suitable for non-normal underlying distributions.

In the Kruskal–Wallis test the original scores are first ranked and an ANOVA analysis is then carried out on the ranks. As with Wilcoxon's rank sum test, ranking of the observations must deal with ties. The sums of squares are based on these ranks, and the test statistic is based on a ratio of the among-samples variability in ranks and the within-samples variability in ranks.

All observations, x_{ij}, are assigned ranks, r_{ij}, and therefore the usual sums of squares can be calculated for the rank scores, r_{ij}. For brevity, the expressions for each are provided in Table 11.8, a general one-way ANOVA table, on the basis of ranks.

The quantities in the ANOVA table based on ranks represent similar quantities as the ANOVA table based on the original scores:

r_{ij} is the rank for individual i in group j
n_j is the sample size for group j

$$n = \sum_{j=1}^{k} n_j \text{ is the total sample size}$$

$\bar{r}_j$ is the average rank for group j

$$s_j^2 = \frac{\sum_{i=1}^{n_j} (r_{ij} - \bar{r}_j)^2}{n_j - 1} \text{ is the variance of ranks in group } j.$$

$\bar{r}$ is the average rank over all groups (the grand mean rank), which can be simplified as:

$$\bar{r}_. = \frac{n+1}{2}.$$

The omnibus test statistic, X^2, follows a χ^2 distribution with $k - 1$ df. If the omnibus test is rejected the pairs of groups can be evaluated using a Bonferroni-type approach. This requires the assumption that the ranks are normally distributed. As with the parametric one-way ANOVA, a minimally significant difference in ranks can be calculated for this purpose as:

$$\text{MSD} = z_{1-(\alpha/2c)} \sqrt{V_{\text{W,ranks}} \left(\frac{1}{n_1} + \frac{1}{n_2} \right)}.$$

For the sake of this example, we use the data from the parametric ANOVA example to illustrate the Kruskal–Wallis test. If it seems at all strange to use the same data for both examples, a parametric analysis and a nonparametric analysis, it is worth noting that a nonparametric analysis is always appropriate for a given dataset meeting the requirements at the start of the chapter. Parametric analyses are not always appropriate for all datasets.

Table 11.8   General one-way ANOVA table for ranks (Kruskal–Wallis test)

Source	Sum of squares	Degrees of freedom	Mean square	χ^2
Among samples	$\sum_{j=1}^{k} n_j(\bar{r}_j - \bar{r}_.)^2$ $= SSA_{ranks}$	$k - 1$	$\dfrac{\sum_{j=1}^{k} n_j(\bar{r}_j - \bar{r}_.)^2}{k - 1}$ $= V_{A,\,ranks}$	$V_{A,ranks}/V_{W,ranks}$
Within samples	$\sum_{j=1}^{k} (n_j - 1)s_j^2$ $= SSW_{ranks}$	$n - k$	$\dfrac{\sum_{j=1}^{k} (n_j - 1)s_j^2}{n - k}$ $= V_{W,\,ranks}$	
Total	$\sum_{j=1}^{k}\sum_{i=1}^{n_j} (r_{ij} - \bar{r})^2$ $= SST_{ranks}$	$n - 1$	$\dfrac{\sum_{j=1}^{k}\sum_{i=1}^{n_j} (r_{ij} - \bar{r})^2}{n - 1}$ $= V_{T,\,ranks}$	

Statistical analysis

The analysis begins with ordering all 15 observations. Note that statistical software packages order and rank the observations and do the ANOVA for you. The ordered observations from lowest to highest across the three groups are as follows:

10 mg					-7	-6	-6	-6		-5
20 mg		-9	-9				-8	-8			-6
30 mg	-10	-10	-9		-8	-8				

Then ranking each observation, accounting for ties as described for the one-way ANOVA, the following ranks are obtained:

10 mg						10	12.5	12.5	12.5		15
20 mg		4	4				7.5	7.5			12.5
30 mg	1.5	1.5	4		7.5	7.5				

The within-samples average ranks are:

$\bar{r}_{10} = 12.5$

$\bar{r}_{20} = 7.1$

$\bar{r}_{30} = 4.4$.

And the grand mean rank:

$\bar{r}_. = 8$.

The within-samples variances (of ranks) are:

$s_{10}^2 = 4.63$

$s_{20}^2 = 12.18$

$s_{30}^2 = 9.05$.

The among-samples mean square is calculated as:

$$V_{A,ranks} = \frac{5(12.5 - 8)^2 + 5(7.1 - 8)^2 + 5(4.4 - 8)^2}{2} = 85.05.$$

The within-samples mean square (mean square error) is calculated as:

$$V_{W,ranks} = \frac{4(3.13) + 4(12.18) + 4(9.05)}{12} = 8.12.$$

Finally, the test statistic is the ratio of these two:

$85.05/8.12 = 10.48$.

We note that the test statistic is greater than the critical value of 5.991 (2 df with an α level of 0.05), so the null hypothesis is rejected.

The next step is to decide which groups (three comparisons) are different with respect to their location. For this purpose the MSD is calculated as:

$$\text{MSD} = z_{0.992} \sqrt{8.12\left(\frac{1}{5} + \frac{1}{5}\right)} = 2.41\sqrt{8.12\left(\frac{1}{5} + \frac{1}{5}\right)} = 4.34.$$

The differences in mean ranks are displayed in Table 11.9. Differences in mean ranks that are greater than the MSD are considered significantly different.

Table 11.9   Absolute differences in mean ranks

	20 mg	30 mg
10 mg	5.4	8.1
20 mg		2.7

Interpretation and decision-making

As the difference in mean ranks exceeds the MSD for the comparison of 10 vs 20 mg and 10 vs 30 mg, we can conclude that these distributions differ in location. This testing procedure ensured that the overall type I error did not exceed 0.05. To interpret the clinical relevance of the differences detected by the test requires some additional point estimates. As the initial procedure was a nonparametric one, the differences in sample means are not appropriate. A more reasonable choice would be to compare the medians as an estimate of the treatment effect.

The nonparametric one-way ANOVA can be quite useful in a number of settings. The most obvious is when reasonable judgment does not allow you to conclude that the distributional assumptions for the one-way parametric ANOVA will hold. Another instance is when the data available for analysis are only ordinal (for example, like a rank) such that the difference between two values does not hold the same meaning as an interval scaled random variable.

There are a number of nonparametric analysis methods dealing with continuous data. The last statistical method included in this chapter is to be used when the continuous outcome is time to an event.

11.14 Hypothesis test of the equality of survival distributions: Logrank test

In Chapter 8 we described analyses to estimate the survival distribution of time to an adverse event. The survival function is the probability that an individual survives (that is, does not experience the event) longer than time t:

$S(t) = P(\text{individual survives longer than } t)$.

In Chapter 10 the use of this method was discussed in terms of estimating the median survival time for participants in a clinical trial. The median survival time can be helpful as a single summary statistic that defines a typical survival time. However, survival distributions may deviate at various points in time. In this section we present the logrank test, which can be used to test the equality of two or more survival distributions. This is not the only test that can be used for this purpose, but it is a natural extension of a method that we have already described and so we have chosen to discuss it.

A test of the equality of two survival distributions would be expressed in terms of the null hypothesis:

$H_0: S_1(t) = S_2(t)$.

If there is sufficient evidence to reject the null hypothesis the alternate hypothesis would be favored:

$H_A: S_1(t) \neq S_2(t)$.

If, in the context of the survival distribution we consider all of the times at which an event occurred and index them as $t(1) < t(2) < t(3) \ldots < t(H)$, it is possible to create a 2×2 classification table for event times $t(h)$, where $h = 1, 2, 3, \ldots, H$ in which the numbers of individuals with and without the event of interest are displayed for each group. Table 11.10 is a sample cross-classification table for time h.

Table 11.10   Cross-classification table of treatment and event at time h

Event?	Group 1	Group 2	Total
Yes	m_{1h}	m_{2h}	m_h
No	$n_{1h} - m_{1h}$	$n_{2h} - m_{2h}$	$n_h - m_h$
	n_{1h}	n_{2h}	n_h

Given the familiar set-up of this contingency table it may not surprise you that we can use the methods of the stratified (Mantel–Haenszel) χ^2 test to define a test statistic. Each of the distinct event times is treated as a stratum, just as we treated investigative centers as strata earlier. The test statistic for the logrank test is:

$$X^2_{LR} = \frac{\left(\sum\limits_{h=1}^{H} \dfrac{n_{h1} \, n_{h2}}{n_h} (\hat{p}_{h1} - \hat{p}_{h2}) \right)^2}{\sum\limits_{h=1}^{H} \dfrac{n_{h1} \, n_{h2}}{n_h - 1} \bar{p}_h \bar{q}_h}.$$

As before, the proportion of observations with the characteristic of interest at time h for the two independent groups is denoted by $\hat{p}_{h1}$ and $\hat{p}_{h2}$, respectively. The overall proportion of individuals with the characteristic of interest within each time h is denoted by $\bar{p}_h$. The overall proportion of individuals without the characteristic of interest within each time h is denoted by $\bar{q}_h = 1 - \bar{p}_h$.

When the sample size is reasonably large ($n > 30$), the test statistic X^2_{LR} follows a χ^2 distribution with 1 df. Values of the test statistic that lie in the critical region are those with $X^2_{LR} > \chi^2_{1,1-\alpha}$, that is, values of χ^2 with 1 df that cut off the upper tail area of α.

To illustrate an example, we use the data from Chapter 9 with some modifications. Although the event of interest in that case was an adverse event, a safety parameter, we can treat it this time as an efficacy parameter.

Event of interest

The event of interest is return to a state of normal blood pressure (by some measure). The treatment administered to the group demonstrating earlier event times would be considered the better treatment.

Design

In this 10-day study of a novel antihypertensive, hypertensive study participants were randomly assigned to test treatment or placebo (10 in each group). They were monitored once a day (in the evening) to measure their resting SBP. The primary endpoint of the study was the time (days) to return to a normal blood pressure.

Data

The event times for the placebo and active groups are provided below ("C" indicates a censored observation):

Placebo: 3(C) 4 5 8 8 8   10(C) 10(C) 10(C) 10(C)
Active: 2   3 3 4 4 4   10(C) 10(C) 10(C) 10(C).

The unique times at which events occurred (not censored observations) are on days 2, 3, 4, 5, and 8. Table 11.11 represents the required contingency tables for the logrank test.

Table 11.11   Contingency table of treatment by event at each event time

Day 2: Normal SBP?	Active	Placebo	Total
Yes	1	0	1
No	9	10	19
	10	10	20

Day 3: Normal SBP?	Active	Placebo	Total
Yes	2	0	2
No	7	10	17
	9	10	19

Day 4: Normal SBP?	Active	Placebo	Total
Yes	3	1	4
No	4	8	12
	7	9	16

Day 5: Normal SBP?	Active	Placebo	Total
Yes	0	1	1
No	4	7	11
	4	8	12

Day 8: Normal SBP?	Active	Placebo	Total
Yes	0	3	3
No	4	4	8
	4	7	11

Note that on day 2 there were 10 participants at risk for the event in the active group. On day 2 one participant in the active group had the event of interest and is therefore removed from the number at risk at later time points. At day 3 there were nine remaining in the active group, two of whom experienced the event, leaving seven in the "risk set" for later times. On day 3 one placebo participant was censored, meaning that day 3 was the last known time at which the participant had not experienced the event. This person is removed from the risk set for later times. The tables are filled out in a similar manner for all times at which the events occurred. The important thing to remember with these contingency tables is that the number in each group decreases for later time points when the individual either had the event or was censored.

The test statistic can be computed by hand, but software is the ideal method, especially for more than a handful of event times. The numerator part of the test statistic would be calculated as:

$$\left[\frac{(10)(10)}{20}(0.10 - 0) + \frac{(9)(10)}{19}(0.22 - 0) + \ldots + \frac{(4)(7)}{11}(0 - 0.43) \right]^2$$

$$= 1.90.$$

The denominator would be calculated as:

$$\frac{(10)(10)}{19}(0.05)(0.95) + \frac{(9)(10)}{18}(0.11)(0.89) + \ldots + \frac{(4)(7)}{10}(0.27)(0.73)$$

$$= 2.286.$$

The test statistic is calculated as the ratio of the two:

$$\chi^2_{LR} = \frac{1.90}{2.286} = 0.831.$$

Interpretation and decision-making

As we saw in Table 10.5, the critical value for the test at an α level of 0.05 is 3.841. As the value of the test statistic $0.831 < 3.841$ there is not enough evidence to reject the null hypothesis.

Small studies such as this can be difficult to interpret. There is a suggestion that the times to response may be shorter with the active treatment, but the hypothesis test did not suggest that the variation seen was attributable to anything but chance given the sample size.

11.15 Review

1. In a therapeutic exploratory trial comparing a single dose of a new analgesic to placebo, 17 individuals were treated with the new analgesic (test treatment) and 15 were treated with the placebo (control). The participants reported the severity of their pain 6 hours after dental surgery using a visual analog scale (VAS). Pain scores on this scale range from 0 to 100, where 0 = "no pain" and 100 = "very severe pain." The mean (SD) pain score in the test treatment group ($n = 17$) was 18 (7). The mean (SD) score in the control group ($n = 15$) was 24 (8). Investigators would like to know if the mean VAS pain score is different between the two populations assumed to be represented by the two samples of study participants.

   (a) What are the null and alternate hypotheses?
   (b) Assume $\alpha = 0.05$. What are the values of the rejection region?
   (c) What assumptions are necessary for the use of the t test?
   (d) What is the value of the test statistic?
   (e) What is your interpretation of the hypothesis test?

2. This ANOVA table represents data from a study of an analgesic. The variable of interest is a pain score (higher values mean greater pain).

Source	SS	df	MS	F
drug	99.89459	2	*	*
Error	*	30	*	
Total	338.57355	32		

   (a) Write in the missing values of the ANOVA table (denoted with *).
   (b) In this study, how many treatments were tested?
   (c) What are the null and alternate hypotheses?
   (d) How many individuals were studied?
   (e) What is the critical region for a test with $\alpha = 0.05$?
   (f) What is the statistical conclusion and interpretation of the hypothesis test?

3. Consider an ANOVA with four treatment groups (30 participants in each), placebo, and three doses of an investigational drug: Low, medium, and high.

(a) What are the null and alternate hypotheses?

(b) What assumptions must be made for the ANOVA?

(c) If the omnibus F test is significant, what are the pairwise comparisons that would be of interest?

(d) Why would Tukey's test be useful to evaluate the pairwise comparisons in (b)?

(e) Assume the mean square within-samples is 20. What is the value of the minimum significant difference – Tukey (MSD_T) that would determine whether pairs of treatments were significantly different?

4. In what situations would the Kruskal–Wallis test be appropriate?

11.16 References

Schork MA, Remington RD (2000). *Statistics with Applications to the Biological and Health Sciences*, 3rd edn. Upper Saddle River, NJ: Prentice-Hall.

Turner JR (2007). *New Drug Development: Design, methodology, and analysis*. Hoboken, NJ: John Wiley & Sons.

12

Additional statistical considerations in clinical trials

12.1 Introduction

The previous chapters have provided you with an introduction to statistical methods and analyses that are commonly used in pharmaceutical clinical trials, with an emphasis on therapeutic confirmatory trials. Although we certainly have not covered all of the analyses that can be conducted in these trials, those that we have discussed have given you a solid foundation that will also enable you to understand the basics of other analyses.

Throughout our discussions we have illustrated the importance of selecting the appropriate analytical strategy that best serves the objective of a given trial. There is hardly a single statistical method that always applies to a given study design or type of data: Rather, the choice of the analytical strategy for a given trial is the result of statistical considerations, clinical judgments, and regulatory standards.

In this chapter we highlight additional statistical considerations relevant to therapeutic confirmatory trials, and other study designs that also provide important information upon which to base decision-making. These additional insights and information build upon the material presented so far. As this chapter is largely conceptual rather than computational, we have included a number of references to guide your further reading.

12.2 Sample size estimation

An important part of study design is the "determination" of the required sample size. Before starting, we should note that we prefer the term "estimation" to the terms "determination" and "calculation" of a sample size. Although a mathematical calculation is certainly performed here, the values that are put into the appropriate formula are chosen by the researcher.

It is also appropriate to note that not all clinical trials utilize formal sample size estimation methods. In many instances (for example, FTIH studies) the sample size is determined on the basis of logistical constraints and the size of the study thought to be necessary to gather sufficient evidence (for example, pharmacokinetic profiles) to rule out unwanted effects. However, when the objective of the clinical trial (for example, a superiority trial) is to claim that a true treatment effect exists while at the same time limiting the probability of committing type I or II errors (α and β), there are computational methods used to estimate the required sample size. The use of formal sample size estimation is required in therapeutic confirmatory trials, this book's major focus, and strongly suggested in therapeutic exploratory trials.

12.2.1 Sample size for continuous outcomes in superiority trials

Consider the simple case of a superiority trial of an investigational drug (the test treatment) being compared with placebo with respect to a continuous outcome (for example, change from baseline SBP). The null hypothesis typically tested in such a trial and its complementary alternate hypothesis are:

H_0: $\mu_{TEST} - \mu_{PLACEBO} = \Delta$

H_A: $\mu_{TEST} - \mu_{PLACEBO} \neq \Delta$.

There are a number of values of the treatment effect (delta or Δ) that could lead to rejection of the null hypothesis of no difference between the two means. For purposes of estimating a sample size the power of the study (that is, the probability that the null hypothesis of no difference is rejected given that the alternate hypothesis is true) is calculated for a *specific* value of Δ. In the case of a superiority trial, this specific value represents the minimally clinically relevant difference between groups that, if found to be plausible on the basis of the sample data through construction of a confidence interval, would be viewed as evidence of a definitive and clinically important treatment effect.

Another way of stating this is that, if the true difference in population means is as large as a specific value of Δ proposed as clinically important, we would like to find the sample size such that the null hypothesis would be rejected $(1 - \beta)\%$ of the time. The sample size must also be chosen so that α is maintained at an acceptably low value.

The sample size formula required to test (two-sided) the equality of two means from random variables with normal distributions is:

$$n \text{ per group} = \frac{2\sigma^2(Z_{1-\alpha/2} + Z_\beta)^2}{\Delta^2}.$$

In this equation:

- n is the sample size per group
- σ^2 is the assumed variance
- $Z_{1-\alpha/2}$ is the value of the Z distribution that defines an area of size $\alpha/2$ in the upper tail of the Z distribution
- Z_β is the value of the Z distribution that defines an area of size β in the lower tail of the Z distribution
- Δ is the difference in means that we would like to detect, if it exists, by virtue of rejecting the null hypothesis.

Both α and β are design parameters, and are chosen at the discretion of those designing the trials. In confirmatory trials, α is 0.05 and β is typically 0.10 or 0.20 (meaning that the study has 90% or 80% power, respectively). The choices of σ and Δ are not quite as straightforward, because the range of possible values is outside the direct control of the study planner. The standard deviation σ must be estimated using (any) available data, and the value of the treatment effect Δ is determined using clinical judgment.

It is important to note that, all other things being equal, the following statements are true:

- The required sample size increases as the variance increases.
- The required sample size increases as the size of the treatment effect decreases.
- The required sample size increases as α decreases.
- The required sample size increases as the power $(1 - \beta)$ increases.

This sample size formula can be illustrated with the following example. Suppose that, in exploratory therapeutic trials of a new antihypertensive, the standard deviation for the between-treatment difference in mean change from baseline SBP was estimated to be 50 mmHg. After reviewing the literature and consulting with regulatory authorities, it is agreed that a between-treatment group difference in mean change from baseline (that is, the treatment effect) of at least 20 mmHg would be considered a clinically important benefit of a new drug to treat hypertension. The study sponsor is planning a confirmatory trial comparing the test drug with a placebo and would like to have an excellent chance (90%) of claiming that the treatment effect is not zero if the drug is as efficacious as they believe. From the expression above, the sample size required per group is:

$$n = \frac{2(50)^2(1.96 + 1.645)^2}{20^2}$$

= 133 per group for a total of 266 individuals.

This sample size estimate would be described in the study protocol in this manner:

A total of 266 participants (133 per group) will be randomized in this study in a 1:1 ratio to test and placebo. Assuming a common standard deviation of 50 mmHg, this sample size will provide 90% power to detect a between-group difference in mean change from baseline of at least 20 mmHg using a two-sided test of size $\alpha = 0.05$.

The power of the study is the probability of rejecting the null hypothesis of no difference in means, assuming that the true difference is at least 20 mmHg and the estimated variance is correct. As we have seen in this book, all estimates have sampling variation associated with them. Therefore, it can be helpful to see how the power to detect a difference of 20 mmHg varies as a function of sample size using three different values of the standard deviation. The impact of these two factors on the power can be seen in Figure 12.1, a graphical display called a power curve. Figure 12.1 is a compelling illustration of the importance of the assumed value of the standard deviation. Consider that, in the design of the study in our worked example, the assumed standard deviation of 50 mmHg led to a sample size of 133 per group for a power of 90% to detect the important difference of 20 mmHg. If the standard deviation was underestimated such that it was really 70 mmHg, the study would really only have 64% power to detect the difference that was considered important. Of course, this cannot be known in advance of a trial, but a post hoc examination of the study data, and a possible re-estimation of the standard deviation, can better inform future trials and increase the probability that they will be successful.

12.2.2 Sample size for binary outcomes in superiority trials

We have encountered a number of statistical methods used to test the difference between two population proportions. Suppose that we are interested in estimating the sample size for a superiority trial of an investigational drug (the test treatment), which will be compared with placebo with respect to a binary outcome, for example, proportion of individuals attaining a goal SBP. The null hypothesis and its complementary alternate hypothesis typically tested in such a trial are:

$$H_0: p_{TEST} - p_{PLACEBO} = 0.$$
$$H_A: p_{TEST} - p_{PLACEBO} \neq 0.$$

As in Chapter 10, the population proportions for each of two independent groups are represented by p_{TEST} and $p_{PLACEBO}$. Just as for the case of continuous outcomes, the power of the study is calculated for a *specific* value of $\Delta = p_{TEST} - p_{PLACEBO}$, a value that is considered the minimally clinically relevant difference (CRD).

The sample size formula required to test (two-sided) the equality of two population proportions used here is cited from Fleiss et al. (2003).

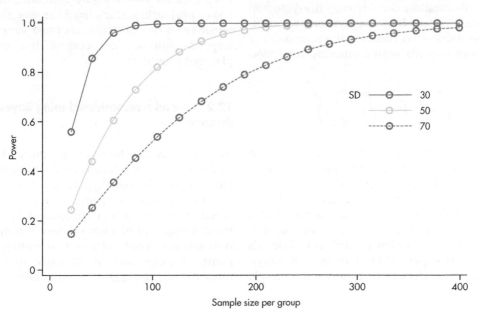

Figure 12.1 Power curve ($\Delta = 20$ mmHg) as a function of sample size (n) for $\sigma = 30$ mmHg, 50 mmHg, and 70 mmHg

The calculation involves two parts. The first makes use of a normal approximation:

$$n' = \frac{(Z_{1-\alpha/2}\sqrt{2\bar{p}\bar{q}} + Z_\beta\sqrt{p_{TEST}q_{TEST} + p_{PLACEBO}q_{PLACEBO}})^2}{(\Delta)^2},$$

where:

$$\Delta = p_{TEST} - p_{PLACEBO},$$

$$\bar{p} = \frac{p_{TEST} + p_{PLACEBO}}{2},$$

$$\bar{q} = 1 - \bar{p},$$

$$q_{TEST} = 1 - p_{TEST},$$

and

$$q_{PLACEBO} = 1 - p_{PLACEBO}.$$

Note that the sample size depends not only on the value of Δ, but also on the individual proportions themselves. The implication of this is that the sponsor must make a reasonable estimate of the response in the placebo group (that is, $p_{PLACEBO}$) and then postulate a value of Δ that is clinically relevant. The corresponding value of p_{TEST} can be obtained by subtraction. This first sample size estimate (n') can be improved through the use of a continuity correction, which gives more accurate results when a discrete distribution (in this case the binomial distribution) is used to approximate a continuous distribution (in this case the normal). The sample size formula with continuity correction is:

$$n \text{ per group} = \frac{n'}{4}\left(1 + \sqrt{1 + \frac{4}{n'|\Delta|}}\right)^2.$$

In a confirmatory efficacy trial the study sponsor would like to evaluate a test treatment (an anti-hypertensive) versus placebo with respect to a binary outcome of attaining a goal SBP $\leq$ 140 mmHg. After reviewing several sources of data the sponsor estimates that the placebo response will be around 0.20 (that is, 20% of individuals will attain the goal without medical therapy). The sponsor would like to estimate the sample size required to detect a difference in response rates of 0.20 – that is, the postulated value of the response for test treatment is 0.40. As the study is a confirmatory trial, 90% power is recommended and the test will be a two-sided test with $\alpha = 0.05$.

Substituting these values into the formula for the per-group sample size, we obtain:

$$n' = \frac{(1.96\sqrt{2(0.30)(0.70)} + 1.645\sqrt{(0.40)(0.60) + (0.20)(0.80)})^2}{(0.20)^2} = 306.$$

With a continuity correction the result is:

$$n = \frac{306}{4}\left(1 + \sqrt{1 + \frac{4}{306(0.20)}}\right)^2 = 316 \text{ individuals per group.}$$

This sample size estimate would be described in the study protocol in this manner:

A total of 632 individuals (316 per group) will be randomized in this study in a 1:1 ratio to the test treatment and the placebo treatment. Assuming a placebo response rate of 20%, this sample size will provide 90% power to detect a between-group difference in response rates of 20% using a two-sided test with $\alpha = 0.05$.

As for continuous data, a power curve can be generated for a number of scenarios for binary outcomes. As seen in Figure 12.2, the power of a test of proportions (for a fixed value of Δ) is quite sensitive to the particular assumed value of the response rate in the control (for example, placebo) group.

12.2.3 α and β reconsidered using Bayes' theorem

After a study has been completed, a statistical analysis provides a means either to reject or to fail to reject the null hypothesis. The statistical conclusion will, in part, be used to justify whether or not further investment is made in the development of a test product. A sound business strategy would dictate that further investment be made only if objective information from the study suggests it. Inferential statistics

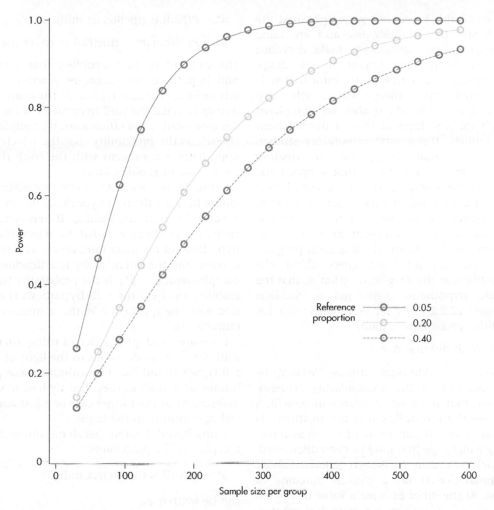

Figure 12.2   Power curve ($\Delta = 0.10$) as a function of sample size (n) for $p_{TEST} = 0.05$, $p_{TEST} = 0.20$, and $p_{TEST} = 0.40$

(for example, a hypothesis test) is the appropriate means to differentiate a real effect from a chance effect. For the remainder of this section we investigate the wisdom of adopting such a policy, using an approach similar to that described by Lee and Zelen (2000). In particular, the remainder of this section will address the following two questions:

1. How likely is the sponsor to be misled by the result of the statistical conclusion from a hypothesis test with design parameters α and β?
2. What is the role of accumulating evidence about the true treatment effect on the credibility of results from a hypothesis test?

Throughout this book we have emphasized the role of Statistics in designing and analyzing studies that enable sponsors to make decisions about the future development of new drugs. When developing a new drug, information is accumulated over time, with each step informing the next. As studies are completed through various stages of clinical development (FTIH studies, therapeutic exploratory studies, and one or more therapeutic confirmatory studies) evidence is gathered that supports the efficacy of the new drug. This is true only if new studies are planned because such a promise exists. Hence we assume over time, with the accumulation of new information, that various scientists involved in the development program *could* make an informed guess about the probability that the drug works (that is, that the alternate hypotheses considered in Sections 12.2.1 and 12.2.2 really represent the truth). Let us call this probability, τ (tau).

τ = probability that $\Delta \neq 0$.

However, as additional studies would be conducted only if the accumulating evidence suggested that there was a treatment benefit, τ represents the probability that the treatment is truly effective. We can think of $\tau = 0$ as representing a molecule that has just been discovered, for which no evidence has been generated about its ultimate effect on a clinical outcome of interest. At the other extreme a value of $\tau = 0.8$ represents a drug for which a great deal of information has been collected and most of the data support a beneficial effect of the treatment. Values of τ around 0.5 may represent a drug for which some (or limited) data support a treatment benefit.

Consider the following probabilities, which express the likelihood of the true state of affairs given the statistical conclusion at the end of the study:

$\alpha^* = P(\text{Null is true}|\text{Reject null})$

$\beta^* = P(\text{Alternate is true}|\text{Fail to reject the null})$.

The value α^* is the probability that a rejected null hypothesis (for example, p value $\leq \alpha$) is misleading. That is, it represents the chance that, having rejected the null hypothesis of no effect, the treatment is not efficacious. Its complement, $(1 - \alpha^*)$, is the probability that the rejected null hypothesis is consistent with the truth (that is, the treatment is efficacious).

Similarly, the value β^* is the probability that failure to reject the null hypothesis (for example, p value $> \alpha$) is misleading. It represents the chance that, having failed to reject the null hypothesis of no effect (and acting as if the null is true), the treatment really is efficacious. The complement, $(1 - \beta^*)$, is the probability that our inability to reject the null hypothesis is consistent with the truth (that is, the treatment is not efficacious).

If we are to adopt a policy of using inferential statistics to make decisions in the light of uncertainty, we would like to minimize these probabilities, α^* and β^*, as they directly lead to wasted investment in the former case or a lost commercial opportunity in the latter.

Using Bayes' theorem (recall our discussions in Chapter 6), the probability,

$\alpha^* = P(\text{Null is true}|\text{Reject null})$,

can be written as:

$$\alpha^* = P(\text{Reject null} \mid \text{Null is true}) \frac{P(\text{Null is true})}{P(\text{Reject null})}.$$

Recall also from Chapter 6 that the marginal probability of an event can be expressed as a series of conditional probabilities as long as the conditional events are mutually exclusive and exhaustive. This allows us to express the probability,

$$P(\text{Reject null}) = P(\text{Reject null}) \mid \text{Null is true}) \, P(\text{Null is true}) + P(\text{Reject null}) \mid \text{Alternative is true})P(\text{Alternative is true}).$$

Finally, putting this entire expression together we have:

$$\alpha^* = \frac{P(\text{Reject null}) \mid \text{Null is true})P(\text{Null is true})}{P(\text{Reject null}) \mid \text{Null is true})P(\text{Null is true}) + P(\text{Reject null}) \mid \text{Alternative is true})P(\text{Alternative is true})}.$$

This probability can then be expressed as a function of the design parameters, α and β, and the estimated probability that the alternative is true, τ:

$$\alpha^* = \frac{\alpha(1 - \tau)}{\alpha(1 - \tau) + (1 - \beta)\tau}.$$

Bayes' theorem and algebra can be used in a similar fashion to obtain the following expression for β*:

$$\beta^* = \frac{\beta\tau}{\beta\tau + (1 - \alpha)(1 - \tau)}.$$

We can use these two expressions to answer the questions posed at the beginning of this section. The first of these is:

> How likely is the sponsor to be misled by the result of the statistical conclusion from a hypothesis test?

The short answer is that it depends on the power (and therefore the sample size) of the study. To illustrate this, assume that the value of the design parameter α is dictated by regulatory concerns, which is reasonable especially in confirmatory trials. Further, before a new study is completed there is still some doubt as to whether the new treatment is efficacious, such that the value of τ is conjectured to be 0.5. Resulting values of the error rates, α* and β*, are presented in Table 12.1 as a function of the power (or, equivalently, β) of the study.

The key message from Table 12.1 is that the probability of both errors decreases with increases in statistical power. A study planned with power of 0.5 and a statistical decision to reject the null (for example, because *p* value ≤ 0.05) yields a probability of 0.09 that the two treatments are not significantly different. In contrast, a study with power 0.9 and the same outcome (to reject the null) yields a probability of 0.05 that the two treatments are really significantly different. Even though the statistical test has indicated that further investment should be considered because the test treatment appears to be efficacious, the underpowered study leads to an unwise decision 1.8 times (0.09/0.05) more often than the conventionally powered study. Similar statements can be made about unwisely abandoning an efficacious product by examining the values of β*. Another way of stating this is that the greater the statistical power for a study, the more reliable the decisions made as a result.

Now consider the second question:

> What is the role of accumulating evidence about the true treatment effect on the credibility of results from a hypothesis test?

To address this question, the error rates, α* and β*, are presented in Table 12.2 as a function of τ (a measure of the likelihood the treatment is efficacious) with power 0.9 and α = 0.05, typical values for highly powered studies. An examination of a couple of cases will help to answer this question.

When τ = 0 there is a great deal of uncertainty about the probability that the treatment is efficacious. This situation may apply when there is no experience with the test treatment or some experience with mixed or poor results. When a statistically significant result leading to rejection of the null hypothesis has been observed in this situation, the sponsor will be misled into thinking that the drug is effective when it really is not with probability 0.33. On the other hand,

Table 12.1 Error rates α^* and β^* as a function of β ($a = 0.05$ and $\tau = 0.5$)

β	1 − β (power)	α*	1 − α*	β*	1 − β*
0.5	0.5	0.09	0.91	0.34	0.66
0.4	0.6	0.08	0.92	0.30	0.70
0.3	0.7	0.07	0.93	0.24	0.76
0.2	0.8	0.06	0.94	0.17	0.83
0.1	0.9	0.05	0.95	0.10	0.90

Table 12.2   Error rates α^* and β^* as a function of τ ($\alpha = 0.05$ and $1 - \beta = 0.9$)

τ	α^*	$1 - \alpha^*$	β^*	$1 - \beta^*$
0.1	0.33	0.67	0.01	0.99
0.3	0.11	0.89	0.04	0.96
0.5	0.05	0.95	0.10	0.90
0.7	0.02	0.98	0.20	0.80
0.9	0.01	0.99	0.49	0.51

failure to reject the null hypothesis in this situation will mislead the sponsor who abandons development with probability 0.01.

Once some studies have been completed and evidence has been gathered to support the efficacy of the new treatment, the value of τ may be around 0.5. This value represents at least moderate evidence that the treatment is truly efficacious. When a statistically significant result leading to rejection of the null hypothesis has been observed in this situation, the sponsor will be misled into thinking that the drug is effective when it really is not, with probability only 0.05. This reflects previous experience, which has shown that the treatment provides a benefit. Failure to reject the null hypothesis will mislead the sponsor who then abandons development as a result, with probability 0.10. Again, this probability reflects previous experience because the new evidence contradicts the prior belief that the treatment is efficacious so that acting on the new study result may be misleading.

The case where $\tau = 0.9$ represents nearly certain knowledge. It is hard to understand why any additional data would be required in this instance. However, an examination of the error rates α^* and β^* in this situation is illuminating. Rejection of the null hypothesis would come as no surprise so that such a result would rarely be misleading. Failure to reject the null hypothesis would come as a surprise because it is almost known with certainty that the null is false. Thus, this information is too bad to be true and acting on it is unwise.

The probability τ is analogous to the underlying prevalence of disease in a population. In the setting of diagnostic testing, α^* and β^* refer to the positive and negative predictive values of a test. As illustrated in Chapter 6, when evaluating a diagnostic test, even high values of sensitivity and specificity can lead to skepticism about a positive test when the prevalence of the underlying disease is low.

In a similar manner, τ should serve to temper the enthusiasm of study sponsors who have observed a new positive study result, especially early in development programs. It can be used to calibrate the credibility of statistical results. Without sufficient prior information about the treatment even a statistically significant result can lead to poor (and expensive) business decisions. When a sponsor desires either to continue or to discontinue development of a new drug as a result of a study, the results in this section point to the importance of power. Despite their other benefits, exploratory therapeutic trials, which tend to be small in size (and therefore have low power), are poor studies on which to make business decisions. Small, early clinical studies may provide some evidence on which to base future research, including τ. However, once that is done, there is no substitute for definitive, highly powered studies in appropriate populations, using acceptable clinically relevant endpoints. In short, power, a statistical design parameter, has a **direct** bearing on the quality of decision-making. We believe that recognition of this relationship is very much underappreciated, and that it has a profound bearing on the way sound business decisions should be made.

12.2.4 Importance of collaboration in sample size estimation

Sample size estimation requires the input of a number of specialists involved with the development of new drugs. The estimate of the standard deviation can be informed by exploratory therapeutic trials of the same drug or by literature reviews of similar drugs. Synthesis of these data from a number of sources requires statistical and clinical judgments. As was seen in Figure 12.1 the estimate of the standard deviation has an important effect on the sample size. Study teams should understand the sources of variability in the response variable and attempt to minimize unwanted variability.

The definition of the minimally clinically relevant difference of interest involves clinical, medical, and regulatory experience and judgments. The appropriate sample size formula depends on the test of interest and should take into account the need for multiple comparisons (either among treatments or with respect to multiple examinations of the data). The project statistician provides critical guidance in this area.

It is appropriate to note here that in some instances the sample size may not be completely dictated by the statistical requirements for a given power calculation. The ICH has published a guidance document (ICH Guidance E1, 1994) applicable to drugs given chronically. This guidance specifies the minimum number of individuals who should be exposed for certain periods of time so that potential adverse events (AEs) may come to light before the drug is marketed. The need for a larger safety database may supersede the sample size required to demonstrate a statistically significant and clinically relevant treatment effect.

In summary, sample size estimation requires the input of a number of disciplines involved in the design of clinical trials.

12.3 Multicenter studies

A certain number of participants need to be recruited for any given trial. In Section 12.2 we discussed sample size estimation, which takes into account a number of considerations that are important not only to the statistician but also to the clinical scientist and the regulator. Once determined, the value produced by this process of estimation is incorporated into the study protocol.

We have seen that relatively small numbers of participants are recruited for early phase trials (perhaps 20–80 in FTIH studies and 200–300 in early Phase II studies), and relatively larger numbers are recruited for therapeutic confirmatory trials (perhaps 3000–5000). It is relatively easy to recruit between 20 and 80 participants at a single investigational site. Indeed, as we noted in Section 7.3, conducting a FTIH study at a single center enhances consistency with respect to management of participants, study conduct, and assessment of AEs, and provides for frequent and careful monitoring of study participants. However, it is not feasible to recruit 3000–5000 participants at a single investigational site, so multicenter studies are typical at this stage of clinical development programs.

As for so many of the topics that we have discussed, multicenter studies have both advantages and disadvantages. Let us consider the disadvantages first and then focus on the advantages. The major disadvantage relates to the logistic demands of coordinating a multicenter trial. The rarer the medical condition of interest in the trial, the more sites that will probably be needed because fewer individuals will likely be available at each site. It is not unusual to have between 50 and 100 investigational sites participating in some trials. These sites may be scattered across a country and, increasingly, they may be scattered across several countries and continents. This occurrence has many consequences, including:

- All investigational sites must obtain approval from their investigational review board (IRB) to conduct their portion of the trial.
- The drug products used in the trial must be shipped to all sites, which may entail dealing with customs and import/export controls.
- If some sites speak different languages, all relevant issues must be addressed (for example, translating the informed consent form into each language).
- All principal investigators (one from each site) and certain members of their staff must receive training that will attempt to ensure consistency of all methodology used in the trial. Investigator meetings are held accordingly.
- Multicenter studies benefit from (rely on) the use of central labs to analyze certain samples taken during the trial (for example, blood samples). This is a complex shipping problem, especially when samples must be transported to the central laboratory under certain conditions and very quickly from distant locations.

Each of the above considerations adds considerably to the total cost of a multicenter trial.

From a statistical point of view, while every attempt is made to standardize the implementation of study methodology at all sites, perfect standardization is not a realistic expectation. Although simpler is usually better, study protocols often become complex during their development, and different investigational sites will likely differ in their implementation of some procedural aspects. This occurrence introduces extraneous variability into data collected and analyzed. Extensions of some of the analysis methods described in this book can be used to account for center-to-center variability, including multi-way ANOVA models for continuous variables, stratified χ^2 tests for categorical variables, and stratified log-rank tests for time-to-event analyses. Various other methodological controls can be introduced in an attempt to minimize such extraneous variability, but the success of any control strategy is unlikely to be perfect.

For these and other reasons, we believe that, if it were possible to conduct a trial requiring 3000–5000 participants at a single investigational site, sponsors would do so, even though this statement is at odds with the commonly cited major advantage of multicenter trials, which is that they enable greater generalization of results obtained from the trial. It is statistically possible to assess the treatment effect at each investigational site as well as assessing it using the data from all sites, although a given site needs to have reasonable enrollment for the treatment effect calculated from its participants to be meaningful. If similar treatment effects are observed at sites that tended to enroll relatively older individuals, relatively younger ones, ethnically homogeneous samples, ethnically heterogeneous samples, with less or more experience of treating the designated indication, and so forth, it is reasonable to have a certain degree of faith that the treatment effect is generalizable to the eventual patient population if and when the drug is approved for marketing.

12.4 Analysis populations

Various analysis populations for clinical trial data can be defined and are used in statistical analyses, including:

- The intent-to-treat (ITT) population: This comprises all participants in a clinical trial who were randomized to a treatment group, regardless of whether any data were actually collected from them.
- The safety population: This is a subset of the ITT population, defined as the population of participants who received at least one dose of a study treatment.
- The per-protocol population (also known as the efficacy or evaluable population): This is also a subset of the ITT population, and comprises individuals whose participation and involvement in the trial were considered to comply with significant requirements and activities detailed in the study protocol. Participants would typically be excluded from the per-protocol population if they exhibited poor dosing compliance, missed a number of clinic visits, or used prohibited medications that may interfere with the evaluation of the test treatment.

Both the ITT and the safety populations can be used in the analysis of safety data. The ITT and per-protocol population are typically used in the analysis of efficacy data.

12.4.1 Using both ITT and per-protocol populations in efficacy analyses

In therapeutic confirmatory trial efficacy, the same analyses are typically conducted twice, using data from the ITT population and data from the per-protocol population (see Turner, 2007). The analyses conducted using the ITT population are considered to be the primary analyses because ITT analysis provides a conservative strategy in the sense that it tends to bias against finding the results that the researcher "hopes" for, particularly in the case of superiority trials. The conservative nature of ITT analysis is deemed particularly appropriate when attempting to demonstrate the efficacy of an investigational drug because these data do not favor the desired outcome. Then, if there is compelling evidence of the drug's efficacy, this evidence will be particularly noteworthy. The ITT population is the most appropriate sample population from which to make inferences to the population of patients who may receive the drug if and when it receives marketing approval.

Having conducted primary analyses using the ITT population it is then appropriate to conduct secondary analyses using the per-protocol population, the subset of participants whose participation in the trial was compliant with the study protocol. This analysis is regarded as less conservative than ITT analysis because analysis of the per-protocol population may maximize the opportunity to demonstrate efficacy: The per-protocol population is the population in which the treatment is likely to perform best.

Regulatory authorities are encouraged if the results from the ITT efficacy analysis and the per-protocol efficacy analysis are similar, and their overall confidence in the trial results is increased. However, if they are not similar, questions may be raised as to why they are not. Some of these questions are (Turner, 2007):

- Is the per-protocol population a lot smaller than the ITT population (it will almost certainly be somewhat smaller)?
- If so, were there a lot of major protocol violations?
- Were a lot of participants removed for the same protocol violation?
- Were many of the participants with protocol violations enrolled at the same investigative site?
- Are there any systematic problems in the conduct of the trial?

All of the issues addressed by these questions can reduce the regulatory reviewers' overall confidence in the trial's findings.

12.4.2 Proper and improper subgroup analysis

Investigators may be interested to examine potential differences among groups of participants according to some characteristic. For example, there may be differences in the response to treatment according to age. An analysis to investigate such a phenomenon could involve separate analyses for participants aged 18–34, 35–54, 55–74, and 75 years and older. Similar analyses could be presented in which participants are grouped according to some measure of disease severity. Results such as these should be interpreted with caution because the more subgroups that are examined the greater the chance of discovering a false positive (recall our earlier discussions of multiple comparisons).

Although we have not discussed this topic, differences in treatment effects may be tested to see if they are homogeneous across the various subgroups. This test is called a test of the treatment-by-subgroup (for example, treatment by age) interaction. It is useful because it can rule out, using a hypothesis test, apparent differences among subgroups of subgroups that really represent random variation. Citing from the ICH Guidance E9 (1994, p 27):

The treatment effect itself may also vary with subgroup or covariate – for example, the effect may decrease with age or may be larger in a particular diagnostic category of subjects. In some cases such interactions are anticipated or are of particular prior interest (e.g. geriatrics), and hence a subgroup analysis, or a statistical model including interactions, is part of the planned confirmatory analysis. In most cases, however, subgroup or interaction analyses are exploratory and should be clearly identified as such; they should explore the uniformity of any treatment effects found overall. In general, such analyses should proceed first through the addition of interaction terms to the statistical model in question, complemented by additional exploratory analysis within relevant subgroups of subjects, or within strata defined by the covariates. When exploratory, these analyses should be interpreted cautiously; any conclusion of treatment efficacy (or lack thereof) or safety based solely on exploratory subgroup analyses are unlikely to be accepted.

These cautions having been noted, some unexpected subgroup findings may actually reveal important findings that should be further investigated in additional studies. This can be especially important when there is evidence of different safety profiles among subgroups. Matthews (2006) distinguished between two sorts of subgroup formation, and hence analysis:

- a limited number of subgroups identified *a priori* with an apparent biological/clinical reason for the difference of interest
- subgroups whose apparent importance is retrospective, and arises only as a result of doing analyses.

If the treatment effect appears to differ across subgroups identified in the first way, the phenomenon "should be taken much more seriously" than if the subgroups came to light via the second process (Matthews, 2006, p 171).

12.5 Dealing with missing data

For various reasons there are often participants in a trial for whom a complete set of data is not collected. This is the province of missing data. When conducting efficacy analyses we need to address this issue, and the way(s) in which it is addressed can influence the regulatory reviewers' interpretation of the analyses presented. The issue of missing data is problematic in clinical research because humans have complex lives. Human participants may choose to leave a study early or be unable to attend a specific visit, both situations leading to missing data. Nonclinical research involves tighter experimental control in which the subjects (animals) do not have the ability voluntarily to leave the study early.

Piantadosi (2005) observed that there are only three generic analytic approaches to addressing the issue of missing data:

1. Disregard the observations that contain a missing value.

2. Disregard a particular variable if it has a high frequency of missing values.
3. Replace the missing values by some appropriate value.

The last of these approaches is called imputation of missing values. As Piantadosi (2005, p 400) commented, although this approach sounds a lot like "making up data," when done properly it may be the most sensible strategy. While techniques for addressing missing data can be technically difficult, one commonly used, simple imputation method is called last observation carried forward (LOCF). In a study with repeated measurements over time, the most recent observation replaces any subsequent missing observations (Piantadosi, 2005).

An assumption of such an imputation strategy is that the future course of the individual's condition can reasonably be predicted by the last known state. If participants in the test group drop out of the study more often than those on placebo because the test treatment has failed, such an assumption may not be realistic. It is possible that participants who dropped out for treatment failure actually got worse than when they left the study. A commonly proposed strategy is to use a number of imputation methods and see how the analysis results change as a result. If the results of this sensitivity analysis suggest that the overall conclusion remains the same, it is less important how the missing data are managed.

Differential rates of loss to follow-up among groups or high rates in any single group complicate the management of missing data. Strategies that minimize the chance that participants will leave a study prematurely should be considered at the design and protocol writing stage, and incorporated in the protocol as appropriate.

A number of approaches to dealing with missing data are described by Molenberghs and Kenward (2007).

12.5.1 The importance of study conduct and study monitoring

While there are widely accepted methodologies for dealing with missing data, it is certainly preferable to have as many "actual" data as possible. This simple point underscores the critical nature of study conduct. All procedures detailed in the study protocol need to be followed, and all data required need to be collected to the greatest degree possible (there will always be occasional genuine reasons why this was not possible in a specific situation).

This need for as complete a dataset as possible underscores the importance of the clinical monitor. Two related and critical responsibilities of clinical monitors are to ensure that all sites in the trial follow the study protocol, and to check that the required data are recorded as and when they should be. A good monitor will spot the absence of recorded data sooner rather than later, which considerably increases the likelihood of locating and subsequently recording those data.

12.6 Primary and secondary objectives and endpoints

A given trial is conducted to collect optimum quality data with which to answer an identified and important research question. The data collected are intended to provide the most accurate answers to the research questions posed. A study protocol will often include both primary and secondary objectives, and also the associated primary and secondary endpoints.

12.6.1 The primary objective and endpoint

Turner (2007) noted that, in a very real sense, all the clinical studies that are conducted before a therapeutic confirmatory trial is undertaken have one purpose: To allow the primary objective in the therapeutic confirmatory trial to be stated as simply as possible. An objective that can be stated simply can be tested simply, that is, in a straightforward and unambiguous manner. This is a highly desirable attribute in a primary objective.

By the time a therapeutic confirmatory trial is appropriate it should be possible to state a single primary objective (or perhaps two if the sponsor really feels that this is appropriate) that is clinically relevant and biologically plausible. Having stated this primary objective, deciding upon the primary endpoint should be straightforward. Deciding on the appropriate study design and the associated statistical analyses should also be straightforward. Throughout this book we have focused on the development of a new antihypertensive drug. The primary objective of a therapeutic confirmatory trial in this therapeutic area will be to determine if the investigational drug does indeed lower blood pressure, and the associated endpoint(s) may be a certain magnitude reduction in systolic blood pressure (SBP), diastolic BP (DBP), or both.

At the analysis stage of the trial this endpoint provides the focus for rigorous statistical analysis and interpretation (Machin and Campbell, 2005). Formal hypothesis testing will be employed to determine the presence or absence of a statistically significant difference between the mean decrease seen in the drug treatment group and that seen in the control group. In addition, the clinical significance of the treatment effect will be addressed.

Having a single primary objective has an additional advantage in a study. It means that sample-size estimation can be based on that objective and the associated estimated treatment effect of interest (recall our discussion of sample-size estimation in Section 12.2). Having multiple primary endpoints requires adjustments for multiplicity and can be difficult to interpret if only one of multiple primary endpoints is found to have a statistically significant effect.

12.6.2 Secondary objectives and endpoints

In addition to the primary objective, a study may have a small number of secondary objectives. A secondary endpoint will be associated with each secondary objective. For example, assessments of quality of life may fall under the category of secondary objectives. (In some studies quality of life may be the primary objective: It is simply used here as a realistic example.) Quality of life (QoL) is an extremely important consideration, and particularly so in long-term pharmaceutical therapy. Even if a disease or condition cannot be cured, keeping the symptomatology at acceptable levels can be considered a tremendous success.

Formal hypothesis testing is less likely to occur for secondary endpoints. Descriptive statistics are more likely to be presented. It is also possible that findings of particular interest may lead to a primary objective in a subsequent trial. That is, these data are more suited to hypothesis formation than hypothesis testing. It is important to emphasize here that data leading to the formation of a hypothesis cannot be used to test that hypothesis: As just noted, a new dataset must be generated.

12.6.3 How many objectives should we list?

The number of objectives that should be incorporated in any clinical trial is often a topic of considerable debate among study teams (Turner, 2007). Some members will likely argue that, while taking all the trouble to conduct the trial, why not collect as much data as possible and ask as many questions as possible? This approach leads to a large number of study objectives, sometimes broken down into primary objectives, secondary objectives, and even tertiary objectives. It is certainly legitimate in some studies to be interested in more than one primary endpoint and possibly in several secondary endpoints. However, from a statistical point of view, increasing the number of objectives leads to serious problems, and it can compromise the weight of any particular piece of evidence that is eventually presented to regulatory agencies.

In Chapter 11 we discussed the issue of multiple comparisons and multiplicity in the context of pairwise treatment comparisons following a significant omnibus F test. When we adopt the 5% significance level ($\alpha = 0.05$), by definition it is likely that a type I error will occur when 20 separate comparisons are made. That is, a statistically significant result will be "found" by chance alone. The greater the number of objectives presented in a study protocol, the greater the number of comparisons that will be

made at the analysis stage, and the greater the chance of a type I error. Machin and Campbell (2005) commented: "If there are too many endpoints defined, the multiplicity of comparisons then made at the analysis stage may result in spurious statistical significance."

The concern of multiplicity can also apply to studies in which data are examined during the study at interim time points. Interim analyses are discussed in Section 12.9.

12.7 Evaluating baseline characteristics

It is common practice in analyses of clinical data to inspect the distributions of baseline characteristics – for example, demographics and measures of disease severity – through the use of descriptive summary statistics. This is an important analysis because it helps to describe the sample representing the target population of interest. If the sample is representative of the target population the inferences drawn from the study will be considered relevant.

Sometimes the baseline homogeneity of these characteristics is assessed using a hypothesis test, for example, an omnibus F-test from a one-way ANOVA testing for differences in age. If a "significant" result is found, some researchers might offer this as evidence that something went awry with the randomization process. However, this view has two problems: One is that multiple hypothesis tests can lead to spurious findings or "false positives;" the second is that, on any given single instance, a proper randomization cannot ensure that this possibility does not occur. What randomization can ensure is that, on average, over all possible randomizations, distributions of baseline characteristics will be homogeneous across groups. This result is all that is required for proper statistical inferences. Senn (1997) emphasized that "inferential statistics calculated from a clinical trial make an allowance for differences between patients and that this allowance will be correct on average if randomization has been employed." It is worth noting that standard errors represent such allowances.

When there is evidence to suggest a baseline imbalance with respect to a characteristic that may influence an important outcome of the study, such as the primary efficacy endpoint, some investigators choose to examine the effect of this factor in additional statistical analyses. Possible approaches to this would include ANOVA or analysis of covariance (ANCOVA) in which a continuous variable (for example, age) is adjusted for in assessing the main effect of interest, that is, the treatment effect for the primary outcome variable.

Such a step is not required from a statistical point of view, as a result of the role of a properly executed randomization process, but it can be comforting if it supports the clinical relevance of the effect after adjustment for the baseline covariate. If there are specific explanatory factors that are suspected of having an effect on the outcome of interest at the start of a study, it is advisable to incorporate them into the overall study design (for example, through stratified randomization). A brief discussion of this topic has been published by Roberts and Torgerson (1999). The EMEA CPMP has also published a guidance document on baseline covariates (EMEA CPMP 2003).

12.8 Equivalence and noninferiority study designs

The goal of equivalence trials is to demonstrate that a new (test) drug (T) and an active comparator drug (C) are "equivalent" or have a similar effect. This means that, in the best-case scenario, the test treatment is trivially better than the reference treatment and, in the worst, it is tolerably worse.

Equivalence trials are important when it would be unethical to compare the test treatment with an inactive control, and when comparing the test with the control for equivalent efficacy with a superior safety profile for the test drug. The difference between groups that we believe to be "trivially better" or "tolerably worse" is called the equivalence margin. Defining the equivalence margin is not an easy task and requires input from regulatory authorities. The definition of the equivalence margin is required in estimating a sample size for such a

study and it must be decided upon in advance of the study and detailed in the study protocol.

Noninferiority trials are very similar to equivalence trials in the manner of their statistical approach. In noninferiority trials the objective is to demonstrate that the test drug is no worse than – that is, not inferior to – the control. Assuming that the test drug had some other benefit, such as better tolerability or safety or cost, a claim of noninferiority could mean that the effect for the test drug is trivially worse than the control. The design, including the choice of the noninferiority margin, must be agreed to with regulatory authorities and provided in the study protocol. A guidance document published by the EMEA CPMP (2000) addresses issues related to interpreting data from superiority studies for noninferiority claims, although it is our opinion that such a practice is rarely justified.

12.8.1 Why the hypothesis-testing strategies are different in these designs

The research questions in equivalence and noninferiority trials are different from those used in superiority trials. Hypothesis testing strategies that are so frequently used in superiority trials do not serve the needs of these designs well. As Matthews (2006, p 199) commented: "Failing to establish that one treatment is superior to the other is not the same as establishing their equivalence." In other words, obtaining a nonsignificant p value in a superiority trial does not demonstrate that the two treatments are the same. As we shall see, conventional p values have no role in establishing equivalence or noninferiority.

12.8.2 Use of confidence intervals for inferences

Given that the research questions in these trials are different from those used in superiority trials, the formats of the null and alternate hypotheses are also different. The research question associated with an equivalence trial is: Does the test drug demonstrate equivalent efficacy compared with the comparator drug? The null hypothesis, stated in terms of differences in population means, is:

$$H_0: |\mu_{TEST} - \mu_{CONTROL}| \geq \delta_{equivalence}.$$

The alternate hypothesis is:

$$H_A: |\mu_{TEST} - \mu_{CONTROL}| < \delta_{equivalence}.$$

If the null hypothesis is rejected in this case, the conclusion would be that the two population means were within $\delta_{equivalence}$ units of each other. The equivalence margin would be selected such that the two treatments were considered equivalent. If two antihypertensive therapies were compared in this manner, an equivalence margin might be 5 mmHg (a trivial difference). The inferential statistical analysis for equivalence trials typically involves the calculation of a $(1 - \alpha)\%$ confidence interval for the difference in population means. If the lower and upper bounds of the confidence interval are both within the equivalence margin, the conclusion is that we are $(1 - \alpha)\%$ confident that the true difference in population means does not exceed $\delta_{equivalence}$. The conclusions that can be drawn from an equivalence trial are displayed in Figure 12.3.

The research question for a noninferiority trial is stated as: Is the test drug not inferior to the control? The null hypothesis to be tested in this study is:

$$H_0: \mu_{TEST} - \mu_{CONTROL} \geq \delta_{noninferiority}.$$

If the null hypothesis is rejected, the following alternate hypothesis will be favored:

$$H_A: \mu_{TEST} - \mu_{CONTROL} < \delta_{noninferiority}.$$

If the null hypothesis is rejected in this case, the conclusion would be that the population mean for the control treatment did not exceed that for the test group by more than $\delta_{noninferiority}$. The inferential statistical analysis for noninferiority trials typically involves the calculation of a one-sided $(1 - \alpha)\%$ confidence interval for the difference in population means. If the upper bound of the confidence interval is within the noninferiority margin, the conclusion is that we are $(1 - \alpha)\%$ confident that the true difference in population means is less than $\delta_{noninferiority}$. The conclusions that can be drawn from a noninferiority trial are displayed in Figure 12.4.

Equivalence and noninferiority trials may be the only viable means to test a new drug in

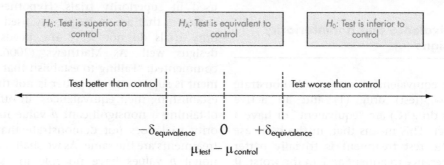

Figure 12.3 Conclusions to be drawn from the difference in population means from an equivalence trial

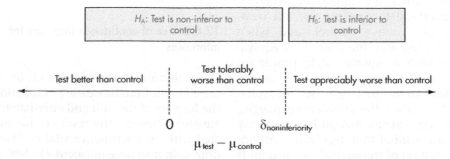

Figure 12.4 Conclusions to be drawn from the difference in population means from a noninferiority trial

certain circumstances. One important consideration in equivalence trials with a single active comparator is to consider what it means to conclude that the test drug is equivalent to the comparator. Not all marketed drugs are efficacious in every study. If the test drug were shown to be equivalent to the control, the test drug would be either efficacious or not efficacious. Which of these outcomes represents the truth depends on how the comparator would have performed had it been tested against a placebo. The ability to establish that a study can distinguish effective treatments from ineffective ones is called assay sensitivity. One way to establish this for equivalence trials is to select a comparator that had demonstrated consistent superiority to a placebo. Another option for equivalence trials in some instances is to include a third placebo arm. This is not possible when the ethics of the situation preclude this possibility. This is yet another illustration of the complexity of designing trials for which the outcomes have universally meaningful interpretations.

12.9 Additional study designs

Other appealing design features in new drug development include those that allow for monitoring of data while the trial is ongoing, and those that permit adaptations during a trial.

12.9.1 Interim analyses

Analyses conducted during a study are called interim analyses. Common uses of interim analyses are as follows:

- re-estimate the study sample size
- evaluate whether or not a study has accumulated sufficient data to stop early for definitive evidence of efficacy, for evidence of harm, or definitive evidence that the trial is unlikely to be successful in terms of its originally planned objectives.

A number of methodologies are available to assist in the quantification of evidence (accounting for type I and II errors) that enable

early stopping of trials. Jennison and Turnbull (1999) provide a detailed description of sequential designs in which data are evaluated periodically for evidence of benefit, harm, or futility. Sequential designs typically involve the use of boundaries for the test statistic that define each of these outcomes.

One complicating factor of interim analyses is that they require the use of a data monitoring committee (DMC), which is independent of the study sponsor and others involved in the study. This is intended to protect the integrity of the clinical trial and to avoid any influence that knowledge of results may have on the future course of the trial. The work of the DMC is dictated by a specific protocol, or charter, written for the purpose of listing responsibilities of all parties and measures undertaken to protect the integrity of the trial. Ellenberg et al. (2003) have written a valuable reference outlining the complex issues associated with DMC involvement in trials.

12.9.2 Adaptive designs

Adaptive designs have become a topic of great interest, as evidenced by a recent Pharmaceutical Research and Manufacturers of America (PhRMA) working group convened to discuss adaptive designs methods. Dragalin (2006) provided an excellent overview of these studies. The ability to modify a study in midcourse may offer significant advantages to pharmaceutical companies, especially given the tremendous investment of time and money required for developing new drugs.

However, the logistical aspects of monitoring data at several points during a study are not trivial. An important concern with interim analyses is to ensure that knowledge of the results, however vague, does not unduly influence or bias the study. Hung et al. (2006, p 572) stated: "When the adaptation in confirmatory trials is extensive, the key hypothesis tested becomes unclear, protection of trial integrity is difficult, the infrastructure that is needed for logistics may be impossible to establish, and evaluation by regulatory agencies may be impossible." Summarizing the opportunities and the challenges of adaptive designs on behalf of the PhRMA working group, Gallo and Krams (2006, p 423) stated that: "We feel that the potential benefits for all involved parties suggested by adaptive designs are too enticing not to make every effort to find out if their promise can be realized." These designs represent an area for emerging research.

12.10 Review

1. Consider a design for an exploratory therapeutic trial of a new antihypertensive drug compared with placebo. It has been agreed that a between-treatment group difference in mean change from baseline (that is, the treatment effect) of at least 20 mmHg in SBP would be considered clinically meaningful. The primary hypothesis must be tested with $\alpha = 0.05$.

   (a) If the standard deviation for the between difference in mean change from baseline SBP is 40 mmHg, what is the required sample size for a test with power of 80%? What is the required sample size for a test with 90% power?

   (b) If the standard deviation for the between difference in mean change from baseline SBP is 60 mmHg, what is the required sample size for a test with power of 80%? What is the required sample size for a test with 90% power?

   (c) How is the estimate of the standard deviation obtained?

2. What are some advantages and disadvantages of using multiple investigational centers in clinical trials?

3. In what ways are noninferiority trials different from superiority trials?

12.11 References

Dragalin V (2006). Adaptive designs: terminology and classification. *Drug Information J* **40**:425–435.

Ellenberg SE, Fleming TR, DeMets DL (2003). *Data Monitoring Committees in Clinical Trials: A practical perspective*. Chichester: John Wiley & Sons.

EMEA Committee for Proprietary Medicinal Products (CPMP) (2000). *Points to Consider on Switching Between Superiority and Non-Inferiority*. London: EMEA.

EMEA CPMP (2003). *Points to Consider on Adjustment for Baseline Covariates*. London: EMEA.

Fleiss JL, Paik MC, Levin B (2003). *Statistical Methods for Rates and Proportions*, 3rd edn. Chichester: John Wiley & Sons.

Gallo P, Krams M (2006). PhRMA working group on adaptive designs: introduction to the full white paper. *Drug Information J* **40**:421–423.

Hung HMJ, O'Neill RT, Wang SJ, Lawrence J (2006). A regulatory view on adaptive/flexible clinical trial design. *Biometr J* **48**:565–573.

ICH Guidance E1 (1994). *The Extent of Population Exposure to Assess Clinical Safety for Drugs Intended for Long-Term Treatment of None-Life-Threatening Conditions*. Available at: www.ich.org (accessed July 1 2007).

Jennison C, Turnbull BW (2000). *Group Sequential Methods with Applications to Clinical Trials*. Boca Raton, IL: Chapman & Hall/CRC.

Lee SJ, Zelen M (2000). Clinical trials and sample size considerations: another perspective. *Statist Sci* **15**: 95–110.

Machin D, Campbell MJ (2005). *Design of Studies for Medical Research*. Chichester: John Wiley & Sons.

Matthews JNS (2006). *Introduction to Randomized Controlled Clinical Trials*, 2nd edn. Boca Raton, FL: Chapman & Hall/CRC.

Molenberghs G, Kenward M (2007). *Missing Data in Clinical Studies*. Chichester: John Wiley & Sons.

Piantadosi S (2005). *Clinical Trials: A methodologic perspective*, 2nd edn. Chichester: John Wiley & Sons.

Roberts C, Torgerson DJ (1999). Understanding controlled trials: baseline imbalance in randomised controlled trials. *BMJ* **319**:185.

Senn S (1997). *Statistical Issues in Drug Development*. Chichester: John Wiley & Sons.

Turner JR (2007). *New Drug Development: Design, methodology, and analysis*. Hoboken, NJ: John Wiley & Sons.

13

Concluding comments

We conclude with two overarching comments that bring together the various topics and considerations that we have discussed throughout the book.

First, when faced with the myriad challenges that occur during drug development, the discipline of Statistics is the knight in shining armor that rides to our assistance and facilitates the collection, analysis, and interpretation of optimum quality data as the basis for rational decision-making at all stages of the process. The discipline of Statistics as operationally defined in this book includes study design, experimental methodology, statistical analysis, and the interpretation of the findings of the trial. Very importantly, the interpretation involves addressing issues of both statistical significance and clinical significance. Our interest in Statistics, then, is a pragmatic one: The discipline provides the best way currently available to conduct clinical development programs.

Second, it is appropriate to remind ourselves that our ultimate interest is in providing a new, biologically active, pharmacological agent that will alter a patient's biology for the better. Statistical analyses can be performed on any kind of data (some extremely influential statistical methods were developed in the agricultural arena). In this book, however, the data of interest are biological data, both desirable biologically therapeutic effects and undesirable biological side-effects. Producing a drug that has an acceptable benefit–risk ratio is a long and complex process, and one in which statistical methodology is invaluable.

It is also good to remind ourselves frequently that the welfare of real patients is our ultimate concern. This may not be the first thought that pops into our heads when we are in the middle of a sample-size estimation calculation for an upcoming clinical trial, or when deciding upon which imputation methodology to use to deal with missing data in a clinical database. Nevertheless, this is why we do these things. The pharmaceutical industry is not immune to controversy; far from it. However, as Turner (2007, p 239) noted: "New drug development is a very complicated and difficult undertaking, but one that makes an enormous difference to the health of people across the globe. It is a noble pursuit."

In this book, set in the context of drug development, we have taught you how to conduct an array of statistical analyses. While teaching such computational skills is appropriate in a statistics textbook, we also hope that we have been successful in providing you with a conceptual understanding of and appreciation for the contribution of the discipline of Statistics to the development of pharmaceutical drugs that may improve the health of your family members, your friends, and yourself.

Reference

Turner JR (2007). *New Drug Development: Design, methodology, and analysis.* Hoboken, NJ: John Wiley & Sons.

Appendices

Statistical tables

Appendix 1

Standard normal distribution areas

z	$P(Z < z)$	$P(Z > z)$	$P(-z < Z < z)$	$P(Z < -z$ or $Z > z)$
0.00	0.50000	0.50000	0.00000	1.00000
0.01	0.50399	0.49601	0.00798	0.99202
0.02	0.50798	0.49202	0.01596	0.98404
0.03	0.51197	0.48803	0.02393	0.97607
0.04	0.51595	0.48405	0.03191	0.96809
0.05	0.51994	0.48006	0.03988	0.96012
0.06	0.52392	0.47608	0.04784	0.95216
0.07	0.52790	0.47210	0.05581	0.94419
0.08	0.53188	0.46812	0.06376	0.93624
0.09	0.53586	0.46414	0.07171	0.92829
0.10	0.53983	0.46017	0.07966	0.92034
0.11	0.54380	0.45620	0.08759	0.91241
0.12	0.54776	0.45224	0.09552	0.90448
0.13	0.55172	0.44828	0.10343	0.89657
0.14	0.55567	0.44433	0.11134	0.88866
0.15	0.55962	0.44038	0.11924	0.88076
0.16	0.56356	0.43644	0.12712	0.87288
0.17	0.56749	0.43251	0.13499	0.86501
0.18	0.57142	0.42858	0.14285	0.85715
0.19	0.57535	0.42465	0.15069	0.84931
0.20	0.57926	0.42074	0.15852	0.84148
0.21	0.58317	0.41683	0.16633	0.83367
0.22	0.58706	0.41294	0.17413	0.82587
0.23	0.59095	0.40905	0.18191	0.81809
0.24	0.59483	0.40517	0.18967	0.81033
0.25	0.59871	0.40129	0.19741	0.80259
0.26	0.60257	0.39743	0.20514	0.79486
0.27	0.60642	0.39358	0.21284	0.78716
0.28	0.61026	0.38974	0.22052	0.77948
0.29	0.61409	0.38591	0.22818	0.77182
0.30	0.61791	0.38209	0.23582	0.76418
0.31	0.62172	0.37828	0.24344	0.75656
0.32	0.62552	0.37448	0.25103	0.74897
0.33	0.62930	0.37070	0.25860	0.74140
0.34	0.63307	0.36693	0.26614	0.73386
0.35	0.63683	0.36317	0.27366	0.72634
0.36	0.64058	0.35942	0.28115	0.71885
0.37	0.64431	0.35569	0.28862	0.71138
0.38	0.64803	0.35197	0.29605	0.70395

z	$P(Z < z)$	$P(Z > z)$	$P(-z < Z < z)$	$P(Z < -z$ or $Z > z)$
0.39	0.65173	0.34827	0.30346	0.69654
0.40	0.65542	0.34458	0.31084	0.68916
0.41	0.65910	0.34090	0.31819	0.68181
0.42	0.66276	0.33724	0.32551	0.67449
0.43	0.66640	0.33360	0.33280	0.66720
0.44	0.67003	0.32997	0.34006	0.65994
0.45	0.67364	0.32636	0.34729	0.65271
0.46	0.67724	0.32276	0.35448	0.64552
0.47	0.68082	0.31918	0.36164	0.63836
0.48	0.68439	0.31561	0.36877	0.63123
0.49	0.68793	0.31207	0.37587	0.62413
0.50	0.69146	0.30854	0.38292	0.61708
0.51	0.69497	0.30503	0.38995	0.61005
0.52	0.69847	0.30153	0.39694	0.60306
0.53	0.70194	0.29806	0.40389	0.59611
0.54	0.70540	0.29460	0.41080	0.58920
0.55	0.70884	0.29116	0.41768	0.58232
0.56	0.71226	0.28774	0.42452	0.57548
0.57	0.71566	0.28434	0.43132	0.56868
0.58	0.71904	0.28096	0.43809	0.56191
0.59	0.72240	0.27760	0.44481	0.55519
0.60	0.72575	0.27425	0.45149	0.54851
0.61	0.72907	0.27093	0.45814	0.54186
0.62	0.73237	0.26763	0.46474	0.53526
0.63	0.73565	0.26435	0.47131	0.52869
0.64	0.73891	0.26109	0.47783	0.52217
0.65	0.74215	0.25785	0.48431	0.51569
0.66	0.74537	0.25463	0.49075	0.50925
0.67	0.74857	0.25143	0.49714	0.50286
0.68	0.75175	0.24825	0.50350	0.49650
0.69	0.75490	0.24510	0.50981	0.49019
0.70	0.75804	0.24196	0.51607	0.48393
0.71	0.76115	0.23885	0.52230	0.47770
0.72	0.76424	0.23576	0.52848	0.47152
0.73	0.76730	0.23270	0.53461	0.46539
0.74	0.77035	0.22965	0.54070	0.45930
0.75	0.77337	0.22663	0.54675	0.45325
0.76	0.77637	0.22363	0.55275	0.44725
0.77	0.77935	0.22065	0.55870	0.44130
0.78	0.78230	0.21770	0.56461	0.43539
0.79	0.78524	0.21476	0.57047	0.42953
0.80	0.78814	0.21186	0.57629	0.42371
0.81	0.79103	0.20897	0.58206	0.41794
0.82	0.79389	0.20611	0.58778	0.41222
0.83	0.79673	0.20327	0.59346	0.40654
0.84	0.79955	0.20045	0.59909	0.40091
0.85	0.80234	0.19766	0.60467	0.39533
0.86	0.80511	0.19489	0.61021	0.38979
0.87	0.80785	0.19215	0.61570	0.38430

z	$P(Z < z)$	$P(Z > z)$	$P(-z < Z < z)$	$P(Z < -z$ or $Z > z)$
0.88	0.81057	0.18943	0.62114	0.37886
0.89	0.81327	0.18673	0.62653	0.37347
0.90	0.81594	0.18406	0.63188	0.36812
0.91	0.81859	0.18141	0.63718	0.36282
0.92	0.82121	0.17879	0.64243	0.35757
0.93	0.82381	0.17619	0.64763	0.35237
0.94	0.82639	0.17361	0.65278	0.34722
0.95	0.82894	0.17106	0.65789	0.34211
0.96	0.83147	0.16853	0.66294	0.33706
0.97	0.83398	0.16602	0.66795	0.33205
0.98	0.83646	0.16354	0.67291	0.32709
0.99	0.83891	0.16109	0.67783	0.32217
1.00	0.84134	0.15866	0.68269	0.31731
1.01	0.84375	0.15625	0.68750	0.31250
1.02	0.84614	0.15386	0.69227	0.30773
1.03	0.84849	0.15151	0.69699	0.30301
1.04	0.85083	0.14917	0.70166	0.29834
1.05	0.85314	0.14686	0.70628	0.29372
1.06	0.85543	0.14457	0.71086	0.28914
1.07	0.85769	0.14231	0.71538	0.28462
1.08	0.85993	0.14007	0.71986	0.28014
1.09	0.86214	0.13786	0.72429	0.27571
1.10	0.86433	0.13567	0.72867	0.27133
1.11	0.86650	0.13350	0.73300	0.26700
1.12	0.86864	0.13136	0.73729	0.26271
1.13	0.87076	0.12924	0.74152	0.25848
1.14	0.87286	0.12714	0.74571	0.25429
1.15	0.87493	0.12507	0.74986	0.25014
1.16	0.87698	0.12302	0.75395	0.24605
1.17	0.87900	0.12100	0.75800	0.24200
1.18	0.88100	0.11900	0.76200	0.23800
1.19	0.88298	0.11702	0.76595	0.23405
1.20	0.88493	0.11507	0.76986	0.23014
1.21	0.88686	0.11314	0.77372	0.22628
1.22	0.88877	0.11123	0.77754	0.22246
1.23	0.89065	0.10935	0.78130	0.21870
1.24	0.89251	0.10749	0.78502	0.21498
1.25	0.89435	0.10565	0.78870	0.21130
1.26	0.89617	0.10383	0.79233	0.20767
1.27	0.89796	0.10204	0.79592	0.20408
1.28	0.89973	0.10027	0.79945	0.20055
1.29	0.90147	0.09853	0.80295	0.19705
1.30	0.90320	0.09680	0.80640	0.19360
1.31	0.90490	0.09510	0.80980	0.19020
1.32	0.90658	0.09342	0.81316	0.18684
1.33	0.90824	0.09176	0.81648	0.18352
1.34	0.90988	0.09012	0.81975	0.18025
1.35	0.91149	0.08851	0.82298	0.17702
1.36	0.91309	0.08691	0.82617	0.17383

z	P(Z < z)	P(Z > z)	P(−z < Z < z)	P(Z < −z or Z > z)
1.37	0.91466	0.08534	0.82931	0.17069
1.38	0.91621	0.08379	0.83241	0.16759
1.39	0.91774	0.08226	0.83547	0.16453
1.40	0.91924	0.08076	0.83849	0.16151
1.41	0.92073	0.07927	0.84146	0.15854
1.42	0.92220	0.07780	0.84439	0.15561
1.43	0.92364	0.07636	0.84728	0.15272
1.44	0.92507	0.07493	0.85013	0.14987
1.45	0.92647	0.07353	0.85294	0.14706
1.46	0.92785	0.07215	0.85571	0.14429
1.47	0.92922	0.07078	0.85844	0.14156
1.48	0.93056	0.06944	0.86113	0.13887
1.49	0.93189	0.06811	0.86378	0.13622
1.50	0.93319	0.06681	0.86639	0.13361
1.51	0.93448	0.06552	0.86896	0.13104
1.52	0.93574	0.06426	0.87149	0.12851
1.53	0.93699	0.06301	0.87398	0.12602
1.54	0.93822	0.06178	0.87644	0.12356
1.55	0.93943	0.06057	0.87886	0.12114
1.56	0.94062	0.05938	0.88124	0.11876
1.57	0.94179	0.05821	0.88358	0.11642
1.58	0.94295	0.05705	0.88589	0.11411
1.59	0.94408	0.05592	0.88817	0.11183
1.60	0.94520	0.05480	0.89040	0.10960
1.61	0.94630	0.05370	0.89260	0.10740
1.62	0.94738	0.05262	0.89477	0.10523
1.63	0.94845	0.05155	0.89690	0.10310
1.64	0.94950	0.05050	0.89899	0.10101
1.65	0.95053	0.04947	0.90106	0.09894
1.66	0.95154	0.04846	0.90309	0.09691
1.67	0.95254	0.04746	0.90508	0.09492
1.68	0.95352	0.04648	0.90704	0.09296
1.69	0.95449	0.04551	0.90897	0.09103
1.70	0.95543	0.04457	0.91087	0.08913
1.71	0.95637	0.04363	0.91273	0.08727
1.72	0.95728	0.04272	0.91457	0.08543
1.73	0.95818	0.04182	0.91637	0.08363
1.74	0.95907	0.04093	0.91814	0.08186
1.75	0.95994	0.04006	0.91988	0.08012
1.76	0.96080	0.03920	0.92159	0.07841
1.77	0.96164	0.03836	0.92327	0.07673
1.78	0.96246	0.03754	0.92492	0.07508
1.79	0.96327	0.03673	0.92655	0.07345
1.80	0.96407	0.03593	0.92814	0.07186
1.81	0.96485	0.03515	0.92970	0.07030
1.82	0.96562	0.03438	0.93124	0.06876
1.83	0.96638	0.03362	0.93275	0.06725
1.84	0.96712	0.03288	0.93423	0.06577
1.85	0.96784	0.03216	0.93569	0.06431

z	P(Z < z)	P(Z > z)	P(−z < Z < z)	P(Z < −z or Z > z)
1.86	0.96856	0.03144	0.93711	0.06289
1.87	0.96926	0.03074	0.93852	0.06148
1.88	0.96995	0.03005	0.93989	0.06011
1.89	0.97062	0.02938	0.94124	0.05876
1.90	0.97128	0.02872	0.94257	0.05743
1.91	0.97193	0.02807	0.94387	0.05613
1.92	0.97257	0.02743	0.94514	0.05486
1.93	0.97320	0.02680	0.94639	0.05361
1.94	0.97381	0.02619	0.94762	0.05238
1.95	0.97441	0.02559	0.94882	0.05118
1.96	0.97500	0.02500	0.95000	0.05000
1.97	0.97558	0.02442	0.95116	0.04884
1.98	0.97615	0.02385	0.95230	0.04770
1.99	0.97670	0.02330	0.95341	0.04659
2.00	0.97725	0.02275	0.95450	0.04550
2.01	0.97778	0.02222	0.95557	0.04443
2.02	0.97831	0.02169	0.95662	0.04338
2.03	0.97882	0.02118	0.95764	0.04236
2.04	0.97932	0.02068	0.95865	0.04135
2.05	0.97982	0.02018	0.95964	0.04036
2.06	0.98030	0.01970	0.96060	0.03940
2.07	0.98077	0.01923	0.96155	0.03845
2.08	0.98124	0.01876	0.96247	0.03753
2.09	0.98169	0.01831	0.96338	0.03662
2.10	0.98214	0.01786	0.96427	0.03573
2.11	0.98257	0.01743	0.96514	0.03486
2.12	0.98300	0.01700	0.96599	0.03401
2.13	0.98341	0.01659	0.96683	0.03317
2.14	0.98382	0.01618	0.96765	0.03235
2.15	0.98422	0.01578	0.96844	0.03156
2.16	0.98461	0.01539	0.96923	0.03077
2.17	0.98500	0.01500	0.96999	0.03001
2.18	0.98537	0.01463	0.97074	0.02926
2.19	0.98574	0.01426	0.97148	0.02852
2.20	0.98610	0.01390	0.97219	0.02781
2.21	0.98645	0.01355	0.97289	0.02711
2.22	0.98679	0.01321	0.97358	0.02642
2.23	0.98713	0.01287	0.97425	0.02575
2.24	0.98745	0.01255	0.97491	0.02509
2.25	0.98778	0.01222	0.97555	0.02445
2.26	0.98809	0.01191	0.97618	0.02382
2.27	0.98840	0.01160	0.97679	0.02321
2.28	0.98870	0.01130	0.97739	0.02261
2.29	0.98899	0.01101	0.97798	0.02202
2.30	0.98928	0.01072	0.97855	0.02145
2.31	0.98956	0.01044	0.97911	0.02089
2.32	0.98983	0.01017	0.97966	0.02034
2.33	0.99010	0.00990	0.98019	0.01981
2.34	0.99036	0.00964	0.98072	0.01928

z	$P(Z < z)$	$P(Z > z)$	$P(-z < Z < z)$	$P(Z < -z \text{ or } Z > z)$
2.35	0.99061	0.00939	0.98123	0.01877
2.36	0.99086	0.00914	0.98173	0.01827
2.37	0.99111	0.00889	0.98221	0.01779
2.38	0.99134	0.00866	0.98269	0.01731
2.39	0.99158	0.00842	0.98315	0.01685
2.40	0.99180	0.00820	0.98360	0.01640
2.41	0.99202	0.00798	0.98405	0.01595
2.42	0.99224	0.00776	0.98448	0.01552
2.43	0.99245	0.00755	0.98490	0.01510
2.44	0.99266	0.00734	0.98531	0.01469
2.45	0.99286	0.00714	0.98571	0.01429
2.46	0.99305	0.00695	0.98611	0.01389
2.47	0.99324	0.00676	0.98649	0.01351
2.48	0.99343	0.00657	0.98686	0.01314
2.49	0.99361	0.00639	0.98723	0.01277
2.50	0.99379	0.00621	0.98758	0.01242
2.51	0.99396	0.00604	0.98793	0.01207
2.52	0.99413	0.00587	0.98826	0.01174
2.53	0.99430	0.00570	0.98859	0.01141
2.54	0.99446	0.00554	0.98891	0.01109
2.55	0.99461	0.00539	0.98923	0.01077
2.56	0.99477	0.00523	0.98953	0.01047
2.57	0.99492	0.00508	0.98983	0.01017
2.58	0.99506	0.00494	0.99012	0.00988
2.59	0.99520	0.00480	0.99040	0.00960
2.60	0.99534	0.00466	0.99068	0.00932
2.61	0.99547	0.00453	0.99095	0.00905
2.62	0.99560	0.00440	0.99121	0.00879
2.63	0.99573	0.00427	0.99146	0.00854
2.64	0.99585	0.00415	0.99171	0.00829
2.65	0.99598	0.00402	0.99195	0.00805
2.66	0.99609	0.00391	0.99219	0.00781
2.67	0.99621	0.00379	0.99241	0.00759
2.68	0.99632	0.00368	0.99264	0.00736
2.69	0.99643	0.00357	0.99285	0.00715
2.70	0.99653	0.00347	0.99307	0.00693
2.71	0.99664	0.00336	0.99327	0.00673
2.72	0.99674	0.00326	0.99347	0.00653
2.73	0.99683	0.00317	0.99367	0.00633
2.74	0.99693	0.00307	0.99386	0.00614
2.75	0.99702	0.00298	0.99404	0.00596
2.76	0.99711	0.00289	0.99422	0.00578
2.77	0.99720	0.00280	0.99439	0.00561
2.78	0.99728	0.00272	0.99456	0.00544
2.79	0.99736	0.00264	0.99473	0.00527
2.80	0.99744	0.00256	0.99489	0.00511
2.81	0.99752	0.00248	0.99505	0.00495
2.82	0.99760	0.00240	0.99520	0.00480
2.83	0.99767	0.00233	0.99535	0.00465

z	P(Z < z)	P(Z > z)	P(-z < Z < z)	P(Z < -z or Z > z)
2.84	0.99774	0.00226	0.99549	0.00451
2.85	0.99781	0.00219	0.99563	0.00437
2.86	0.99788	0.00212	0.99576	0.00424
2.87	0.99795	0.00205	0.99590	0.00410
2.88	0.99801	0.00199	0.99602	0.00398
2.89	0.99807	0.00193	0.99615	0.00385
2.90	0.99813	0.00187	0.99627	0.00373
2.91	0.99819	0.00181	0.99639	0.00361
2.92	0.99825	0.00175	0.99650	0.00350
2.93	0.99831	0.00169	0.99661	0.00339
2.94	0.99836	0.00164	0.99672	0.00328
2.95	0.99841	0.00159	0.99682	0.00318
2.96	0.99846	0.00154	0.99692	0.00308
2.97	0.99851	0.00149	0.99702	0.00298
2.98	0.99856	0.00144	0.99712	0.00288
2.99	0.99861	0.00139	0.99721	0.00279
3.00	0.99865	0.00135	0.99730	0.00270
3.01	0.99869	0.00131	0.99739	0.00261
3.02	0.99874	0.00126	0.99747	0.00253
3.03	0.99878	0.00122	0.99755	0.00245
3.04	0.99882	0.00118	0.99763	0.00237
3.05	0.99886	0.00114	0.99771	0.00229
3.06	0.99889	0.00111	0.99779	0.00221
3.07	0.99893	0.00107	0.99786	0.00214
3.08	0.99896	0.00104	0.99793	0.00207
3.09	0.99900	0.00100	0.99800	0.00200
3.10	0.99903	0.00097	0.99806	0.00194
3.11	0.99906	0.00094	0.99813	0.00187
3.12	0.99910	0.00090	0.99819	0.00181
3.13	0.99913	0.00087	0.99825	0.00175
3.14	0.99916	0.00084	0.99831	0.00169
3.15	0.99918	0.00082	0.99837	0.00163
3.16	0.99921	0.00079	0.99842	0.00158
3.17	0.99924	0.00076	0.99848	0.00152
3.18	0.99926	0.00074	0.99853	0.00147
3.19	0.99929	0.00071	0.99858	0.00142
3.20	0.99931	0.00069	0.99863	0.00137
3.21	0.99934	0.00066	0.99867	0.00133
3.22	0.99936	0.00064	0.99872	0.00128
3.23	0.99938	0.00062	0.99876	0.00124
3.24	0.99940	0.00060	0.99880	0.00120
3.25	0.99942	0.00058	0.99885	0.00115
3.26	0.99944	0.00056	0.99889	0.00111
3.27	0.99946	0.00054	0.99892	0.00108
3.28	0.99948	0.00052	0.99896	0.00104
3.29	0.99950	0.00050	0.99900	0.00100
3.30	0.99952	0.00048	0.99903	0.00097
3.31	0.99953	0.00047	0.99907	0.00093
3.32	0.99955	0.00045	0.99910	0.00090

z	P(Z < z)	P(Z > z)	P(−z < Z < z)	P(Z < −z or Z > z)
3.33	0.99957	0.00043	0.99913	0.00087
3.34	0.99958	0.00042	0.99916	0.00084
3.35	0.99960	0.00040	0.99919	0.00081
3.36	0.99961	0.00039	0.99922	0.00078
3.37	0.99962	0.00038	0.99925	0.00075
3.38	0.99964	0.00036	0.99928	0.00072
3.39	0.99965	0.00035	0.99930	0.00070
3.40	0.99966	0.00034	0.99933	0.00067
3.41	0.99968	0.00032	0.99935	0.00065
3.42	0.99969	0.00031	0.99937	0.00063
3.43	0.99970	0.00030	0.99940	0.00060
3.44	0.99971	0.00029	0.99942	0.00058
3.45	0.99972	0.00028	0.99944	0.00056
3.46	0.99973	0.00027	0.99946	0.00054
3.47	0.99974	0.00026	0.99948	0.00052
3.48	0.99975	0.00025	0.99950	0.00050
3.49	0.99976	0.00024	0.99952	0.00048
3.50	0.99977	0.00023	0.99953	0.00047
3.51	0.99978	0.00022	0.99955	0.00045
3.52	0.99978	0.00022	0.99957	0.00043
3.53	0.99979	0.00021	0.99958	0.00042
3.54	0.99980	0.00020	0.99960	0.00040
3.55	0.99981	0.00019	0.99961	0.00039
3.56	0.99981	0.00019	0.99963	0.00037
3.57	0.99982	0.00018	0.99964	0.00036
3.58	0.99983	0.00017	0.99966	0.00034
3.59	0.99983	0.00017	0.99967	0.00033
3.60	0.99984	0.00016	0.99968	0.00032
3.80	0.99993	0.00007	0.99986	0.00014
3.82	0.99993	0.00007	0.99987	0.00013
3.84	0.99994	0.00006	0.99988	0.00012
3.86	0.99994	0.00006	0.99989	0.00011
3.88	0.99995	0.00005	0.99990	0.00010
3.90	0.99995	0.00005	0.99990	0.00010
3.92	0.99996	0.00004	0.99991	0.00009
3.94	0.99996	0.00004	0.99992	0.00008
3.96	0.99996	0.00004	0.99993	0.00007
3.98	0.99997	0.00003	0.99993	0.00007
4.00	0.99997	0.00003	0.99994	0.00006
4.02	0.99997	0.00003	0.99994	0.00006
4.04	0.99997	0.00003	0.99995	0.00005
4.06	0.99998	0.00002	0.99995	0.00005
4.08	0.99998	0.00002	0.99995	0.00005
4.10	0.99998	0.00002	0.99996	0.00004
4.12	0.99998	0.00002	0.99996	0.00004
4.14	0.99998	0.00002	0.99997	0.00003
4.16	0.99998	0.00002	0.99997	0.00003
4.18	0.99999	0.00001	0.99997	0.00003
4.20	0.99999	0.00001	0.99997	0.00003

z	$P(Z < z)$	$P(Z > z)$	$P(-z < Z < z)$	$P(Z < -z$ or $Z > z)$
4.22	0.99999	0.00001	0.99998	0.00002
4.24	0.99999	0.00001	0.99998	0.00002
4.26	0.99999	0.00001	0.99998	0.00002
4.28	0.99999	0.00001	0.99998	0.00002
4.30	0.99999	0.00001	0.99998	0.00002
4.32	0.99999	0.00001	0.99998	0.00002
4.34	0.99999	0.00001	0.99999	0.00001
4.36	0.99999	0.00001	0.99999	0.00001
4.38	0.99999	0.00001	0.99999	0.00001
4.40	0.99999	0.00001	0.99999	0.00001
4.42	1.00000	0.00000	0.99999	0.00001
4.44	1.00000	0.00000	0.99999	0.00001
4.46	1.00000	0.00000	0.99999	0.00001
4.48	1.00000	0.00000	0.99999	0.00001
4.50	1.00000	0.00000	0.99999	0.00001
4.52	1.00000	0.00000	0.99999	0.00001
4.54	1.00000	0.00000	0.99999	0.00001
4.56	1.00000	0.00000	0.99999	0.00001
4.58	1.00000	0.00000	1.00000	0.00000
4.60	1.00000	0.00000	1.00000	0.00000

Appendix 2

Percentiles of t distributions

Degrees of freedom (df)	Area in the symmetric central region $P(-t < T < t)$				
	0.80	0.90	0.95	0.99	0.999
	Area to the left of t: $P(T < t)$				
	0.90	0.95	0.975	0.995	0.9995
1	3.078	6.314	12.71	63.66	636.6
2	1.886	2.920	4.303	9.925	31.60
3	1.638	2.353	3.182	5.841	12.92
4	1.533	2.132	2.776	4.604	8.610
5	1.476	2.015	2.571	4.032	6.869
6	1.440	1.943	2.447	3.707	5.959
7	1.415	1.895	2.365	3.499	5.408
8	1.397	1.860	2.306	3.355	5.041
9	1.383	1.833	2.262	3.250	4.781
10	1.372	1.812	2.228	3.169	4.587
11	1.363	1.796	2.201	3.106	4.437
12	1.356	1.782	2.179	3.055	4.318
13	1.350	1.771	2.160	3.012	4.221
14	1.345	1.761	2.145	2.977	4.140
15	1.341	1.753	2.131	2.947	4.073
16	1.337	1.746	2.120	2.921	4.015
17	1.333	1.740	2.110	2.898	3.965
18	1.330	1.734	2.101	2.878	3.922
19	1.328	1.729	2.093	2.861	3.883
20	1.325	1.725	2.086	2.845	3.850
21	1.323	1.721	2.080	2.831	3.819
22	1.321	1.717	2.074	2.819	3.792
23	1.319	1.714	2.069	2.807	3.768
24	1.318	1.711	2.064	2.797	3.745
25	1.316	1.708	2.060	2.787	3.725
26	1.315	1.706	2.056	2.779	3.707
27	1.314	1.703	2.052	2.771	3.690
28	1.313	1.701	2.048	2.763	3.674
29	1.311	1.699	2.045	2.756	3.659
30	1.310	1.697	2.042	2.750	3.646
31	1.309	1.696	2.040	2.744	3.633
32	1.309	1.694	2.037	2.738	3.622
33	1.308	1.692	2.035	2.733	3.611
34	1.307	1.691	2.032	2.728	3.601
35	1.306	1.690	2.030	2.724	3.591

Degrees of freedom (df)	Area in the symmetric central region $P(-t < T < t)$				
	0.80	0.90	0.95	0.99	0.999
	Area to the left of t: $P(T < t)$				
	0.90	0.95	0.975	0.995	0.9995
36	1.306	1.688	2.028	2.719	3.582
37	1.305	1.687	2.026	2.715	3.574
38	1.304	1.686	2.024	2.712	3.566
39	1.304	1.685	2.023	2.708	3.558
40	1.303	1.684	2.021	2.704	3.551
45	1.301	1.679	2.014	2.690	3.520
50	1.299	1.676	2.009	2.678	3.496
60	1.296	1.671	2.000	2.660	3.460
70	1.294	1.667	1.994	2.648	3.435
80	1.292	1.664	1.990	2.639	3.416
90	1.291	1.662	1.987	2.632	3.402
100	1.290	1.660	1.984	2.626	3.390
120	1.289	1.658	1.980	2.617	3.373
140	1.288	1.656	1.977	2.611	3.361
160	1.287	1.654	1.975	2.60	3.352
180	1.286	1.653	1.973	2.603	3.345
200	1.286	1.653	1.972	2.601	3.340
220	1.285	1.652	1.971	2.598	3.335
240	1.285	1.651	1.970	2.596	3.332
260	1.285	1.651	1.969	2.595	3.328
280	1.285	1.650	1.968	2.594	3.326
300	1.284	1.650	1.968	2.592	3.323

Appendix 3

Percentiles of χ^2 distributions

Degrees of freedom (df)	Area to the left of X^2: $P(X < X^2)$			
	0.90	0.95	0.99	0.999
1	2.706	3.841	6.635	10.828
2	4.605	5.991	9.210	13.816
3	6.251	7.815	11.345	16.266
4	7.779	9.488	13.277	18.467
5	9.236	11.070	15.086	20.515
6	10.645	12.592	16.812	22.458
7	12.017	14.067	18.475	24.322
8	13.362	15.507	20.090	26.124
9	14.684	16.919	21.666	27.877
10	15.987	18.307	23.209	29.588
11	17.275	19.675	24.725	31.264
12	18.549	21.026	26.217	32.909
13	19.812	22.362	27.688	34.528
14	21.064	23.685	29.141	36.123
15	22.307	24.996	30.578	37.697
16	23.542	26.296	32.000	39.252
17	24.769	27.587	33.409	40.790
18	25.989	28.869	34.805	42.312
19	27.204	30.144	36.191	43.820
20	28.412	31.410	37.566	45.315
21	29.615	32.671	38.932	46.797
22	30.813	33.924	40.289	48.268
23	32.007	35.172	41.638	49.728
24	33.196	36.415	42.980	51.179
25	34.382	37.652	44.314	52.620
26	35.563	38.885	45.642	54.052
27	36.741	40.113	46.963	55.476
28	37.916	41.337	48.278	56.892
29	39.087	42.557	49.588	58.301
30	40.256	43.773	50.892	59.703
35	46.059	49.802	57.342	66.619
40	51.805	55.758	63.691	73.402
45	57.505	61.656	69.957	80.077
50	63.167	67.505	76.154	86.661
55	68.796	73.311	82.292	93.168
60	74.397	79.082	88.379	99.607
70	85.527	90.531	100.43	112.32

Degrees of freedom (df)	Area to the left of X^2: $P(X < X^2)$			
	0.90	0.95	0.99	0.999
80	96.578	101.88	112.33	124.84
90	107.57	113.15	124.12	137.21
100	118.50	124.34	135.81	149.45
110	129.39	135.48	147.41	161.58
120	140.23	146.57	158.95	173.62
130	151.05	157.61	170.42	185.57
140	161.83	168.61	181.84	197.45
150	172.58	179.58	193.21	209.26
160	183.31	190.52	204.53	221.02
170	194.02	201.42	215.81	232.72
180	204.70	212.30	227.06	244.37
190	215.37	223.16	238.27	255.98
200	226.02	233.99	249.45	267.54

Appendix 4

Percentiles of F distributions ($\alpha = 0.05$)

(ddf)	Numerator degrees of freedom (ndf)								
	1	2	3	4	5	6	7	8	9
1	161.4	199.5	215.7	224.6	230.2	234.0	236.8	238.9	240.5
2	18.51	19.00	19.16	19.25	19.30	19.33	19.35	19.37	19.38
3	10.13	9.55	9.28	9.12	9.01	8.94	8.89	8.85	8.81
4	7.71	6.94	6.59	6.39	6.26	6.16	6.09	6.04	6.00
5	6.61	5.79	5.41	5.19	5.05	4.95	4.88	4.82	4.77
6	5.99	5.14	4.76	4.53	4.39	4.28	4.21	4.15	4.10
7	5.59	4.74	4.35	4.12	3.97	3.87	3.79	3.73	3.68
8	5.32	4.46	4.07	3.84	3.69	3.58	3.50	3.44	3.39
9	5.12	4.26	3.86	3.63	3.48	3.37	3.29	3.23	3.18
10	4.96	4.10	3.71	3.48	3.33	3.22	3.14	3.07	3.02
11	4.84	3.98	3.59	3.36	3.20	3.09	3.01	2.95	2.90
12	4.75	3.89	3.49	3.26	3.11	3.00	2.91	2.85	2.80
13	4.67	3.81	3.41	3.18	3.03	2.92	2.83	2.77	2.71
14	4.60	3.74	3.34	3.11	2.96	2.85	2.76	2.70	2.65
15	4.54	3.68	3.29	3.06	2.90	2.79	2.71	2.64	2.59
16	4.49	3.63	3.24	3.01	2.85	2.74	2.66	2.59	2.54
17	4.45	3.59	3.20	2.96	2.81	2.70	2.61	2.55	2.49
18	4.41	3.55	3.16	2.93	2.77	2.66	2.58	2.51	2.46
19	4.38	3.52	3.13	2.90	2.74	2.63	2.54	2.48	2.42
20	4.35	3.49	3.10	2.87	2.71	2.60	2.51	2.45	2.39
21	4.32	3.47	3.07	2.84	2.68	2.57	2.49	2.42	2.37
22	4.30	3.44	3.05	2.82	2.66	2.55	2.46	2.40	2.34
23	4.28	3.42	3.03	2.80	2.64	2.53	2.44	2.37	2.32
24	4.26	3.40	3.01	2.78	2.62	2.51	2.42	2.36	2.30
25	4.24	3.39	2.99	2.76	2.60	2.49	2.40	2.34	2.28
26	4.23	3.37	2.98	2.74	2.59	2.47	2.39	2.32	2.27
27	4.21	3.35	2.96	2.73	2.57	2.46	2.37	2.31	2.25
28	4.20	3.34	2.95	2.71	2.56	2.45	2.36	2.29	2.24
29	4.18	3.33	2.93	2.70	2.55	2.43	2.35	2.28	2.22
30	4.17	3.32	2.92	2.69	2.53	2.42	2.33	2.27	2.21
40	4.08	3.23	2.84	2.61	2.45	2.34	2.25	2.18	2.12
50	4.03	3.18	2.79	2.56	2.40	2.29	2.20	2.13	2.07
60	4.00	3.15	2.76	2.53	2.37	2.25	2.17	2.10	2.04
70	3.98	3.13	2.74	2.50	2.35	2.23	2.14	2.07	2.02
80	3.96	3.11	2.72	2.49	2.33	2.21	2.13	2.06	2.00
90	3.95	3.10	2.71	2.47	2.32	2.20	2.11	2.04	1.99
100	3.94	3.09	2.70	2.46	2.31	2.19	2.10	2.03	1.97
110	3.93	3.08	2.69	2.45	2.30	2.18	2.09	2.02	1.97
120	3.92	3.07	2.68	2.45	2.29	2.18	2.09	2.02	1.96

(ddf)	10	12	15	20	25	30	40	60	80	100	120
						Numerator degrees of freedom (ndf)					
1	241.9	243.9	245.9	248.0	249.3	250.1	251.1	252.2	252.7	253.0	253.3
2	19.40	19.41	19.43	19.45	19.46	19.46	19.47	19.48	19.48	19.49	19.49
3	8.79	8.74	8.70	8.66	8.63	8.62	8.59	8.57	8.56	8.55	8.55
4	5.96	5.91	5.86	5.80	5.77	5.75	5.72	5.69	5.67	5.66	5.66
5	4.74	4.68	4.62	4.56	4.52	4.50	4.46	4.43	4.41	4.41	4.40
6	4.06	4.00	3.94	3.87	3.83	3.81	3.77	3.74	3.72	3.71	3.70
7	3.64	3.57	3.51	3.44	3.40	3.38	3.34	3.30	3.29	3.27	3.27
8	3.35	3.28	3.22	3.15	3.11	3.08	3.04	3.01	2.99	2.97	2.97
9	3.14	3.07	3.01	2.94	2.89	2.86	2.83	2.79	2.77	2.76	2.75
10	2.98	2.91	2.85	2.77	2.73	2.70	2.66	2.62	2.60	2.59	2.58
11	2.85	2.79	2.72	2.65	2.60	2.57	2.53	2.49	2.47	2.46	2.45
12	2.75	2.69	2.62	2.54	2.50	2.47	2.43	2.38	2.36	2.35	2.34
13	2.67	2.60	2.53	2.46	2.41	2.38	2.34	2.30	2.27	2.26	2.25
14	2.60	2.53	2.46	2.39	2.34	2.31	2.27	2.22	2.20	2.19	2.18
15	2.54	2.48	2.40	2.33	2.28	2.25	2.20	2.16	2.14	2.12	2.11
16	2.49	2.42	2.35	2.28	2.23	2.19	2.15	2.11	2.08	2.07	2.06
17	2.45	2.38	2.31	2.23	2.18	2.15	2.10	2.06	2.03	2.02	2.01
18	2.41	2.34	2.27	2.19	2.14	2.11	2.06	2.02	1.99	1.98	1.97
19	2.38	2.31	2.23	2.16	2.11	2.07	2.03	1.98	1.96	1.94	1.93
20	2.35	2.28	2.20	2.12	2.07	2.04	1.99	1.95	1.92	1.91	1.90
21	2.32	2.25	2.18	2.10	2.05	2.01	1.96	1.92	1.89	1.88	1.87
22	2.30	2.23	2.15	2.07	2.02	1.98	1.94	1.89	1.86	1.85	1.84
23	2.27	2.20	2.13	2.05	2.00	1.96	1.91	1.86	1.84	1.82	1.81
24	2.25	2.18	2.11	2.03	1.97	1.94	1.89	1.84	1.82	1.80	1.79
25	2.24	2.16	2.09	2.01	1.96	1.92	1.87	1.82	1.80	1.78	1.77
26	2.22	2.15	2.07	1.99	1.94	1.90	1.85	1.80	1.78	1.76	1.75
27	2.20	2.13	2.06	1.97	1.92	1.88	1.84	1.79	1.76	1.74	1.73
28	2.19	2.12	2.04	1.96	1.91	1.87	1.82	1.77	1.74	1.73	1.71
29	2.18	2.10	2.03	1.94	1.89	1.85	1.81	1.75	1.73	1.71	1.70
30	2.16	2.09	2.01	1.93	1.88	1.84	1.79	1.74	1.71	1.70	1.68
40	2.08	2.00	1.92	1.84	1.78	1.74	1.69	1.64	1.61	1.59	1.58
50	2.03	1.95	1.87	1.78	1.73	1.69	1.63	1.58	1.54	1.52	1.51
60	1.99	1.92	1.84	1.75	1.69	1.65	1.59	1.53	1.50	1.48	1.47
70	1.97	1.89	1.81	1.72	1.66	1.62	1.57	1.50	1.47	1.45	1.44
80	1.95	1.88	1.79	1.70	1.64	1.60	1.54	1.48	1.45	1.43	1.41
90	1.94	1.86	1.78	1.69	1.63	1.59	1.53	1.46	1.43	1.41	1.39
100	1.93	1.85	1.77	1.68	1.62	1.57	1.52	1.45	1.41	1.39	1.38
110	1.92	1.84	1.76	1.67	1.61	1.56	1.50	1.44	1.40	1.38	1.36
120	1.91	1.83	1.75	1.66	1.60	1.55	1.50	1.43	1.39	1.37	1.35

Appendix 5

Values of q for Tukey's HSD test ($a = 0.05$)

v	2	3	4	5	6
4	3.92649	5.04024	5.75706	6.28702	6.70644
5	3.63535	4.60166	5.21848	5.67312	6.03290
6	3.46046	4.33902	4.89559	5.30494	5.62855
7	3.34392	4.16483	4.68124	5.06007	5.35909
8	3.26115	4.04101	4.52880	4.88575	5.16723
9	3.19906	3.94850	4.41490	4.75541	5.02352
10	3.15106	3.87676	4.32658	4.65429	4.91202
11	3.11265	3.81952	4.25609	4.57356	4.82295
12	3.08132	3.77278	4.19852	4.50760	4.75015
13	3.05529	3.73414	4.15087	4.45291	4.68970
14	3.03319	3.70139	4.11051	4.40661	4.63854
15	3.01432	3.67338	4.07597	4.36699	4.59474
16	2.99800	3.64914	4.04609	4.33269	4.55681
17	2.98373	3.62796	4.01999	4.30271	4.52365
18	2.97115	3.60930	3.99698	4.27629	4.49442
19	2.95998	3.59274	3.97655	4.25283	4.46846
20	2.95000	3.57794	3.95829	4.23186	4.44524
21	2.94102	3.56463	3.94188	4.21300	4.42436
22	2.93290	3.55259	3.92704	4.19594	4.40547
23	2.92553	3.54167	3.91356	4.18045	4.38831
24	2.91880	3.53170	3.90126	4.16632	4.37265
25	2.91263	3.52257	3.89000	4.15337	4.35831
26	2.90697	3.51417	3.87964	4.14146	4.34511
27	2.90174	3.50643	3.87009	4.13047	4.33294
28	2.89690	3.49918	3.86125	4.12030	4.32167
29	2.89240	3.49263	3.85304	4.11087	4.31121
30	2.88822	3.48651	3.84540	4.10208	4.30147
31	2.88432	3.48065	3.83828	4.09389	4.29238
32	2.88068	3.47525	3.83162	4.08622	4.28389
33	2.87726	3.47019	3.82537	4.07904	4.27592
34	2.87405	3.46544	3.81951	4.07230	4.26844
35	2.87103	3.46097	3.81400	4.06595	4.26141
36	2.86818	3.45676	3.80880	4.05997	4.25477
37	2.86550	3.45278	3.80389	4.05432	4.24851
38	2.86296	3.44902	3.79925	4.04898	4.24258
39	2.86055	3.44546	3.79486	4.04392	4.23697
40	2.85827	3.44208	3.79069	4.03913	4.23165
41	2.85610	3.43888	3.78673	4.03457	4.22659

v	2	3	4	5	6
42	2.85404	3.43582	3.78296	4.03024	4.22179
43	2.85208	3.43292	3.77938	4.02611	4.21721
44	2.85020	3.43015	3.77596	4.02217	4.21284
45	2.84842	3.42751	3.77270	4.01842	4.20868
46	2.84671	3.42499	3.76958	4.01483	4.20469
47	2.84508	3.42257	3.76660	4.01140	4.20089
48	2.84352	3.42026	3.76375	4.00812	4.19724
49	2.84203	3.41805	3.76102	4.00497	4.19375
50	2.84059	3.41592	3.75839	4.00195	4.19040
51	2.83921	3.41389	3.75588	3.99906	4.18719
52	2.83789	3.41193	3.75346	3.99627	4.18410
53	2.83662	3.41005	3.75104	3.99360	4.18113
54	2.83540	3.40824	3.74886	3.99103	4.17827
55	2.83422	3.40649	3.74677	3.98855	4.17552
56	2.83308	3.40482	3.74475	3.98616	4.17287
57	2.83199	3.40320	3.74268	3.98386	4.17031
58	2.83093	3.40163	3.74075	3.98164	4.16785
59	2.82992	3.40013	3.73889	3.97949	4.16547
60	2.82893	3.39867	3.73709	3.97742	4.16317
61	2.82798	3.39726	3.73535	3.97542	4.16094
62	2.82706	3.39590	3.73367	3.97348	4.15879
63	2.82617	3.39458	3.73204	3.97161	4.15671
64	2.82531	3.39331	3.73047	3.96979	4.15470
65	2.82448	3.39207	3.72894	3.96804	4.15275
66	2.82367	3.39088	3.72746	3.96633	4.15085
67	2.82288	3.38971	3.72603	3.96468	4.14902
68	2.82212	3.38859	3.72464	3.96308	4.14724
69	2.82138	3.38750	3.72329	3.96152	4.14552
70	2.82067	3.38644	3.72198	3.96001	4.14384
71	2.81997	3.38540	3.72071	3.95855	4.14221
72	2.81929	3.38440	3.71947	3.95712	4.14063
73	2.81864	3.38343	3.71827	3.95574	4.13909
74	2.81800	3.38248	3.71710	3.95439	4.13759
75	2.81738	3.38156	3.71596	3.95308	4.13614
76	2.81665	3.38067	3.71485	3.95181	4.13472
77	2.81606	3.37979	3.71377	3.95056	4.13334
78	2.81548	3.37894	3.71273	3.94935	4.13200
79	2.81492	3.37812	3.71170	3.94818	4.13069
80	2.81437	3.37731	3.71071	3.94703	4.12941
81	2.81384	3.37652	3.70973	3.94591	4.12817
82	2.81332	3.37575	3.70879	3.94481	4.12696
83	2.81281	3.37501	3.70786	3.94375	4.12577
84	2.81232	3.37428	3.70696	3.94271	4.12462
85	2.81184	3.37356	3.70608	3.94169	4.12349
86	2.81136	3.37287	3.70522	3.94070	4.12239
87	2.81090	3.37219	3.70438	3.93974	4.12132
88	2.81045	3.37152	3.70356	3.93879	4.12027
89	2.81001	3.37087	3.70276	3.93778	4.11924

v	2	3	4	5	6
90	2.80958	3.37024	3.70197	3.93691	4.11824
91	2.80916	3.36962	3.70121	3.93607	4.11725
92	2.80875	3.36901	3.70046	3.93524	4.11630
93	2.80835	3.36842	3.69972	3.93443	4.11536
94	2.80795	3.36784	3.69901	3.93363	4.11444
95	2.80757	3.36727	3.69830	3.93274	4.11354
96	2.80719	3.36671	3.69762	3.93194	4.11266
97	2.80682	3.36617	3.69694	3.93117	4.11180
98	2.80646	3.36564	3.69628	3.93041	4.11095
99	2.80611	3.36511	3.69564	3.92967	4.11013
100	2.80576	3.36460	3.69501	3.92894	4.10932
101	2.80542	3.36410	3.69439	3.92822	4.10853
102	2.80509	3.36361	3.69378	3.92752	4.10775
103	2.80476	3.36313	3.69318	3.92684	4.10699
104	2.80444	3.36266	3.69260	3.92616	4.10624
105	2.80412	3.36219	3.69203	3.92550	4.10550
106	2.80382	3.36174	3.69147	3.92486	4.10478
107	2.80351	3.36129	3.69092	3.92422	4.10408
108	2.80322	3.36085	3.69038	3.92360	4.10339
109	2.80293	3.36043	3.68984	3.92299	4.10271
110	2.80264	3.36000	3.68932	3.92239	4.10204
111	2.80236	3.35959	3.68881	3.92180	4.10139
112	2.80208	3.35918	3.68831	3.92122	4.10074
113	2.80181	3.35878	3.68782	3.92065	4.10011
114	2.80155	3.35839	3.68733	3.92009	4.09949
115	2.80129	3.35801	3.68686	3.91954	4.09888
116	2.80103	3.35763	3.68639	3.91900	4.09828
117	2.80078	3.35726	3.68593	3.91847	4.09769
118	2.80053	3.35689	3.68548	3.91795	4.09711
119	2.80028	3.35653	3.68503	3.91744	4.09655
120	2.80004	3.35618	3.68460	3.91694	4.09599
121	2.79981	3.35583	3.68417	3.91644	4.09544
122	2.79958	3.35549	3.68375	3.91596	4.09490
123	2.79935	3.35516	3.68333	3.91548	4.09436
124	2.79913	3.35482	3.68292	3.91501	4.09384
125	2.79890	3.35450	3.68252	3.91454	4.09333
126	2.79869	3.35418	3.68213	3.91409	4.09282
127	2.79847	3.35387	3.68174	3.91364	4.09232
128	2.79826	3.35356	3.68135	3.91320	4.09183
129	2.79806	3.35325	3.68098	3.91276	4.09135
130	2.79785	3.35295	3.68061	3.91234	4.09087
131	2.79765	3.35265	3.68024	3.91192	4.09040
132	2.79745	3.35236	3.67988	3.91150	4.08994
133	2.79726	3.35208	3.67953	3.91109	4.08949
134	2.79707	3.35179	3.67918	3.91069	4.08904
135	2.79688	3.35152	3.67883	3.91029	4.08860
136	2.79669	3.35124	3.67849	3.90990	4.08817
137	2.79651	3.35097	3.67816	3.90952	4.08774

v	2	3	4	5	6
138	2.79633	3.35071	3.67783	3.90914	4.08723
139	2.79615	3.35045	3.67751	3.90877	4.08683
140	2.79598	3.35019	3.67719	3.90840	4.08644
141	2.79580	3.34993	3.67687	3.90804	4.08606
142	2.79563	3.34968	3.67656	3.90768	4.08562
143	2.79547	3.34943	3.67626	3.90732	4.08538
144	2.79530	3.34919	3.67596	3.90698	4.08495
145	2.79514	3.34895	3.67566	3.90663	4.08459
146	2.79498	3.34871	3.67537	3.90630	4.08423
147	2.79482	3.34848	3.67508	3.90596	4.08388
148	2.79466	3.34825	3.67479	3.90563	4.08342
149	2.79451	3.34802	3.67451	3.90531	4.08306
150	2.79435	3.34780	3.67423	3.90499	4.08271

Review exercise solutions by chapter

Chapter 5

1.

  a nominal
  b ratio
  c ratio
  d ratio
  e ratio
  f ordinal

3.

  a 63
  b 53
  c 72

Chapter 6

1.

  a $100/200 = 0.5$
  b $30/200 = 0.15$
  c $45/200 = 0.225$
  d $30/45 = 0.67$

3.

  a 0.00135
  b 0.5
  c 0.05
  d 0.00003

9.

  a $t < -1.833$ or $t > 1.833$
  b $t < -3.250$ or $t > 3.250$
  c $t < -2.045$ or $t > 2.045$
  d $t < -3.659$ or $t > 3.659$

10.

  a not reject
  b reject
  c reject
  d not reject

Chapter 8

2.

  a (0.04, 0.21)
  b (0.08, 0.16)

3.

  a (0.10, 0.22)
  b (0.08, 0.24)
  c $Z = 0.74$ therefore we would be 54% confident.

4.

  a (0.005, 0.15)
  b $(-0.01, 0.16)$
  c $(-0.04, 0.19)$

Chapter 9

2.

  a $(-0.745, 1.425)$
  b $(-0.963, 1.643)$
  c $(-1.405, 2.085)$

3.

  a The difference between groups is not statistically significant.

b   The difference between groups is statistically significant and the treatment appears to increase SBP.

c   The difference between groups is statistically significant and the treatment appears to lower SBP.

Chapter 10

3.

a   not rejected
b   rejected
c   rejected
d   rejected
e   not rejected
f   not rejected
g   rejected
h   not rejected

4.

a   0.119
b   0.008
c   0.001
d   0.317

5.

a

	Placebo	Test
Responder	117	152
Non-responder	385	346
	502	498

b $H_0: p_1 - p_2 = 0$
    $H_A: p_1 - p_2 \neq 0$

c   Chi-square test, Fisher's exact test, or z approximation

d   Yes, there is sufficient evidence to reject the null hypothesis ($\alpha = 0.05$). Using the chi-square test the assumptions are that the two groups are independent; responses are mutually exclusive; and the expected cell counts are at least 5 in $> 80\%$ of the cells. The value of the chi-square test statistic is 6.62.

e   The odds ratio $= \dfrac{(152)(385)}{(117)(346)} = 1.45$

Participants exposed to the test treatment are 1.45 times more likely to respond than participants in the placebo group.

Chapter 11

1.

a $H_0: \mu_{TEST} - \mu_{PLACEBO} = 0$
    $H_A: \mu_{TEST} - \mu_{PLACEBO} \neq 0$

b $t < -2.0423$ or $t > 2.042$

c   Independent samples; outcome approximately normally distributed; equal unknown variance

d -2.26

e   Do not reject H_0 since $-2.042 < -0.68 < 2.042$. The mean pain scores are not significantly different between the two groups.

2.

a   SS error $= 238.67896$
    MS Drug $= 49.947295$
    MS Error $= 7.95597$
    $F = 6.28$

b   3

c $H_0: \mu_1 = \mu_2 = \mu_3$
    H_A: at least one pair of population means are unequal

d   33

e $F > 3.32$

f   Reject H_0 since $6.28 > 3.32$. At least one pair of population means is unequal.

3.

a $H_0: \mu_P = \mu_L = \mu_M = \mu_H$
    H_A: at least one pair of population means are unequal

b   Each group represents a simple random sample from relevant populations; observations are independent; outcome is approximately normally distributed; the variance is equal across the populations

c   Placebo vs. low; placebo vs. medium; placebo vs. high; low vs. medium; low vs. high; medium vs. high

d   To control the overall Type I error

e $MSD_T = 3.68639\sqrt{\dfrac{20}{30}} = 3.01$

Chapter 12

4.

a   80% power: 64/group
90% power: 86/group

b   80% power: 143/group
90% power: 191/group

Index

Note: page numbers in *italics* refer to Figures, and those in **bold** to Tables.